THE FLEETING PROMISE OF ART

THE FLEETING PROMISE OF ART

Adorno's Aesthetic Theory Revisited

PETER UWE HOHENDAHL

CORNELL UNIVERSITY PRESS
ITHACA AND LONDON

First published 2013 by Cornell University Press
First printing, Cornell Paperbacks, 2013

Printed in the United States of America

Library of Congress Cataloging-in-Publication Data

Hohendahl, Peter Uwe, author.
    The fleeting promise of art : Adorno's aesthetic theory revisited / Peter
Uwe Hohendahl.
        pages cm
    Includes bibliographical references and index.
    ISBN 978-0-8014-5236-9 (cloth : alk. paper) —
    ISBN 978-0-8014-7898-7 (pbk. : alk. paper)
    1. Adorno, Theodor W., 1903–1969—Aesthetics. 2. Aesthetics,
German—20th century. I. Title.
    B3199.A34H633 2013
    111'.85092—dc23   2013009769

| Cloth printing | 10 | 9 | 8 | 7 | 6 | 5 | 4 | 3 | 2 | 1 |
| Paperback printing | 10 | 9 | 8 | 7 | 6 | 5 | 4 | 3 | 2 | 1 |

Contents

ACKNOWLEDGMENTS

This book has a long and complex history. It grew out of individual but related projects focused on Adorno's aesthetic theory and literary criticism. Some of them were originally conceived as more specific investigations or interventions, written either as essays or book chapters. Chapters 1, 2, 3, and 5 were previously published in somewhat different form. Part of chapter 1 was published in *The Philosophical Forum* (43:3, Fall 2012). Chapter 2 first appeared in a volume edited by Gerhard Richter, *Language without Soil: Adorno and Late Philosophical Modernity* (Fordham University Press, 2010). A version of chapter 3 was originally published in *Cultural Critique* (60, Spring 2005), and chapter 5 first appeared in *New Literary History* (42:1, 2011).

This project could not have been undertaken and completed without encouragement from colleagues and friends. I want to thank Rita Felsky, Gerhard Richter, and the late Jochen Schulte-Sasse for reading drafts of various chapters and providing generous critical feedback. While repeated conversations with Peter Gilgen and Andrew Chignell on problems of aesthetics encouraged me to put Adorno's theory in the larger context of contemporary philosophy, frequent discussions with Paul Fleming inspired me to rethink the nature and relevance of Adorno's literary criticism. Finally, I want to express my gratitude to everyone I worked with at Cornell University Press for their enthusiastic and sustained support. In particular, Peter Potter's advice and assistance have been invaluable.

ABBREVIATIONS

Ä   Theodor W. Adorno. *Ästhetik (1958/59): Nachgelassene Schriften,* Abteilung IV: Vorlesungen, vol. 3. Edited by Erhard Ortland. Frankfurt am Main: Suhrkamp, 2009.

ÄT   Theodor W. Adorno. *Ästhetische Theorie.* Edited by Gretel Adorno and Rolf Tiedemann. 4th ed. Frankfurt am Main: Suhrkamp, 1980.

AT   Theodor W. Adorno. *Aesthetic Theory.* Translated and edited by Robert Hullot-Kentor. Minneapolis: University of Minnesota Press, 1997.

BT   Friedrich Nietzsche. *The Birth of Tragedy and Other Writings.* Translated by Raymond Geuss and Ronald Speirs. Cambridge: Cambridge University Press, 1999.

CJ   Immanuel Kant. *Critique of the Power of Judgment.* Edited by Paul Guyer. Translated by Paul Guyer and Eric Matthews. New York: Cambridge University Press, 2000.

CPR   Immanuel Kant. *Critique of Pure Reason.* Translated by Norman Kemp Smith. New York: St. Martin's Press, 1965.

DE   Max Horkheimer and Theodor W. Adorno. *Dialectic of Enlightenment.* Translated by John Cumming. New York: Herder and Herder, 1972.

IT   Arthur Henkel. "Iphigenie auf Tauris." In *Das deutsche Drama vom Barock bis zur Gegenwart,* edited by Benno von Wiese, 1:170–194. Düsseldorf: Bagel, 1964.

KC   Theodor W. Adorno. *Kant's "Critique of Pure Reason."* Edited by Rolf Tiedemann. Translated by Rodney Livingston. Stanford, CA: Stanford University Press, 2001.

KK   Theodor W. Adorno. *Kants Kritik der reinen Vernunft (1959), Nachgelassene Schriften,* Abteilung IV: Vorlesungen, vol. 4. Edited by Rolf Tiedemann. Frankfurt am Main: Suhrkamp, 1995.

KU   Immanuel Kant. *Kritik der Urteilskraft.* In Kant, *Werke.* 6 vols. Edited by Wilhelm Weischedel. Darmstadt: Wissenschaftliche Buchgesellschaft, vol. 5, 1957.

NL   Theodor W. Adorno. *Notes to Literature.* Translated by Shierry Weber Nicholsen. 2 vols. New York: Columbia University Press, 1991–1992.

OL   Theodor W. Adorno. *Ohne Leitbild: Parva Aesthetica.* Frankfurt am Main: Suhrkamp, 1967.

PMM   Theodor W. Adorno. *Philosophy of New Music.* Edited and translated by Robert Hullot-Kentor. Minneapolis: University of Minnesota Press, 2006.

Pr   Theodor W. Adorno. *Prisms.* Translated by Shierry Weber Nicholsen and Samuel Weber. Cambridge, MA: MIT Press, 1981.

THE FLEETING PROMISE OF ART

INTRODUCTION

A discussion of Adorno's *Aesthetic Theory* is bound to look significantly different today than it would have looked in the early 1990s, especially in North America. At that time, immediately after the end of the Cold War, which had influenced aesthetic debates more than most participants were ready to concede, the discovery of Adorno's posthumous work through translations challenged students of critical theory because of its philosophical density. Reading *Aesthetic Theory* (first published in 1970) required a familiarity with the German dialectical tradition that could not be taken for granted in this country.[1] The explication of Adorno's late work as the culmination of his entire oeuvre demanded close attention to the text and a mode of immanent analysis that opens up a complex structure of arguments. While this work is still continuing and remains by all means necessary, two decades later the general debate on aesthetics has changed so much that a rereading of *Aesthetic Theory* exposes rather different questions and arguments. Seen from the perspective of mainstream philosophical aesthetics, Adorno's work may look even less familiar now than in the 1990s. For instance, his philosophical presuppositions as well as his understanding of the role and function of art are possibly less accepted today than they were then. Likewise, the concept of critique as being at the very core of aesthetic theory and the emphatic notion of a truth content in artworks may find resistance in the contemporary discussion that has embraced a broader understanding of the aesthetic and a more lenient notion of art. Generally speaking, Adorno's hostility toward entertainment, so striking in the culture industry essay of *Dialectic of Enlightenment,* finds less sympathetic readers today than a generation ago. It might even be rejected as cultural conservatism. (Somewhat hastily, as I will show.)

In the present discussion the emphatic demand for aesthetic truth and the call for an exceptional position of the artwork pose stumbling blocks for Adorno's theory. Using the distinction between aesthetic theory in its original (narrow) sense and philosophy of art, those of Adorno's commitments that are more controversial today fall under the rubric of philosophy of art, including its close link to the philosophy of history. Also, Adorno's concerns over the fate of art in a late capitalist society no longer find a general echo in the public sphere. In short, the stakes of Adorno's aesthetic theory, its high expectations as well as its fundamental doubts about the future of art, are sometimes met with suspicion or indifference. Is it an accident that Robert Stecker's textbook, *Aesthetics and the Philosophy of Art* (2005), contains no mention of Adorno, not even in the bibliography? (A fate, incidentally, shared by Hegel and Heidegger.) While Stecker gives Kant a place in the contemporary discussion, the Hegelian tradition, to which Adorno is so clearly indebted, is excluded.

How do we account for this glaring omission and make sense of it in today's theoretical context? To answer this question a more detailed assessment of the contemporary field is necessary, an assessment that will enable a rereading of Adorno within the parameters of the new debate on aesthetics. This assessment will ultimately have to come to terms with the fundamental question: Is Adorno's *Aesthetic Theory* still relevant today? That is, is it a work worth returning to? Let me be clear: this question should not be seen as concealing a dogmatic point. The issue is not the teaching of Adorno, his specific judgments, preferences, and prejudices. Rather, at stake is the relevance of the kind of questions raised in Adorno's work, among them the emphasis on the special status of the artwork for which he uses the term "autonomy," a term that actually covers only in part what is essential to him. The real problem for Adorno is, as Christoph Menke has rightly underscored,[2] the sovereignty of art, its capacity to transcend the aesthetic sphere. As we will see, it is exactly this excess—this supposed special power of the artwork to impact the nonaesthetic sphere—that has come under scrutiny.

The unexpected return of the aesthetic in today's cultural debates implies also a limitation of its scope. While this new horizon acknowledges the autonomy of art, even vigorously defends it, there is less emphasis on the idea of a truth content. In this new environment Adorno's aesthetic theory stands out in a different way than it did in the 1970s, when it was measured against the political aesthetics of Brecht, and in the 1990s, when it was discussed in the context of poststructuralist theories. Seemingly, the return of the aesthetic, which in itself is multifaceted and full of tensions, would encourage the reception of Adorno's late work; yet this support is aligned with a different perspective that gives Adorno a new profile. Possibly his theory has to assert itself in light of aesthetic assumptions that its author treated as problematic. In short, the new impulses in the contemporary discussion, readily associated with names such as Elaine Scarry and Peter de Bolla, require a rereading of *Aesthetic Theory.*[3] Was Adorno's position part of the antiaesthetic that challenged traditional aesthetics, or was he involved in defending the tradition of aesthetic theory from Kant to Hegel? Clearly, Adorno considered the thought of Kant, Schelling, and Hegel as indispensable for contemporary aesthetic theory. At the same time, he asserted the need to critique the tradition as the only method of working out a theory compatible with modern art. This ambiguity, which made it possible to treat Adorno either as a conservative (an appreciator of art) or as a radical (a critic of timeless aesthetic values), takes on a new significance when the importance and the value of the aesthetic sphere is emphatically claimed. It is safe to say that it never occurred to Adorno to consider the aesthetic as a mere ideology in support of modern capitalism, but how does his strong defense of aesthetic autonomy fit into the new discussion? One cannot deny the centrality of the concept of aesthetic experience in *Aesthetic Theory,* yet how does it compare to the ideas of Scarry and de Bolla? Or, to turn the table, can one argue for the universal nature of aesthetic experience or universal aesthetic values and include Adorno in such an argument? These questions put a kind of pressure on Adorno's theory that significantly differs from the political position of the 1970s and 1980s and the deconstructive position of the 1990s. They also suggest a realignment with the philosophical tradition at the expense of the moment of critical self-reflection.

What defines the new aesthetic discourse, at least in part, is the return to the concept of beauty as the central aesthetic issue. Both Scarry and de Bolla underscore the centrality of beauty when considering both artworks and natural objects. For Scarry the presence of beauty is immediate and apparent and has been wrongly accused of political indifference. "But, as I will try to explain," she writes, "these political complaints against beauty are themselves incoherent. Beauty is, at the very least, innocent of the charges against it, and it may even be the case that far from damaging our capacity to attend to problems of injustice, it instead intensifies the pressure we feel to repair existing injustices."[4] Scarry's approach to aesthetics relies rather explicitly on the notion of aesthetic values. That is, the value of the beautiful is never in doubt; if there is a problem with beauty the problem concerns its compatibility with other values—for instance, justice or ethical goodness. With this in mind, she tries to demonstrate that these values can coexist and even support each other. For instance, she argues that the regard for beauty will assist our attention to justice.[5] Whether or not this argument holds true is of less interest here than the fundamental assumption of the existence of (transhistorical) universal values to which human beings can turn in order to enhance their lives. Scarry's main point against the antiaesthetic critique of the 1980s and 1990s is that these universal values do not contradict each other. There is in her mind a "continuity of evidence"[6] that connects the different, independent value spheres. Although there is no causal connection, one can detect an analogy that enables the observer to appreciate the harmony of the whole.

What is striking about Scarry's defense of the aesthetic is its scope, the idea that beauty is part of a larger harmonious configuration of values that is given and readily perceivable to those who want to see. Although she is attentive to the specific character of the aesthetic experience, she is not interested in the fundamental epistemological particularity of the aesthetic experience. Her approach clearly keeps its distance from Kant. Even less can one detect an attempt to come to terms with modern art, especially those features that resist the notion of beauty. It remains unclear whether Scarry considers modern art as simply not concerned with beauty or as an aberration. From Scarry's position, then, Adorno's aesthetic theory looks problematic at best, since he rejects the notion of beauty as a transcendent value and insists instead on the significance of the ugly in the context of modern art. His credo that contemporary art is defined by the color black would hardly be accepted by Scarry.

In the case of de Bolla the gap is not as wide because, like Adorno, he is concerned with artworks and specifically contemporary artworks. His defense of the aesthetic is focused on the importance of artworks. Furthermore, and this would bring him closer to Adorno's understanding, he wants to elaborate the specific nature of aesthetic experience as "distant from other kinds of experiences."[7] In particular, he is interested in the affective aspect of this experience as distinct from the cognitive side (which he does not deny). While he briefly invokes Adorno and believes he shares methodological concerns with him, he misses Adorno's emphasis on the objective aspect of the aesthetic—the concern with the structure of the artwork—which is fundamental to his theory. The shift toward affective criticism by necessity underscores the subjective side, assigning aesthetic value based on the response of the recipient. Aesthetic value, in other words, is defined exclusively in subjective terms; it is imposed on the object rather than found in the actual artwork, as Scarry would argue. However, what de Bolla and Scarry share is the belief in the immediacy of the aesthetic experience. Both would argue that the aesthetic experience is always present and unambiguous in its nature. Both of them resist a hermeneutics of suspicion and the suggestion that the aesthetic experience itself might be ideological (Eagleton, Bourdieu) or that artworks owe their existence to concrete material conditions. Put differently, the autonomy of the aesthetic sphere is taken for granted—either as an objective realm of the beautiful (Scarry) or as a distinct realm of experience (de Bolla). While Scarry stands in the Platonic tradition, de Bolla's approach is closer to Kant, whom he invokes in the last chapter.[8]

The return to aesthetics, as both Scarry and de Bolla claim, amounts to a return to traditional aesthetics, a recourse that denies or eliminates the questions raised during the late twentieth century. This would also apply to the analytical approach of Stecker and others. Yet the question remains whether these decades that followed the publication of *Aesthetic Theory* (1970) can be, so to speak, stricken from the record. Moreover, what would a postcritical aesthetic theory do with Adorno's writings? Could they be redeemed because their author quite consciously developed his own theory in a (critical) dialogue with the tradition, especially with Kant and Hegel? Or would his insistence on the critical nature of the engagement exclude him from the new aesthetic?

Of course, a return to Kant's *Critique of Judgment,* as Jonathan Loesberg and others have shown, does not necessarily amount to a mode of dogmatic thinking in which the historical positionality of the theory is rigorously suppressed. Rather, the importance of Kant for the contemporary discussion can be, in fact should be, approached as part of the larger question of the fate of aesthetics in the age of Enlightenment. As Loesberg puts it, if postmodernism can be defined as a project to break away from the trajectory of the Enlightenment and its consequence in modernism, "all these arguments [of the postmodern critics] have faced a relentless and quite repetitious charge of self-contradiction."[9] He holds against the various strands of poststructuralist criticism that the emphasis on the internal contradictions of any grounded philosophical position has become highly repetitive and has thereby undermined the process of critique itself, since it leaves philosophy in permanent limbo and thought without orientation. In brief, the weakness of poststructuralist critique is, Loesberg tells us, the ineffectiveness of an ongoing exchange of arguments without ever reaching a conclusion. Seen in the light of this countercritique, which is more suggestive than carefully documented and argued, there is today a strong need to rethink the status of aesthetics. This process should move in two opposite directions. On the one hand, it has to confront a dogmatic and uncritical return to the tradition; on the other, it needs to address the radical subversion of the aesthetic in the name of postmodern critique.

In this context it is important to note that when Adorno was beginning to work on *Aesthetic Theory* in the late 1950s he was fully aware of the problematic mentioned above. In his draft introduction of 1959 (later discarded) he outlines the philosophical and historical conditions for a contemporary theory that can escape the dilemma between stale academic traditionalism and radical private subjectivism. Adorno's point of departure in the 1950s is not the traditional question of grounding but the widening gap between the conceptual apparatus of academic aesthetics and the challenges of modern art. More radically, he questions the very possibility of philosophical aesthetics in the context of avant-garde art. It is modern art that challenges academic aesthetics to such an extent that the foundations of aesthetic theory have to be rethought. This question more than any other has resulted in Adorno's *Aesthetic Theory* being branded as a theory of modernism, and as such as potentially outdated by the collapse of high modernism. This branding is unfortunate because it misunderstands Adorno's problem. His point was not to develop a theory specifically for modern art; rather, he maintained that modern art challenged the very possibility of systematic aesthetics *tout court*. Neither aesthetic values nor the feasibility of aesthetic judgments can be taken for granted, which, however, is not the same as arguing that aesthetic concepts are a priori ideological. The difficulty with this position is that it does not neatly and easily fit into the present discourse on aesthetics. The recent reinstatement of the aesthetic, either in its more dogmatic version (Scarry and de Bolla) or in its more self-reflective form (Loesberg), is primarily concerned with the consequences of a hermeneutics of suspicion and especially with the attack on aesthetics as a mere cover for material interests. The countercritique means to rescue the conditions that allow for the possibility of art and aesthetic judgment denied by those who assert that all aesthetic judgments are based on class interest and all artworks are the expression of power. Quite simply, these and similar assertions make it impossible to place the concept of a truth content at the center of a philosophy of art as Adorno does. And yet Adorno left no doubts in his lectures on aesthetics (1958/59) or in his draft introduction of 1959 that neither artworks nor aesthetic judgments were unproblematically available. To the contrary, he made it quite clear that their universality should always be treated as problematic, both at the historical and the epistemological level.

Before considering Adorno's position in more detail, it is important to be clear about the specific claims of the new aesthetics. What is the argument presented in favor of a return to aesthetics apart from a strong rejection of postmodern critiques? And how persuasive are these arguments? In many instances, unfortunately, the countercritique does not go much beyond the assertion that a fundamental critique of the aesthetic sphere is misplaced or reductive without considering the arguments in favor of the critique. Considerably more instructive would be the claim that the hostility toward the aesthetic as something inferior might itself be part of an unacknowledged attachment of poststructuralism to Enlightenment foundationalism, since this argument looks at the exit from critique and the potential restoration of the aesthetic from the internal process of criticism itself. In other words, the critique of poststructuralism examines the weak spots of the critique with an eye on liberation from critical dogmatism. If the resistance to the Enlightenment is at the bottom of poststructuralist critique, then one has to remind oneself that this mode of critique is deeply indebted to the Enlightenment.

In this sense, the call for a necessary return to the aesthetic would take on the form of an argument for an aesthetic a priori in the assessment of the aesthetic sphere. In other words, the sociological (Bourdieu) or political critique (Marx, Foucault) presupposes *ex negativo* an understanding of the possibility of the aesthetic as a condition to make historically oriented critiques. To use a specific example, Bourdieu's critique of Kant's notion of an aesthetic judgment as disinterested by showing that this notion is historically linked to the rise of the bourgeois elite presupposes the Kantian claim of disinterestedness as the decisive distinctive moment of aesthetic judgment.[10] In this context Kant's theory has two functions: on the one hand, it functions as the purest expression of refined upper-class dominant taste; on the other, it operates (transhistorically) as the norm by which different kinds of aesthetic responses can be judged. In his response to Bourdieu, Loesberg wants to show that Bourdieu remains a Kantian despite his critique of Kant. The argument amounts to the claim that philosophical aesthetics (for instance, that of Kant) remains indispensable for adjudicating historical problems such as class distinctions or periodical differences (transition from romanticism to realism, for instance). There must be a core of indispensable concepts that are inherent in the subject matter and therefore fundamental.[11] This formal foundationalism— i.e. the claim that even the severest critique of the aesthetic as a form of ideology or the mere expression of social attitudes is based on the recognition of a philosophical epistemology—leads to a de-emphasis of the historical context of aesthetics, perhaps to the denial of its importance for aesthetic judgments or the exploration of art in general. This position, while possibly attentive to changes in aesthetic theory as they occurred between the early eighteenth and the late twentieth centuries, underscores the immediacy of the aesthetic, its undeniable presence in terms of its sphere of being as well as its own justification. Hence the legitimacy of the aesthetic can be demonstrated in philosophical, abstract terms without regard for external circumstances that influence the mode of aesthetic responses at different times or in different cultures. In other words, if aesthetic theory has a disciplinary home it is in philosophy, where it can always be safely understood within the boundaries of philosophical discourse.

Although the recent discussion in response to postmodernism and the attempts of analytic philosophy promoted by analytic theorists such as Robert Stecker and Noël Carroll to define the nature and the function of aesthetics have largely remained not only separate but also distinct, they share the belief that philosophical reflection has the resources and the power to defend the legitimate claims of the aesthetic in a world that is too complex to offer simple and obvious guidelines for the evaluation of aesthetic phenomena and especially the evaluation of art.[12] One way to accomplish this, but only one way, is a return to Kant. The renewed interest in Kant's *Critique of Judgment,* in clear opposition to the work of poststructuralist critics such as Jacques Derrida and Paul de Man, should be understood as a fundamental shift in the approach to the aesthetic sphere, a shift that was inconceivable merely two decades ago.

The question that is relevant for my study is the impact of the previously mentioned return of the aesthetic on the place of Adorno today. Taking the recent trend as the index of a new configuration, the interpretation of Adorno's aesthetic theory will have to take into account its characteristics, among them the rejection of sociological and historical approaches, the hostility toward ideology critique and deconstruction, and the preference for formalist arguments. In all those aspects Adorno's theory is vulnerable, and yet at the same time it must be said that in each instance Adorno offers a strong defense of his position, one that anticipates the concerns expressed in the present discourse. Moreover, in addressing those concerns he does not simply reject them but reflects on their merits. Indeed, *Aesthetic Theory* is remarkable for offering a highly self-reflective theory that is already aware of and in dialogue with the arguments presented in the recent debate. Adorno demonstrates a critical distance toward a purely sociological method, although he considers and uses sociological arguments. He embraces formalist arguments in the wake of Kant, but keeps his distance from a purely formalist approach, and most of all he has no sympathy for those who would reduce art to dogmatic versions of ideology critique (art is nothing but a reflection of something else), while he carefully considers the ideological aspects of aesthetic production and reception. The result of this stance is a theory of extreme complexity, which cannot be understood without careful attention to dialectical mediation. In the early phase of its reception (the 1970s) this complexity yielded readings that tried to pull out either the formalist, the sociological, or the communicative aspects, as Albrecht Wellmer has noted.[13] Arguing against the reduction of presenting a merely linear argument, Wellmer rightly pointed to the inner link of the central categories of Adorno's theory such as semblance (*Schein*), truth, and reconciliation against Hans Robert Jauss, Peter Bürger, and Karl Heinz Bohrer, who had isolated specific aspects of Adorno's theory in order to improve it.

The "misreadings" of the 1970s underscore the principal difficulties faced by anyone charged with the task of introducing *Aesthetic Theory*. While the late work of Adorno resonates with certain elements of today's discourse—for instance, a renewed appreciation of the aesthetic including concepts such as natural beauty—it remains distant, even hostile, to other assumptions of the present discussion, among them the return to a form of cautious foundationalism. The greatest difficulty, however, may have to do with formal matters, namely the organization and presentation of the material. The very idea of a philosophically argued systematic theory is questioned from the beginning, as the early introduction clearly demonstrated. In his review of existing academic aesthetic theories Adorno comes to the conclusion that the goal of a systematic presentation does not withstand the force of critique. This critique comes from two sides: it is grounded in the extreme situation of modern art, which subverts transhistorical concepts, and it is furthermore caused by the internal limitations of philosophy, i.e. the inability of traditional conceptual language to open up and unfold the meaning of the artwork, which resists the universality of the concept. Philosophical discourse is therefore at a disadvantage when it confronts art; yet at the same time, as Adorno insists, it cannot give itself up, but must follow its own conceptual logic in order to be consistent. For this reason, Adorno dismisses the compromise of the middle-distance (art appreciation), a theory based on *Einfühlung* (a hermeneutics of empathy). Nonetheless, the tension between conceptual systematizing and concrete engagement with the artwork is consciously maintained as a defining characteristic of *Aesthetic Theory*. Put differently, the goal of a philosophically argued aesthetic theory is always already undermined by the nature of the aesthetic phenomena, as much as the aesthetic material, i.e. the history of artworks, is challenged by the inevitable imposition of a conceptual language.

This contradiction finds its expression in the organization of the work itself. The text that Adorno left behind is, I believe, best understood as a sequence of large essays that are exploring the same questions from different perspectives. Their intellectual energy moves them toward a center that remains ultimately invisible. By defining the chapters of *Aesthetic Theory* as essays I do not mean to emphasize only their relative independence vis-à-vis the whole, the fact that they resist a linear argument, but also Adorno's style. What Adorno said in "The Essay as Form" on the structure of the essay also applies to his late work, at least in part. Neither deduction nor induction is considered as the appropriate procedure. The essay does not demonstrate but suggests. Nonetheless, it is as much concerned with questions of truth as the system. On the other hand, Adorno resists the notion that the essay is an artwork and stresses the difference. The essay allows for the use of concepts and arguments to explore its subject matter. In the same vein the parts of *Aesthetic Theory* follow their internal logic without the imposition of a systematic linear argument. Only in this movement, enhanced by Adorno's paratactic style, can the subject matter, namely the nature of aesthetic phenomena, be disclosed.

Adorno did not conceive of his aesthetic theory as a research methodology or as a method of teaching acknowledged insights. Rather, he thought of it as a critical enterprise, although even this tentative definition has to be modified. It establishes its insights through a process of immanent critique that follows its own dialectic. This accounts for its fluidity and the impossibility of defining it in terms of results. In this movement the individual sentence, considered as a statement, cannot present truth, which makes it difficult to demonstrate a point by selecting a quotation. Truth is attained only in the radical intellectual energy of the movement of thought. Therefore it is easy to find contradictions by putting sentences next to each other that have been taken out of their context. Regarded from the perspective of a systematically organized dogma, *Aesthetic Theory* displays a strong tendency toward undermining its own ground in the name of radically questioning the condition of possibility of aesthetic theory. This critique—and this point is crucial—must not be confused with ideology critique, which is certain of its epistemological ground and therefore offers extrinsic criticism. While Adorno is of course familiar with this method and at least partially approves of it as an established practice of Marxist critique, his own version of immanent critique does not presuppose this kind of certainty. In fact, he turns the sharp edge of critique against central ideas of aesthetics, among them the autonomy of art, the notion of aesthetic transcendence, and the concept of originality.

One might expect that Adorno's principle of radical critique would result in a complete break with tradition. But this is not the case. To the contrary, Adorno frequently invokes the notion of a philosophical tradition. References to Kant and Hegel, especially, are very much part of the complex argument. It is important to note that they are not mentioned as representatives of a past that has become theoretically inadequate and therefore a mere foil for contemporary efforts. In clear contrast to a historicist perspective, Adorno critically engages not only Kant and Hegel but also Schelling, Schopenhauer, and especially Nietzsche. His engagement takes on the form of a comparative analysis in which not the weak but the strong points of different positions are brought into focus. Thus he gives as much attention to Kant's formalism as Hegel's content aesthetics, not to mention Nietzsche's analysis of the Apollonian principle of beautiful semblance against the backdrop of the Dionysian principle. In this manner, Adorno's theory is in dialogue with the idealist German philosophical tradition, developing its own profile through a critical appropriation that gains its strength in this encounter. In all instances, however, the method of engagement is personal. There is no attempt to reconstruct the argument of a given position in order to prepare the better argument. Instead, the thought process includes the older ideas and converts them into thoughts that were not necessarily part of the original system. Thus Adorno pushes the tradition beyond its original boundaries, thereby rescuing it from its historical weight and underscoring its relevance for the contemporary discussion. In this respect, Adorno's conception of critique differs from postmodern notions of leaving modernity and modernism behind as an outdated and by now nefarious project, although he makes no attempt to restore the modernist project in the name of reason. It would be more accurate to argue that for Adorno there is no sharp division between the modern and the postmodern work of art. Yet when it comes to the status of an advanced aesthetic theory he is unwilling to relinquish the high demands developed in the engagement with modern art.

Adorno has frequently been accused of (bourgeois) elitism because of his relentless criticism of popular commercialized culture. Certain passages in the culture industry chapter of *Dialectic of Enlightenment* give credence to this accusation in that they do not carefully differentiate between the institutional and the individual aspect, between the moment of "industrial" production and the possible resistance to and subversion of social conformism by the individual work. That said, the notion that Adorno was an unapologetic defender of high culture is simply false because his critique of culture under the sign of advanced capitalism includes institutionalized high culture, an indication that he fully recognized that the moment of reification is no less pronounced in institutionalized high culture than it is in the sphere of popular culture.[14] Therefore Adorno's aesthetic theory has to mark its distance from all forms of cultural production and dissemination that are mediated by the capitalist market. At the same time, there is for Adorno the realization that there is no space outside the market sphere in an advanced capitalist society, which in his opinion was still better than the cultural censorship of Stalinist regimes. Still, it is interesting to note that in his late work, especially in *Aesthetic Theory,* the polemic against popular culture and the culture of state socialism has subsided. Here Adorno focuses on the immanent dynamic of radical aesthetic production, those forms that resist easy appropriation. In particular, the chapter "Society" (AT 225–261) sets up the parameter for such reflection, defining modern art (in the broader sense) as "the determinate negation of a determinate society" (AT 226).

By emphasizing the moment of negation Adorno forcefully addresses the special status of art against sociological notions of mere imitation of social structures. Although artworks are for Adorno the products of social labor, they are not merely produced for their exchange value (which, however, cannot be simply denied in the manner of idealism). It defines the dual character of artworks that they are social facts and aesthetic structures. Thus Adorno notes: "As far as a social function can be predicated for artworks, it is their lack of a function" (AT 227, translation modified). The lack of a specific social function of authentic art assures the autonomy of the artwork and its aesthetic evaluation without denying the moment of social labor in its production. What characterizes Adorno's understanding of the aesthetic, perceived as art rather than nature, is his adamant refusal to accept the conventional opposition of aesthetic and social phenomena. By insisting on their mediatedness he escapes the cage of abstract idealism (Kant) as well as dogmatic materialism (Engels).

It is easy to misread Adorno's stance as mere methodology, as a way of defining an adequate form of sociology of art. While the methodological aspect should not be denied, it fails to capture the core of the Adornian project, which is defined as the unfolding of the artwork's truth content.

As Adorno remarks, "The truth content of artworks, which is indeed their social truth, is predicated on their fetish character" (AT 227). The paradox is this: only the miscognition of the artwork as completely autonomous by denying its base in social labor makes it possible to recognize the truth content of the work. Examined more closely, Adorno's position is radically removed from a pious support of high culture. In fact, one might well argue that Adorno's demand for a truth content, which incidentally does not sit well with postmodern notions of art, will result in a rebuke of institutional high culture, for in its institutional setting the artwork becomes a vehicle of ideology by serving purposes outside its own form. Thus the pathos of propagating the autonomy of art in a public setting can as an instrument of specific institutional interests turn against the very autonomy of the artwork that Adorno's theory defends.

Although Adorno acknowledged the "aging" of modern art, specifically in the case of music, he was unwilling to make concessions and lower the stakes. He dismissed a gradualist approach that allows for transitions from popular art to advanced works of art. This stubbornness has especially irritated those critics who rediscovered popular art as a genuine part of modern democratic mass societies. It is essential, therefore, to understand why this option was not open to Adorno. A positive appreciation of mass culture requires reconsidering the social role of art in terms of communication. The popular work exposes and disseminates the Zeitgeist, thereby articulating public self-understanding through aesthetic means. This function should not be restricted (as Adorno sometimes suggests) to the purpose of social affirmation. Adorno's essential issue, however, is the idea of a truth content as the core of the artwork. The truth content is both immanent (i.e. it must not be defined extrinsically) and specifically aesthetic (i.e. it is ultimately untranslatable into the sphere of philosophy or science). At the same time, the truth is more than the formal correctness of the artwork. Instead, Adorno's conception hints at a metaphysical quality of the artwork, a relationship, even proximity to the absolute that takes the radical work out of the context of ordinary social communication, though by no means out of a social context. Adorno's inability to include mass culture in his aesthetic theory, his latent hostility to any aesthetic product that primarily serves a communicative function, is grounded in the metaphysical aspect of his theory. Although he explicitly rejects the claim that the artwork can express absolute truth, the assertion of a close link between the aesthetic sphere and the concept of truth clearly separates those works that through their formal organization strive toward a truth content from those that merely facilitate intersubjective communication—either in an affirmative or a critical mode. These metaphysical objectives also separate Adorno from a postmodernist remapping of the aesthetic sphere in which the borders between high and popular culture have become deliberately fluid, since strong truth claims for artworks have been given up or at least suspended. Thus postmodernism does not have to rescue popular art; it merely has to acknowledge and reassess the broader range of aesthetic production. In this theoretical context the notion of aesthetic pleasure, a problematic category for Adorno, can make a strong comeback. Once the extraordinary standard of aesthetic form closely connected to modern art has been removed, not only aesthetic pleasure but also other features of premodernist aesthetics can make a new appearance.

Why did Adorno resist this trend? Why did he so energetically defend the special status of radical art? In the 1960s he had no illusions about the fact that he was witnessing the decline of high modernism and its aggressive claims for an aesthetic revolution (that might possibly prepare a political one) with liberative tendencies. In his interpretation of Beckett's *Endgame,* which he uses as the occasion to assess the status of art in general, he leaves no doubt about the lateness of art, its very complicity in bringing about the end of the project of modernity.[15] As Adorno sees it, late modernist art, the way art is practiced by Beckett, is focused on the subversion of its own artistic means. It has reached the state of parody. Thus the truth content of *Endgame* has been reduced to nothing more than the negation of metaphysical truth. The traditional claims of philosophy have become trash. Still, despite what he sees, Adorno is unwilling to draw the conclusion that the defense of art has become meaningless. To the contrary, in *Aesthetic Theory* he holds on to a strong version of radical aesthetics against conservative notions of high culture, on the one hand, and populist notions of mass culture on the other. What motivates this stance is unclear. *Aesthetic Theory* itself remains silent on this score.

I want to suggest that the contemporary situation of philosophy, especially the status of metaphysics, is at least in part responsible for Adorno's position. If philosophy, in Adorno's mind, is no longer capable of offering a coherent defense of the modern world, then this task has moved to art, which is, as Adorno admits, overburdened by this task but cannot refuse it without leaving a major gap in the interpretation of the world. While positivism is capable of explaining the factual order of reality, it is unable to interpret its meaning. Thus for Adorno, art is the remaining strong interpretation of the world, precisely by not copying reality but by addressing it through determinate negation. The rigorous emphasis on the autonomy of art has to be considered together with the requirement to interpret the social world through negation. In short, for Adorno the social and the aesthetic are necessarily linked; social critique can be accomplished through aesthetic critique, through the radical use of the aesthetic material. As much as more recent readings of *Aesthetic Theory* have attempted to separate this link, it is essential to reiterate the dialectic of Adorno's aesthetic and social critique. The more Adorno became convinced that social movements were no longer able to carry out meaningful social change, the more art became the placeholder for such aspirations. The ultimate perspective of aesthetic criticism is a (weak) utopian force that transcends the given social reality, considered by mainstream social science as structurally immutable. In the final analysis it is this utopian moment that defines the direction of Adorno's theory, especially its resistance to mass culture and popular art, both of which he sees as part of the status quo.

The utopian perspective makes it difficult and precarious to "update" Adorno. In genealogical terms, his project is grounded in twentieth-century philosophy, social theory, and art. Those who have tried to move Adorno into the twenty-first century could do so only by breaking up the original configuration of his theory and by shifting the perspective. After the initial attempt of the 1970s, the most important revisions came out of Critical Theory itself during the 1980s and 1990s. While Albrecht Wellmer sought to align Adorno's theory with Habermas's later social theory, Christoph Menke, partly in critical response to Wellmer, attempted to reinvigorate Adorno's theory through a comparison with Derrida. Wellmer's goal was to rescue Adorno by demonstrating his compatibility with Habermas, which implied that Adorno's theory needed adjustment. Menke, on the other hand, wanted to demonstrate that the core of Adorno's aesthetics would become more legible through a dialogue with poststructuralist thought. In both cases parts of Adorno's theory had to be eliminated as no longer viable. Placing the idea of reconciliation at the center of Adorno's theory, Wellmer underscores its ultimate utopian social dimension insofar as the Adornian dialectic of subjectivism and reification and the dialectic of aesthetic semblance and social communication are brought together without, as Wellmer maintains, reaching a synthesis. Adorno's antinomies, which are ultimately grounded in his nominalist position of a subject-oriented epistemology, can be overcome only by transforming his theory in the context of the intersubjective approach developed by Habermas in response to the aporias of the first generation of Critical Theory. More precisely, Wellmer hopes to reconcile Adorno's categories of semblance and truth as the core of his theory with Habermas's notion of communicative rationality. Yet this transformation results in a significant redefinition of the concept of reconciliation. While Adorno uses the concept to portray a possibility (in the future), Wellmer in the wake of Habermas suggests a "provocative latency of a process which begins with 'the transpositive aesthetic experience into symbolic or communicative action' (Jauss)."[16] This positional shift leads to, among other things, a reconsideration of the concept of truth in aesthetics. For Wellmer it becomes necessary to carefully distinguish between truth claims of different spheres. More specifically, Wellmer limits the truth claim of art (in clear contrast to Adorno) to a metaphorical sense. "Neither the truth nor truthfulness can be ascribed to the work of art in a non-metaphorical sense if we are understanding 'truth' and 'truthfulness' in terms of a pragmatically differentiated every-day concept of truth."[17] The discussion of truth in art therefore always requires a conversion of aesthetic experience into communicative action.

While Wellmer attempts a pragmatic transformation of Adorno's category of truth content in an effort to preserve the moment of reconciliation, Menke from the outset drops the social dimension in Adorno as external to the core of his aesthetic theory. In particular, Menke criticizes the concept of negation, which enabled Adorno to read artworks as performing social critique, as being too imprecise to establish a coherent social dimension of art. Still, Menke seeks to retain a revised form of the concept of negation, i.e. the very dialectic that Wellmer, following Habermas, wants to eliminate. By introducing the distinction between autonomy and sovereignty, Menke asserts: "The concept of aesthetic negativity is the key to understanding the twofold definition of modern art in Adorno, of art as both one of several autonomous discourses and a sovereign subversion of the rationality of all discourses."[18] While in this respect Menke remains close to the structure and aim of Adorno's theory, he strongly asserts the need for a fundamental reconstruction of this theory, since in his opinion a textual interpretation will not suffice to defend the Adornian stakes: "Instead, a systematic reconstruction of this theory's basic concepts needs to be undertaken in light of and with the help of other theoretical approaches."[19] De facto, "other approaches" means Derrida's version of deconstruction, and specifically the dialectic of aesthetic experience and critique of reason. Still, Menke, as did Wellmer before him, explicitly returns to a strictly philosophical discourse without regard to the performative aspect of Adorno's text. Ultimately, conceptual clarity is the standard by which Adorno's theory is judged, which means that Menke no longer takes seriously Adorno's anxieties about the principal status of a philosophical discourse. In this respect he follows Habermas, although he disagrees with him with regard to the function of modern art.[20]

As I have tried to show, the challenge to Adorno's *Aesthetic Theory* comes today from different directions. The "return to aesthetics" has shifted the emphasis away from the concept of critique by strongly asserting the unquestionable presence of aesthetic phenomena and simultaneously blocking a general suspicion against art. From a different perspective, philosophical aesthetics in both Germany and the United States, while attentive to the idea of critique, has returned to a more traditional mode of articulation and also reinforced the notion of a systematic treatment of aesthetic questions. In this context aesthetics is one among several fields of inquiry and can claim no special or even enhanced status. In other words, the stakes have been lowered, especially with regard to the role of art. Rereading Adorno's aesthetic theory in this intellectual environment requires a new set of hermeneutic rules. The least interesting approach would be to attempt to rescue his theory dogmatically, i.e. in terms of its explicitly stated opinions and positions. The result would be of mere historical interest. Of considerably greater interest would be an attempt to reconstruct Adorno's questions—to understand the reasons why he positioned himself vis-à-vis the philosophical tradition (Kant, Schelling, Hegel, Marx) the way he did and why he placed the emphasis in his thought on modern art. Finally, of crucial importance is the structure of Adorno's thought itself and its potential engagement with today's discussion. What Adorno said about Kant applies equally to his own work: the most intriguing and important aspects are the contradictions and aporias rather than the solutions presented as dogma.

To put it another way, the search for truth in Adorno is not about the verification or falsification of statements; rather, it comprises a form of critique that is both intrinsic and extrinsic, that works immanently through the text and accepts the challenges coming from the new intellectual environment.

In light of what I have argued above, this book can be seen as a defense of Adorno's aesthetic theory, but it is not an apology. The notion of critique, which is at the core of Adorno's thought, defines also the direction of this rereading. This mode of reading implies that the horizon of Adorno's theory cannot determine the horizon of our engagement with Adorno's oeuvre. Yet it also implies that the claimed return to the aesthetic is not beyond criticism. In fact, a return to Adorno, unfashionable as it may seem today, offers the opportunity for a critical assessment of the present discourse. There are two aspects in particular that deserve critical attention, namely *1* the immediacy of aesthetic experience (as something outside of history) *2* and the resistance to the concept of ideology as a key to the analysis of the aesthetic. A third issue, the revival of the beautiful as a central category, could also be mentioned. What these issues share is the attempt to restore the traditional role of aesthetics within both the philosophical discourse and the field of art criticism. In all these instances Adorno's theory is not well aligned to the claims of the new aesthetics, but it is also true that it does not dogmatically oppose them. Its dialectical character refuses simple and clearly stated answers, which makes it difficult, if not impossible, to lift ideas and concepts from *Aesthetic Theory* to use them in a different context. For this reason my study works within the boundaries of Adorno's theory, at least initially. I do not, however, offer an overview of Adorno's theory, which, given the existing critical literature, is no longer necessary.[21] Instead, I focus on specific issues within Adorno's theory and probe their direction and consistency in close contact with the text, keeping in mind that the performative aspect always needs to be taken into account.

This book is divided into two parts. In the first part I explore theoretical questions. In the second I examine Adorno's literary criticism; more precisely, I explore Adorno's engagement with specific works, authors, and historical periods. The theoretical chapters of part 1 approach *Aesthetic Theory* from different perspectives. In the first chapter I focus on the complex and volatile impact of Kant on Adorno; in the two following chapters I examine specific moments in *Aesthetic Theory,* namely the role of the ugly and the significance of the absolute for Adorno's late theory.

In chapter 1 I explore Adorno's encounter with Kant's Third Critique, which is reflected both in his repeated lecture courses on aesthetics and in *Aesthetic Theory.* Yet Adorno's interest in the *Critique of Judgment* cannot be isolated from his persistent return to Kant after World War II. While it would be misleading to think of Adorno as a Kantian (in fact, he keeps his distance from the neo-Kantians of the early twentieth century), he assigns Kant a crucial role, not only in the German intellectual tradition but in the development of modern thought *tout court.* Kant represents the strengths and weaknesses of early bourgeois philosophy, its methodical rigor and its philosophical naïveté. This ambiguity also applies to Adorno's evaluation of the Third Critique. Its grounding of aesthetics is perceived as pathbreaking, while its understanding of artworks is judged as ultimately unsatisfying compared with the theories of Schelling or Hegel. But what makes Kant's effort truly significant in Adorno's eyes is the epistemological implications—the fact that Kant grounded the quest for the judgment of taste by connecting it with the fundamental questions of the First Critique. The specificity and validity of the judgment of taste becomes epistemologically clear only through a comparison with other types of judgments. Put differently, what Adorno appreciates in Kant is his rigorous formalism, even though it is this same rigorous formalism that ultimately leads Adorno to reject Kant's type of aesthetic theory in favor of speculative thought and a form of aesthetics for which Hegel provided the (incomplete and problematic) example. This tension marks the treatment of these thinkers in the lecture courses as well as in *Aesthetic Theory.* However, the posthumous work gives more weight to Kant's formalism, especially the concept of aesthetic autonomy, than the lectures of 1958/59, which give priority to Hegel. While the lectures end with a severe critique of Kant, *Aesthetic Theory* maintains a precarious balance between Kant and Hegel. But even in the late 1950s Adorno is attracted to Kant's aesthetics by a number of features that set it apart from a psychological approach, among them the universality of the aesthetic judgment, the concept of natural beauty, and, last but not least, the concept of the sublime. Adorno's interpretation of the Kantian sublime (possibly the most significant element of Kant's theory for Adorno) openly transcends the boundaries of

Kant's thought by bringing together the sublime in nature and the experience of art, specifically the experience of romantic works. This unorthodox treatment of Kant is even more pronounced in *Aesthetic Theory,* where the Kantian elements of Adorno's thinking are more thoroughly integrated into his own discourse, which allows Adorno simultaneously to present Kant's theory as an outdated form of aesthetics, unable to do justice to modern art. Briefly stated, Kant's aesthetic judgment, insofar as it is characterized as disinterested pleasure, lacks the seriousness that autonomous art can claim. In the Third Critique there is no emphatic concept of truth content, which stands at the very center of *Aesthetic Theory.* Adorno does not consider as sufficient Kant's attempts to create a link between the artwork and the moral sphere. In this respect he is much closer to Hegel's notion of semblance. Still, for Adorno Kant's theory is indispensable because it sets the standard for the analysis of aesthetic phenomena. Adorno is selective in his reception of the Third Critique and certainly unorthodox in his interpretation, but there is no doubt that he finds in Kant's thought an essential resource for his own theoretical work.

My goal in the Kant chapter is to examine Adorno's complicated relationship to the philosophical tradition in the arena of aesthetics. Adorno assigns to Kant the role of the rigorous defender of aesthetic autonomy on the basis of his formalist and abstract approach to the judgment of taste. But seen from the core of Adorno's theory, this engagement with Kant (and even with Hegel) can be only a preliminary step, since Kant does not yet present an emphatic concept of the artwork, which Adorno needs in order to assert the larger meaning of art. Chapter 2, "The Ephemeral and the Absolute," is concerned precisely with the status of art in late modernism, specifically with Adorno's interpretation of this status. The point of departure is a reading of Adorno that stresses the continuity from *Dialectic of Enlightenment* to *Aesthetic Theory* with respect to the centrality of the concept of reason (*Vernunft*) and its defense vis-à-vis intellectual and social reification. This means that Adorno's aesthetic theory becomes a historically inflected theory of rationality applied to art. The dominant reading of Adorno's theory is to see it as a means to rescue modern art through the use of determinate negation, which establishes art as a critical counterpoint to social reification. Going against this reading, I explore Adorno's abandonment of this position in some sections of *Aesthetic Theory.* This reading is uncomfortable because it threatens the very concept of a meaningful function of art that philosophy is able to elucidate. This, however, also means that the truth content of the modern artwork appears in a different and more problematic light. It seems to be less certain than is commonly assumed. Of course, *Aesthetic Theory* is quite critical of Hegel's concept of the idea as the determining force of the artwork. By underscoring the enigmatic moment of the artwork, its utter resistance to conceptual transformation, Adorno puts up a block against the rational philosophical redemption of the artwork, although he simultaneously holds on to the official program of *Aesthetic Theory,* which proclaims the philosophical retrieval of the artwork. More than once, Adorno states that aesthetic experience must lead to and become philosophy, thereby shifting the truth content to philosophy. Yet at the same time, Adorno embraces the fragility of the artwork, its fleeting nature that remains hostile to the scrutiny of philosophy, which makes it difficult to attach the notion of truth to it. As a result, it can also be asserted that "artworks stand in the most extreme tension to their truth content" (AT 131). Hence given the demand for spiritualization that Adorno supports, the artwork cannot be contained in its aesthetic mode. There is the aspect of the absolute, a theological dimension that cannot be stated in positive terms. Thus Adorno maps a double trajectory for art: on the one hand, he stresses the special stakes of art, its autonomy vis-à-vis social reality; on the other, he contrasts the truth claims of art with the unknown and hidden absolute, thereby emphasizing the artwork's transiency. It is precisely the theological dimension (which to be sure must not be confused with affirmative religion) that sets limits to the immanent value of art, in particular to the notion of aesthetic reconciliation offered by romantic aesthetic theory. For *Aesthetic Theory* the fleeting character of art is a central insight that sets it apart.

While chapter 2 draws attention to complex configurations of the ephemeral nature of the artwork and its truth content, chapter 3, on the function of the ugly in Adorno's theory, centers on the multiple strands in which the notion of the ugly unfolds in *Aesthetic Theory*. The more limited role of the ugly in nineteenth-century aesthetics and the much greater importance of the ugly for a modernist aesthetics are relatively well known, but this by no means exhausts the meaning of the ugly in *Aesthetic Theory*. In the chapter I pay special attention to the link to the primitive and the archaic. Part of the interpretive work of the chapter consists of reconnecting this crucial strand with Adorno's understanding of classical aesthetics and his assessment of modern art. Most revealing in this respect is Adorno's argument against Stravinsky in *The Philosophy of Modern Music,* whom Adorno accuses of regression to classical tonality and of a dangerous flirtation with folk art and the primitive as a means of critiquing modern culture. Thus Adorno distinguishes two modes of the ugly, a positive formalist version utilized by Schoenberg (through the subversion of tonality) and a negative one in Stravinsky when it parades as a celebration of the primitive. Yet, as a closer examination of Adorno's work reveals, he was more deeply involved in the interpretation of primitive, non-European art than expected.

Decisive for the rediscovery of primitive art around 1900 in Germany was the work of the art historian Carl Einstein. Einstein's study of African sculpture (*Negerplastik*) celebrates this art form as authentic in its own right and in opposition to the European canon as well as European aesthetics (the beautiful). At the same time, Einstein highlights legitimate connections between primitive and modern European art, for instance in the case of cubism.[22] Thus he creates a bridge between "primitive" and modern art that Adorno views with suspicion when evaluating Stravinsky's music. Yet the problem of the ugly in archaic art returns in *Aesthetic Theory* when Adorno attempts to differentiate between ritual and art by placing the emphasis on the moment of subjective expression. For Adorno, it is not the ugly characteristics of archaic works that create a problem for the aesthetic but their cultic environment. Art begins when it frees itself from the cultic element "by a leap" (AT 286) that both transforms and preserves the cultic moment. Thus the strong return of the ugly in modern art is more than a critique of conventional beauty at the center of classicism; it also signals the strength of the repressed cultic moment. But the legitimacy of the "marks of the frightening" (AT 287) is not in doubt. The return of horror in modern art stands in for the return of horror in actual history. At the same time, the presence of archaic magic in modern art does not, Adorno asserts, completely determine the work as a whole and certainly not its truth content, which is always open to philosophical inquiry. It remains an important element of modern art insofar as it calls into question the illusion of the beautiful. The parallel to Nietzsche is hard to overlook, but one has to underscore the difference at the same time. Most decidedly Adorno does not favor the return of myth or an aesthetic built on myth. Rather, he admits the archaic and ugly to the realm of art as a reminder of past and present horror. The ugly, in other words, draws attention to the critical function of modern art.

In the two chapters of part 2 I turn to Adorno's engagement with literature. It is important to note, however, that I do not see Adorno's literary essays as mere applications of his aesthetic theory. In fact, a close analysis will show that his literary criticism and *Aesthetic Theory* do not completely match. Because of their unique *Gestalt* as essays, the literary articles develop their own theoretical direction that is close to, but also in tension with, *Aesthetic Theory*. Moreover, the specific occasion for which they were written determined their style and their level of theoretical complexity, especially in instances when a polemical intention influenced the tone and the argument, as it becomes apparent in Adorno's confrontation with Brecht, Lukács, and Sartre. The explicit opposition to different theoretical positions, especially when seen as hostile to his own thought, forces Adorno to sharpen his own argument, but it also allows the conceptions and categories of the opponent to enter his ideas with unexpected consequences.

The tension between Adorno's theoretical work and his literary criticism becomes also visible in the tensions between his social roles as academic teacher and as a critic in the public sphere. While he clearly stood out as a progressive force in the German academy during the 1950s and early 1960s and was recognized as such by the students, his role as a literary critic was more ambiguous. From the perspective of the young generation of postwar authors, organized in the *Gruppe 47,* he could be seen as part of or leaning toward the conservative camp dominated by critics like Friedrich Sieburg, the editor of the literary section of the *Frankfurter Allgemeine Zeitung,* Karl Korn, and Günter Blöcker. What he shared with these journalists was the emphatic defense of aesthetic autonomy against the notion of political commitment. Moreover, his critical interventions against Brecht and Lukács in the context of the Cold War might also suggest proximity to the conservative forces in the early Federal Republic. Adorno was quite aware of his distance from the literary and critical trends of postwar Germany. In his 1953 radio essay on literary criticism he reflected on the situation of the émigré who returns to his home country after a long period of absence. What irritated Adorno most about the postwar literary configuration was the lack of a critical public sphere comparable to that of Weimar. This critique, anticipating the later work of Habermas, shows

Adorno's position in a different light, because his polemic was potentially
also directed against the opinion leaders on the right for whom the restoration of cultural values was of paramount importance.

Within the institutional organization of postwar literary criticism in
West Germany, Adorno remained ultimately an isolated figure without
firm attachment to the three major camps. His concept of critique, as it
was forcefully developed in his essay "Cultural Criticism and Society,"[23]
precluded any attachment to the conservative camp, which was the target
of his intervention, but also distanced him from the preferences of the liberal camp for abstract norms. More promising was the partial proximity to
the New Left of the 1960s. Yet even in this case, the demand of the young
generation for political commitment in the sphere of art aroused Adorno's
suspicion. Again, Adorno found himself mischaracterized as a liberal intellectual who misreads the historical development, as for instance when
Hans Magnus Enzensberger emphatically labeled the older generation of
left intellectuals (including Adorno) as completely out of touch with the
recent political development of the Federal Republic. For Enzensberger
the political impotence of Critical Theory had become apparent.[24] The
tenor of Adorno's late work, especially *Aesthetic Theory,* was influenced
by the confrontation with the New Left, although Adorno resisted the use
of open polemic. By the time of his death, in 1969, the consensus of public
opinion in West Germany was that Adorno's discourse no longer grasped
the new situation and that his philosophy of art in particular did not reflect
contemporary aesthetic issues. It was more than a decade before this sense
of untimeliness disappeared, and it took another decade for the English-
speaking world to take notice of Adorno's posthumous work.

The two chapters of part 2 follow separate and diverging trajectories in
engaging with Adorno's literary criticism. While chapter 4 examines the
theoretical problem of realism and representation in Adorno, chapter 5
focuses on a canonical German author, namely Goethe, and the controversial role of the concept of classicism in German literary history. In each
case the complex argument leads Adorno beyond the strict confines of his
theory. From the perspective of *Aesthetic Theory,* the problem of realism is,
strictly speaking, a minor issue, having no significant role to play either in
normative or descriptive terms. Adorno's Goethe essay, on the other hand,
engages a category that is hardly compatible with the modernist teaching
of *Aesthetic Theory.* Classicism invokes notions of tradition and canonicity,

both of them regarded as highly problematic in Adorno's late work. Still, Adorno's essay on Goethe's play *Iphigenia in Tauris* is anything but a polemic. Polemical overtones are strictly limited to academic Goethe criticism, and even in this case Adorno makes explicit and implicit exceptions, acknowledging contributions that at least approximate his own critical standards. At the same time, Adorno left no doubt that his essay (originally a public lecture) was meant as a public intervention, namely an attempt to develop a self-reflective critical concept of classicism that subverts its own premises. One rather unexpected aspect of Adorno's essay is its praise of Goethe's attachment to the court of Weimar, the very biographical decision in Goethe's life that earned him the hostility of progressive critics. The other surprising aspect is its form of reading. While Adorno in "On Lyric Poetry and Society" had insisted on a formalist approach to poetry,[25] his engagement with the play relies heavily on elements of its content, for instance the constellation of the characters as well as specific moments of the plot. Even biographical facts are taken into consideration to demonstrate the extraordinary nature of Goethe's play that in Adorno's reading ultimately subverts the very notion of a cultural hegemony of Europe. For this reason it is Thoas, the barbarian king, and not Iphigenia, the Greek priestess, who has the last word, not only in the play but also in Adorno's reinterpretation of Goethe's critique of cultural imperialism. By shifting the critical emphasis from the Greeks to Thoas, Adorno lifts the drama out of its original German historical context, and opens up a dimension of meaning that calls into question the notion of cultural superiority conventionally linked to the concept of German classicism without dismissing it as pure ideology.

While Adorno's Goethe essay was primarily concerned with the question of the national literary tradition, his critical assessment of the concept of realism, obviously a familiar arena of academic criticism, widens the scope, selecting its examples from European literature with an emphasis, as one might expect, on the French nineteenth-century novel. Two short essays on Balzac offer Adorno an opportunity for a reconsideration of realism. Although his name is never mentioned in those essays, it is difficult to overlook the unacknowledged presence of Lukács, who is the opponent of Adorno's reassessment. Lukács's heavy emphasis on the critical significance of bourgeois realism can be seen as the initial provocation, a provocation to which Adorno finally responded in "Extorted Reconciliation," one of Adorno's sharpest polemics against an author whose early work had left a permanent imprint on his thought. In this confrontation the question of realism was of course only a minor issue compared with Adorno's defense of modernism. Still, the critique of Lukács's *Wider den mißverstandenen Realismus* (1958, in English as *Realism in Our Time*) obliges Adorno to sketch a concept of realism, respectively a theory of literary representation. More specifically, the question is: How does the nineteenth-century novel represent the social world?

As one would expect, Adorno resists Lukács's notion of the novel as a reflection of social reality because it violates the concept of determinate negation. Put differently, Adorno is unwilling to accept the concept of a simple parallel between social reality, as the sociologist might define it, and reality as it is presented in a realist novel. For him, therefore, the function of the nineteenth-century novel is not to accurately portray the social life of that time. Of course, we have to remind ourselves that Lukács equally rejected such a conception as mere superficial imitation. In his view the actual power of the great nineteenth-century realists was grounded in their ability to transcend mere imitation and make visible instead the deeper structure of the social world narrated in the novels. Still, in the wake of Marx and Engels, Lukács was holding on to the possibility of an aesthetic reproduction of the social world in which we live by specific artistic means that allow an aesthetically and theoretically correct reflection of reality. In fact, Lukács would claim that aesthetic reflection reveals a deeper meaning than the efforts of the social sciences with the exception of Marxian theory. Everything depended, of course, on the correct method of literary production.

Fully aware of Lukács's approach, Adorno chooses a different path in his essays on Balzac. While ultimately not denying the truth of Balzac's novels, he forcefully distances himself from the conventional understanding of these works as realistic and brings into the foreground elements that undermine the established reception, which Lukács, although in a more sophisticated model, affirms. Reading Balzac's *Lost Illusions,* Adorno points to a pattern of overdetermined social connections, calling it a delusion of references (*Beziehungswahn*), in which the pathology of nineteenth-century reality becomes legible. At the same time, Adorno very much insists (in proximity to Lukács) that Balzac in his novels discloses social structures of his period, i.e. the period of the early phase of high capitalism. This, however, means that the problem of representation cannot be avoided, and without using the term, Adorno's Balzac essays very much explore the link between presentation (style, configuration of characters, importance of objects and social institutions) and social reality. Following Marxian theory, Adorno credits Balzac with a higher degree of truth by creating a fictional world that follows its own laws, thereby precisely disclosing the social totality of the early nineteenth century. In short, the concept of representation enters Adorno's theory through the backdoor, especially in his readings of Balzac that are motivated, against Lukács, by an antirealist bias. Nonetheless, the problem of representation of a reality outside the artwork is not only acknowledged by Adorno but rather carefully examined in these essays. What is avoided, to be sure, is the heavy hand of the Lukácsian reflection theory.

Against this backdrop, the strident polemic against Lukács in "Extorted Reconciliation" (1958) appears in a different light. Despite the unforgiving attack on Lukács and his concept of realism (especially socialist realism), one cannot overlook a common ground when it comes to the notion of literary representation, which logically presupposes the distinction between an independently existing outside reality and the aesthetic world in the artwork. In fact, in Balzac's literary representations of French society Adorno perceives a totality that escapes scientific analysis. Compared with the orientation of *Aesthetic Theory,* the prominence of representation in some of Adorno's literary essays comes as a surprise, for in his strictly theoretical work Adorno plays down the importance of such a model. Specifically, in "On Lyric Poetry and Society," where Adorno presents a theory of the sociological analysis of poetry, he strictly rejects a representation model. Instead, here as in *Aesthetic Theory,* Adorno emphasizes the moment of negation and the rigorous exclusion of social facts from the poem: the poem does not reflect the social conditions. The tension between the Balzac essays and his theoretical position point to the essayistic mode of Adorno's thought. Systemic consistency is ultimately less important than the spirit of rigorous critical thinking that strives to unfold its radical possibilities.

Still, it is by no means impossible to establish a theoretical frame that encompasses both the emphasis on expression in the lyric poetry essay and the focus on representation in the Balzac essays, even though Adorno did not attempt to work this out in purely theoretical terms in these pieces. However, the long section "Society" in *Aesthetic Theory* clarifies Adorno's understanding of a critical sociology of art and also, in nonpolemical terms, the difference between his approach and that of Lukács. In terms of its conceptual apparatus, the society section is surprisingly indebted to Marxian thought. Returning to the dialectic of forces of production and relations of production, Adorno places the emphasis on the forces of production. More specifically, he examines aesthetic production not as linked to the relations of production but to the forces of production, thereby dismissing a reflection model, which determines Lukács's later theory. The gain of Adorno's interpretation of Marxist theory is a higher degree of freedom in defining the social role of art. Seen as pure force of production (*reine Produktionskraft,* ÄT 335), aesthetic production stands outside the fixed relations of production. As Adorno notes, "Artworks are the plenipotentiaries of things that are no longer distorted by exchange, profit, and the false claim of degraded humanity" (AT 227). Therefore, compared with the notion of the primary significance of the forces of production, the difference between representation and expression becomes secondary. While Adorno shuns the conventional conception of realism, without using the term, he leaves room for the category of representation, which brings him closer to Lukács again than he is ready to admit. Although this may appear surprising in light of his fierce polemic against *Realism in Our Time,* we have to remind ourselves that Adorno always acknowledged and remained loyal to the method of *The Theory of the Novel.* While this early work of Lukács is indifferent to the concept of realism, its philosophical schema of history contains the notion of representation.

The relevance of Adorno's philosophy of history for his conception of representation, already visible in the polemic against Lukács, becomes critical in *Aesthetic Theory.* In the discussion of the novel form, in particular its modernist version, Adorno emphasizes the problem of meaning (*Sinn*). Meaning is connected to representation but not constructed as imitation of sensual facts. In the history of the novel, as Adorno constructs it, its final stage in the works of Beckett has reduced the sensual world to a minimum, raising the question of whether meaning can be generated at all. But precisely this legitimate concern demonstrates the nexus between the concept of representation and the notion of meaning. The reduction of the phenomenal world in late modernist novels becomes an index of the decreased meaning of this world. This also defines their truth content. However, the truth content of the artwork rests on its autonomy, i.e. its clear separation from empirical reality. Therefore the model of the monad seems to prohibit the notion of representation. It is critical to realize that this is not the case, since the monad, while windowless, already contains the outside world in itself as the other. Thus Adorno's definition of the artwork as a monad makes representation not only possible but necessary to disclose meaning and articulate the truth content, which requires but also transcends formal organization (*Stimmigkeit*). While Adorno consistently battles reflection theory he also confronts a solipsistic notion of art, the idea that artworks can be explained only as subjective expression.

Part I

1

Human Freedom and the Autonomy of Art

The Legacy of Kant

If Adorno had died in 1949 instead of 1969, he would be remembered today primarily as the coauthor, with Max Horkheimer, of *Dialectic of Enlightenment*. That is, he would be remembered as a fierce critic of the European Enlightenment including Immanuel Kant. What Adorno and Horkheimer had to say about Kant in this pathbreaking study was mostly negative and hostile. Kant makes an appearance in the second chapter, along with the Marquis de Sade, where the authors want to demonstrate that the sage of Königsberg is very much part of a trajectory that began in the seventeenth century and ultimately resulted in the triumph of fascism in Europe. The dialectic of the Enlightenment consists precisely of the intimate but obscured connection between rationalism and fascism. In the development of modern philosophy from Bacon to Carnap, Kant is part of the transformation of reason into positivist rationality, which is the other side of the same coin better known as the mythic irrationalism of fascism. In a more conventional historical reconstruction (for instance that of Ernst Cassirer) Kant would have been evoked as the rationalist opponent of this irrationalism, as the defender of humanism and progress. Instead, Adorno and Horkheimer saw Kant as part of the very reduction of reason that prepared the way for the ultimate historical catastrophe.

Some of the same ideas recur in Adorno's later writings. There are occasional moments when Adorno emphasizes his distance from Kant, a certain impatience with Kant's *Bürgerlichkeit* and lack of radical philosophical reflection, but for the most part Adorno's assessment of Kant is much more positive in his postwar writings. This remarkable return to Kant is by no means limited to a specific field of philosophy. Rather, Adorno's renewed engagement with Kant is equally concerned with his epistemology, his moral philosophy, and his aesthetic theory, which will be at the center of my analysis. It is important to grasp the broad spectrum of Adorno's rereading of Kant as well as the interconnectedness of his attempts to revive the interest in Kant in various fields of philosophy.

My intention here is not to dwell on the reasons for Adorno's surprising return to Kant. The new engagement was probably related, at least in part, to his teaching obligations at the University of Frankfurt. He was expected to offer lecture courses and seminars that would cover the German philosophical tradition. For instance, he offered one lecture course in 1959 on Kant's *Critique of Pure Reason* and another one in 1963 entitled "Problems in Moral Philosophy," which focused largely on Kant. To a lesser degree his lectures on metaphysics (1965) and on aesthetics (1958/59) dealt with Kant's thought as eminently relevant for the present. If a critical reassessment of the German intellectual tradition was at the center of Adorno's postwar pedagogy in Frankfurt, Kant clearly occupied a prominent place, rivaled only by Hegel, who also received Adorno's renewed attentions. The full extent of his engagement with Kant became visible only more recently when his posthumous writings, including his lectures, were published.

Although Adorno's rereadings by no means signaled a dogmatic return to a Kantian framework, even a cursory review of these writings betrays a significant change in Adorno's thinking, one that occurred after his return to Germany in 1950. Now Kant appears as a central figure with power to restore confidence in the German tradition. At the very least, Adorno considered it vital to inform a new generation of students of the philosophical importance of Kant. But there's more to it than that. It is clear that Adorno did not mean to return to the neo-Kantians of the early twentieth century. While they are sometimes mentioned (among them his own teacher Hans

Cornelius), their positions are not validated. As we will see, it becomes important for Adorno to reframe the approach to Kant by marking his distance from the neo-Kantians. This effort is particularly strong in his lectures on Kant's First Critique, where he has to navigate carefully between the latent positivism of a neo-Kantian reading and a radical metaphysical reading of Heidegger that is closer to (but not identical with) his own efforts. Precisely for this reason the distance from Heidegger has to be underlined.

Adorno's lectures on Kant's *Critique of Pure Reason* in particular demonstrate his intent to explore aspects of Kantian thought that the neo-Kantians had neglected or pushed into the background as no longer relevant. Again and again, Adorno explains to his audience that he is not interested in a dogmatic introduction or a pure reconstruction of Kant's epistemological position. His discussion of Kant's epistemology is intended to recover the foundations of Kant's thought, foundations that would be equally relevant for a sustained discussion of ethics and aesthetics. For Adorno, the essential Kant is articulated in the First Critique. When it comes to aesthetic theory, Kant's *Critique of Judgment* is recognized as an important text, but ultimately not as important as Hegel's aesthetics. In other words, for Adorno's own aesthetic theory the insights of Kant's First Critique turn out to be more valuable and demanding than Kant's discussion of the artwork. In the final analysis, Adorno fundamentally disagrees with Kant's approach to art, which means that he can make only selective use of Kant's Third Critique.

For the reasons mentioned above, any discussion of Adorno's postwar reading of Kant has to begin with the *Critique of Pure Reason*. In this chapter, however, I will restrict myself to a reconstruction of Adorno's approach and a discussion of the central themes. It should be noted at the outset that Adorno is much less interested in Kant's solutions than Kant's questions and the internal contradictions that are the result of addressing these questions. Put differently, he means to examine Kant's response to the problems he inherited from his predecessors (i.e. the German metaphysical tradition and the radical skepticism of Hume) as options that determined the later history of philosophy. By later history of philosophy Adorno means the idealism of Fichte, Schelling, and Hegel on the one hand, and the positivism of scientific philosophy on the other (which, by the way, means that he implicitly acknowledges twentieth-century logical positivists as legitimate heirs of Kant). The tension between these contradicting positions is, as Adorno insists, the enigma of Kant, the reason why we have to return to his texts. His rereading of the First Critique especially explores the metacritical level, because a reading at this level enables the reader to understand the structure of Kant's thought rather than the mere truth and legitimacy of certain positions. For this reason Adorno proceeds selectively and is highly unorthodox in his own emphasis.

Adorno is aware that even among his students familiarity with Kant cannot be taken for granted after the Third Reich. Therefore, one important task of his lectures was to lay the ground for a critical reception of Kant's epistemology, but he also understood that such grounding must avoid continuing the neo-Kantian interpretation of Kant. Adorno describes the task in the following manner: "So what I would like to do is to retranslate this philosophy from a codified, ossified system back into the kind of picture that results from a sustained X-ray examination," and he continues by insisting that Kant should be understood as a force field (*Kraftfeld*) where the careful reader finds extraordinary forces of experience (*Erfahrung*) behind the abstract concepts.[1] By emphasizing the concept of experience Adorno prepares a double move: he breaks up the conventional history of philosophy, which is constructed along the lines of concepts and ideas, and he creates a stronger link between philosophy and related cultural experiences and institutions—for instance, music or literature. Thus Adorno is not simply attempting to restore the lost authority of Kant's First Critique; he means to explicate the problems Kant faced at the level of concrete historical experiences.

For Adorno the *Critique of Pure Reason* turns out to be the decisive turning point in modern history; namely, the point when certain fundamental metaphysical questions (e.g. the proof of God) are critically questioned in such a manner that they are subsequently removed from serious philosophical inquiry—even though they may remain central issues in other areas of inquiry such as modern theology (Karl Barth), where the sharp contrast between knowledge and faith (*Glaube*) points back to Kant's epistemology. With Kant, Adorno insists, reason reaches the point where it systematically reflects on its own use and its limitations but not yet on its own preconditions. In this respect, Adorno suggests, Kant remains naive. Kant's famous opening question, "How are synthetic judgments *a priori* possible?" presupposes that synthetic judgments are a priori possible, a ground that remains unquestioned. This unquestioned ground in Kant is precisely what Adorno wants to explore—although his goal is not to refute and dismiss Kant but to problematize philosophy.

While Adorno respects and praises Kant's epistemology for its technical thoroughness, his lectures are ultimately not interested in technical thoroughness. Not unlike Heidegger, Adorno searches for and critically explains the metaphysical ideas that Kant means to assert by demonstrating the limits of reason. Yet this interest must not be misunderstood as a simple return to the metaphysical tradition. Adorno's analysis of reason (in the wake of *Dialectic of Enlightenment*) focuses on the moment of logical identity, the most basic move of philosophy that has remained intact since Aristotle. As Adorno notes, it does not occur to Kant to question the rules of formal logic (KC 14). If critical philosophy is assigned the task of questioning the presuppositions of knowledge, then the concept of reason cannot be treated as a given and becomes ultimately uncertain as well. However, Adorno rejects this quest for the ultimate ground as an illusion (*Fundierungswahn*) and therefore appreciates Kant's more modest program to establish the proper use and the limits of reason, although this appreciation remains somewhat ambivalent, since there are also those moments when he distances himself from Kant's thought as undialectical. For Adorno, Kant's rigorous philosophical honesty comes to the fore in the sustained tension between the elements that move toward the unity of reason and the acceptance of the "consciousness of the heterogeneous, the block, the limit" (KC 18). These two sides are working toward and against each other (*sich aneinander abarbeiten*).[2]

Adorno does not follow the Kantian text in his lectures, but organizes them around a number of themes that he considers defining. Among them we encounter (a) metaphysics, (b) the nature of the transcendental, (c) the subject/object relationship, (d) constituens and constitution, and (e) the limit of knowledge. In my remarks I will focus exclusively on Adorno's reflections on metaphysics in Kant and the problem of constitution. It goes without saying that my treatment can only be schematic. Adorno does not show much interest in restating the obvious: that Kant pursues a thorough critique of the older metaphysical tradition in the wake of Hume's skepticism. Instead, Adorno underscores the methodological and formal aspect in Kant's efforts to define the limits of understanding (*Verstand*). In his fifth lecture Adorno explicates the peculiar nature of Kant's critique. It does not simply prohibit metaphysical statements or take a position on the importance of the concept of God. As Adorno points out, "Direct propositions of this kind are prohibited here because the *Critique of Pure Reason* is concerned not with objects as such, not even the objects of metaphysics, but simply, as Kant puts it, with our faculty to obtain knowledge of such objects" (KC 47). Kant does not dogmatically deny the existence of God, as did the atheists for instance. He merely demonstrates the impossibility of such judgments. Adorno points to the peculiar notion that one can critique metaphysical positions as rationally unfounded and at the same time one can read this critique as enabling a different form of metaphysics. In the later part of the same lecture it becomes clear that Adorno looks at Kant from the vantage point of his successors and critics such as Fichte and Hegel, who, encouraged by the implications of Kantian thought, rescued the concept of speculation from Kant's negative verdict.

As much as Adorno appreciates the Kantian type of formal critique, ultimately he is not satisfied with Kant's method and its results. From Adorno's perspective, Kant's philosophy remains incomplete because its author refused (on formal, rational grounds) to transcend the sphere of experience. Against this position Adorno refers to Hegel in order to demonstrate the need for speculative thought. Hegel, as Adorno insists, does not deny the validity of Kant's analysis (the contradictions of reason when it transcends experience) but he gives it a new and different "value" (KC 49). The contradiction of limited experimental and unlimited speculative knowledge is the powerful motor for the creation of knowledge: "such contradictions are actually the organ, the medium, in which what we think of as knowledge is constituted" (KC 49).

At this point the deeper motivation for Adorno's inquest becomes visible. Kant's First Critique as the paradigmatic modern model that defines the possibility of rational knowledge gives him the opportunity to explore the nature of philosophical thought, its deeper aspects that remain inaccessible in an orthodox interpretation that simply follows Kant's argument. Kant's argument is of interest to Adorno primarily as evidence for the problematic of modern thought. Differently put, Adorno does not present himself as a Kantian or want to persuade his audience to become Kantians. Rather, the study of the *Critique of Pure Reason* is the path to critical thought. The aim of his teaching is what he calls "its hidden content and its hidden puzzles" (KC 52). If one then raises the question what the hidden content of Kant's philosophy could be, Adorno introduces the concept of autonomy of reason, the fact that it is only reason itself that can question control and justify itself (KC 54–55, KK 87).

Not surprisingly, therefore, Adorno returns to this problematic in those later lectures that deal with the tension between *constituens* and *constitutum*, the moment of constituting the object and the given object that we find as already constituted. When Kant discusses the process of understanding, he stresses, as Adorno insists, the subjective side, the consciousness of the subject (KC 140, KK 212); in other words, he underscores the moment of freedom and autonomy rather than the impact of the object on the consciousness. For Adorno, the proof for this thesis is Kant's discussion of causality, especially his engagement with Hume.[3] Using Kant's definition of causality (CPR 125 = A 91, B 124), Adorno argues that this definition performs a circle and then maintains that "causality in Kant must be understood in terms of this synthesis and not in terms of something inherent in objects themselves" (KC 141). In other words, in Adorno's reading causality is grounded in consciousness rather than the relationship between objects.

One might expect that Adorno would take this feature of Kant's theory as proof of the autonomy of the subject, but this is not the case. Instead, Adorno laments the distance between subject and object, the fact that Kant's concepts are imposed on the objects by the subject rather than unfolding within the objects. Thus universality in Kant is, according to Adorno, produced "simply by the constitution of the human subject that comprehends things in this way and no other. It stands in stark contrast to the objective concept of reason such as can be found with exemplary force in traditional philosophy in the thought of Plato. For Plato ascribes a rationality to things themselves" (KC 143).

The contrast between the Kantian subject and its power of synthesis (which is purely formal) and the concept of reason (*logos*) of the tradition is more than a mere historical point. The real question for Adorno is: How can the universality of conceptual understanding be constituted? Who or what is the *constituens*? For Kant the answer is clear: the transcendental subject. Adorno, however, probes this answer and suspects that a consensus of all human beings is actually based on an aggregation of empirical subjects. Kant's transcendental subject is, Adorno argues, the result of abstraction from empirical subjects. Hence, behind the abstract subject we find an empirical subject. But, of course, for Kant this empirical subject is merely constituted by the transcendental subject. Adorno rejects Kant's procedure as circular and opposes Kant's position because it refuses to acknowledge the important role of the collective empirical subject. In technical terms, Adorno holds that Kant should have treated the concept of the subject as a *Reflexionsbegriff* rather than a logical presupposition. More important, Adorno fundamentally questions subjective idealism, treating it as theoretically possible but as philosophically unsatisfactory. This critique includes Kant's successors, especially Fichte, who tried to overcome Kant's problem by creating a "gigantic, absolute subject which encompasses both these concepts—*constituens* and *constitutum*" (KC 147). Against this position Adorno maintains a dialectical approach in which the constituent moment cannot be thought without the constituted moment, which is supposed to be constituted by the constituting subject. At the same time, Adorno underscores that a mere reversal of the two moments—i.e. a dogmatic materialist position—would be equally unsatisfactory. In both instances Adorno would speak of a dogmatic *Fundierungswahn*.

As we have seen, Adorno's interpretation of Kant's First Critique is not defined in terms of a reconstruction of Kant's epistemological position; it has broader ramifications that come into the foreground when Adorno engages the Kantian text. Obviously, there is no intent to return to Kant or to use Kant's epistemology as a basis for a new system. At the same time, there can be no doubt about the seriousness of Adorno's engagement. This insight leads us to the question: What is the purpose? There is no simple answer. To some extent, as we have already seen, his efforts are related to the needs of the German students at that time to familiarize themselves with their philosophical tradition. But there is clearly more involved. Kant is assigned a special place for two reasons: on the one hand, his articulation of the fundamental philosophical problems is seen as especially powerful and persuasive because Kant does not try to cover up the tensions and contradictions of his thought. On the other, his writings on particular topics, for instance ethics and aesthetics, are still of relevance today. In his last work, *Aesthetic Theory,* Adorno repeatedly expresses his sense of indebtedness to Kant, in a more pronounced way in fact, than in his lectures of 1958/59, where he explicitly defines himself as a student of Hegel's aesthetic theory.

After Adorno's return to Germany in 1950, he offered his lecture course on aesthetic theory in frequent intervals, the first time in 1950. He repeated the course in the winter term of 1950/51, and once again in the winter term of 1955/56. When he offered the course once more in the winter term of 1958/59 his lectures were recorded. These recordings became the basis for the book edition (2009). At this point, Adorno was already firmly committed to a book-length manuscript on aesthetics and drafted the first introduction (which was published in 1970 as a supplement to the first edition of *Aesthetic Theory*). The comparison of the old introduction with the lectures makes it evident that Adorno used the lecture course to advance his project by trying out ideas in a public forum. Compared with the almost completed text of the book, the lectures of 1958/59 are still tentative, without the same intellectual and linguistic density that characterizes the later writings. Still, many of the basic elements and themes are already in evidence, among them the tension between a Kantian and a Hegelian approach. However, in the lectures the priority is given to Hegel, whom Adorno acknowledges as a major influence on his own theoretical position. The frequent substantive references to Hegel, especially in the second half of the lecture course, are evidence of a considerable affinity of Adorno to Hegel that is based on shared predispositions. By contrast, the relationship to Kant is more distant. Toward the end of the course he offers a fundamental critique of Kant's approach, a critique so severe that one wonders why Kant is given much attention at all. Kant is reproached for his subjectivism, for discussing the artwork from the perspective of its reception, i.e. the judgment of taste, rather than real involvement that develops the concepts from the inside of the artwork. In other words, Kant's judgment of taste, although universal in its claim, remains extrinsic and thereby fails to disclose the essence of the artwork.

Adorno's resistance to Kant's *Critique of Judgment* has two levels. On a commonsense level, Adorno feels that Kant is indeed too close to the "wide-spread vulgar opinion…that Kant has tried to reduce aesthetics in general to subjective categories, that is to sensations."[4] Against this criticism Adorno is ready to defend Kant with the argument that the vulgar approach overlooks the moment of differentiation in Kant's concept of the subject (and subjectivity). But even if one grants that Kant consistently differentiates between the empirical and the transcendental judgments, his understanding of aesthetic judgments, Adorno claims, remains unsatisfactory. For Adorno the deficiency is a result of Kant's epistemology in general, namely the claim "that reality should be constituted in general by the interplay of sensuous data and forms of consciousness, be it either the so-called forms of 'perception' or the so-called categorical forms through which we constitute objects" (Ä 320). The subject required for this process is the transcendental subject. In the sphere of art, however, we are not dealing with a transcendental but an empirical subject, both on the side of aesthetic production and reception. In other words, in Adorno's terminology the realm of art is the constituted rather than the constituent moment. Hence the aesthetic subject, the subject that can experience artworks, cannot be identical with the transcendental subject; it is in the words of Adorno "a subject saturated with historical experience" (Ä 321). In short, the Kantian assumption that the aesthetic object is perceived by a pure subject capable of universal judgments misses the actual reality of aesthetic phenomena. For this reason Adorno concludes that it is impossible to ground aesthetic theory in the subject alone: "the impossibility of grounding aesthetics in mere subjectivity" (Ä 321). Only an objective turn can overcome this deficit. As Adorno emphasized in his critique of Kant's epistemology, a dialectical understanding of the subject-object relationship is needed.

Given Adorno's severe critique of Kant's approach to aesthetic phenomena, which would of course include Kant's theory of taste, it is difficult to understand why Adorno gives Kant's Third Critique considerable amount of attention. Still, there are a number of themes and concepts that remain of great importance to Adorno, although he rejects Kant's basic position. First of all, Adorno is in complete agreement with Kant that aesthetic judgments must be more than mere individual statements based on the sensibility of the individual recipient. The dignity and essence of the artwork requires more than a sensuous response. For this reason even today Kant's analysis of the beautiful remains an essential aspect of aesthetic theory. In addition, there are two themes in the Third Critique that attract Adorno in particular, namely the concepts of natural beauty and the sublime. Finally, Adorno, possibly in the wake of Schiller, pays attention to Kant's concept of play (*Spiel*).

Of course, Adorno is completely aware that nineteenth-century aesthetics, beginning with Hegel, eliminated the concept of natural beauty from aesthetic theory, as he is also aware that Kant restricts the concept of the sublime to nature. It is not too difficult to grasp the link between these two themes. Adorno means to problematize the categorical separation between nature and the work of art, although his own theory underscores the fact that artworks are produced and are therefore part of social labor. In both instances it is the inner organization of Adorno's theory that encourages the specific engagement with Kant, notwithstanding fundamental disagreements.

How important the concept of natural beauty is for Adorno becomes evident in his lecture course, where he begins in the second lecture to explicate the topic, and develops it more extensively in the third. In order to recuperate the beauty of nature Adorno has to confront Hegel, for whom, because he insists on the spiritual essence of art, natural beauty receives a low priority (Ä 40). Given the contrast between spirit and beauty, which is merely attached to the objects in nature and lacks the dignity of artworks, since for Hegel these are linked to the realm of ideas, Adorno is by no means averse to this argument; in fact, he himself adopts it in a differentiated manner, but he opposes the suppression of nature that he finds in Hegel's aesthetic. Why? For one thing, Adorno is skeptical of the "privileged position of man" (Ä 41) implied in Hegel's position; moreover, as he argues in the third lecture, he emphasizes the significance of reconciliation with nature as a vital theme. This aesthetic recovery of nature, however, has little to do with a sentimental cult of nature in late romanticism. Rather, it is the ephemeral aspect of nature, its lack of conceptual clarity, that attracts Adorno (Ä 48). For Kant, whose transcendental subject is purely formal, there is no need to downgrade nature as antispiritual. In aesthetic terms, artworks are not categorically more valuable than natural objects. Adorno would hardly support Kant's claim that an immediate interest in the beauty of nature is an index of a good soul (*gute Seele*) and that one could discern a moral feeling if this interest becomes habitual, but he is engaged in a reevaluation of nature as an aesthetic object outside the realm of social production. Whereas Kant insists on the close link between natural beauty and a moral habitus/attitude,[5] Adorno underscores the link between natural beauty and the experience of potential reconciliation. It is not accidental that Adorno uses Benjamin's concept of the aura (*Aura*) to describe this experience (Ä 45). At the same time, we have to note that the concept of an aesthetic experience leads Adorno back to the artwork, which means that he denies the strict separation of artwork and nature, at least in the discussion of aesthetic experience.

Adorno's strong interest in the sublime demonstrates this dissolution of the boundary between art and nature. His reading of Kant's theory of the sublime deliberately transcends the Kantian frame by extending the concept to artworks, while Kant thinks of the sublime exclusively in terms of natural phenomena. Furthermore, Kant differentiates carefully between natural beauty and the sublime as a distinction between form and size (*Größe*), quality and quantity, while Adorno de-emphasizes the distinction. Similarly, Kant underscores the peculiar nature of the impact of sublime phenomena in nature: they stimulate admiration or reverence (*Achtung*) rather than a feeling of pleasure. Unlike Kant, Adorno means to bring into close contact, if not to fuse, the experience of beauty and the sublime in nature. He does this by fundamentally reversing the order. While Kant treats nature as the primary phenomenon to which art is related, Adorno argues that the aesthetic experience of nature may be secondary, a late experience. The aesthetic experience of nature presupposes that mankind has lost its primal fear of nature. As Adorno notes, "In this sense it is not accidental that the theory of natural beauty has essentially integrated aesthetic theories coming from the sphere of art" (Ä 50). This supposed impact of aesthetic experience on the experience of nature requires an unorthodox rereading of Kant's concept of the sublime, especially the dynamic-sublime.

In the section on the dynamic-sublime (CJ §28–29) Kant discusses the overwhelming power of nature on the one hand and the fear (*Furcht*) felt by human beings on the other. This kind of the sublime is the result of a situation where the force of nature is so powerful that humans feel threatened. As Kant notes, "Thus, for the aesthetic power of judgment nature can count as a power, thus as dynamically sublime, only insofar as it is considered an object of fear" (CJ §28, 144). However, Kant points out that we are unable to recognize nature as sublime as long as we have reason to be afraid. Only when we are safe, but can observe the destructive power of nature—for instance, a thunderstorm or a volcano—we experience nature as sublime. Thus Kant foregrounds the specific psychological effect of this situation: it encourages a greater "strength of our soul" (CJ §28, 144) than normal because we are confronted with the superhuman vastness and strength of natural forces. "[It] gives us the courage to measure ourselves against the apparent all-powerfulness of nature" (CJ §28, 145). For Kant the point of this exchange is precisely the reverse of the initial situation. Where human beings initially experience fear because of the real threat, they are now at a distance that allows them to reconsider the power of nature in comparison with the power of reason (*Vernunftsvermögen*). Now, by comparison, the sensual world becomes small. Reason provides a "non-sensible standard, which has that very infinity under itself as a unit against which everything in nature is small, and thus found in our own mind a superiority over nature itself even in its immeasurability" (CJ §28, 145). This significant reversal enables Kant to offer a more precise definition of the dynamic-sublime. It is not caused by the extraordinary power of nature per se, but rather by the intellectual resistance of the human observer, who reflects on the ultimate superiority of reason (*Vernunft*). Mankind, although physically weaker than nature, has the intellectual, specifically moral power to overcome its original fear. Thus Kant concludes: "Thus nature is here called sublime merely because it raises the imagination to the point of presenting those cases in which the mind can make palpable to itself the sublimity of its own vocation even over nature" (CJ §28, 145). It is worth noting that Kant extends the experience of the sublime to the religious experience of God. Against the common notion of a necessary human submission under the all-powerful God Kant argues that even in the relationship to God distance and freedom are needed to recognize the sublime character of God (CJ §28, 147). He concludes: "An entirely free judgment is requisite" (CJ §28, 147).

Adorno's interpretation picks up on the aspect of initial fear and later safety as a precondition for the experience of the sublime, reading it, as one would expect, as a moment of man's domination over nature, while the moral aspect, which is clearly central to Kant's argument, is not foregrounded. Instead, Adorno creates a link between the sublime and romantic art. This suggestion contains two significant aspects. It aestheticizes the experience of nature and it historicizes the sublime as a specifically modern experience, beginning in the late eighteenth century, for instance with the Storm and Stress movement. As Adorno explains, "What [Kant] attributes to the ocean or the mountains is that moment that has penetrated art as the new element, for instance in the music of Beethoven, with which Kant of course could not be familiar" (Ä 51).

Adorno rightly considers Kant's understanding of the artwork as influenced by the aesthetic production of the early and mid-eighteenth century in which the aspects of the pleasant and measured dominated. Here art is given its due aesthetic attention through the judgment of taste but there is no experience of high seriousness, i.e. the very experience that Adorno is looking for. The sublime experience, however, contains precisely this moment of high seriousness that the reception of modern art requires. By transporting the sublime experience from nature to art (which Kant excludes) Adorno gains an element that he feels is missing in Kant's aesthetic theory. More specifically, Adorno reads the sublime experience as dissonant, as moving back and forth between fear and freedom, submission and resistance. It is this dissonance that for Adorno characterizes all modern art, changing thereby the concept of beauty. Adorno summarizes his argument as follows:

> And if all art, in order to be beautiful, in order to provide some happiness, had to be necessarily and unalterably also dissonant, then the dissonant character of all modern art in a broad sense is essentially the expression of a dialectic that Kant found in natural beauty, because this dialectic was not yet present in the art of his time, which, however, is already beginning to transcend natural beauty and gestures toward the sphere of beauty in art, which alone has jurisdiction in this matter. (Ä 54)

In Adorno's reading the insufficient moment of Kant's theory of art is compensated by his theory of the sublime, which translates it into the experience of modern art, in which the reconciliation between nature and man can be articulated in a "a kind of pictorial reconciliation" (Ä 53).

The purpose of Adorno's revisionist interpretation of Kant's theory of the sublime is apparent: it enables Adorno to rescue Kant's Third Critique for the understanding of modern art, i.e. a form of art that transcends the categories proposed in the "Analytic of the Beautiful" as essential for the autonomy of art. Still, Adorno does not engage this part in detail, since it reflects a concept of art that he judges as premodern. Kant's strong assertion that the arena of aesthetic experience (in the modern sense) is strictly separate from cognition makes it more difficult to raise the question of truth, which is central to Plato as well as Hegel. The judgment of taste is, Kant claims, based on a feeling of pleasure and displeasure and as such not involved in the subsumption of an object under a concept (*Verstand*). At the same time, one has to note that later sections of the Third Critique, especially the section "The Dialectic of the Aesthetic Power of Judgment," make an effort to overcome the rigid separation.

As noted, Adorno's interest in the analytic of the beautiful is primarily guided by his own emphasis on the autonomy of art, while the judgment of taste is considered as a fundamentally misplaced subjective approach to art. Instead, Adorno focuses on the sublime because this move allows him to create a much closer link between nature and art. In this perspective art participates in the process of human development in a considerably stronger form than the Kantian model allows. But it is not the case that Kant was unaware of this question and overlooked it, as the section "The Dialectic of the Aesthetic Power of Judgment" demonstrates. Especially in §59 Kant discusses the link between beauty and morality (*Sittlichkeit*). Here Kant claims "that the beautiful is the symbol of the morally good" (CJ §59, 227) and explicates this claim by arguing that the proper taste transcends the level of the mere sensations, ascending to a certain "ennoblement and elevation above the mere receptivity for a pleasure from sensible impressions" (CJ §59, 227). The crucial question is how this link can be sustained philosophically, since the aesthetic and the moral sphere are, in Kant's system, fundamentally different. Kant describes this connection as an analogy (CJ §28, 227). His argument provides four steps that enable the transition from a judgment of taste to a moral judgment. The first one states the immediate nature of the aesthetic judgment. The second one underscores the necessary lack of any interest in the judgment. The third step proposes the decisive move by foregrounding the freedom of the *Einbildungskraft* as linked to the *Gesetzmäßigkeit* of reason. Kant speaks of an *Einstimmigkeit*. The fourth step states the parallel between aesthetic and moral judgment insofar as both are understood as universal. As a result Kant argues:

> Taste as it were makes possible the transition from sensible charm to the habitual moral interest without too violent a leap by representing the imagination even in its freedom as purposively determinable for the understanding and teaching us to find a free satisfaction in the objects of the senses even without any sensible charm. (CJ §59, 228)

Why did Adorno not make use of this argument, an argument that would provide a bridge from the sensual to the spiritual realm? Why did he resist the concept of the symbol as a means to make the transition? I suspect there are two reasons. First of all, Kant's claim is too narrowly focused on the moral meaning of artworks, thereby reducing the quest for truth to a quest for moral values. Moreover, Kant's concept of the symbol, as it is explicated in §59, is highly specific and rather narrow. The symbol is an intuition that indirectly represents a concept. Specifically, Kant distinguishes between schemata and symbols, defining the latter as indirect presentation of concepts. The examples that Kant provides make it quite clear that he speaks of what is commonly called allegories. In short, Kant's attempt to provide greater significance to the artwork leads him back to the concept, a path that Adorno is not prepared to follow. By comparison, Kant's concept of the sublime appears to offer a more promising path to Adorno's notion of *Geist* as the core of the modern artwork, because Kant notes: "One can describe the sublime thus: it is an object (of nature) the representation of which determines the mind to think of the unattainability of nature as a representation of ideas" (CJ §29, 151). While Kant's argument leads again to the moral sphere by way of "*Gemüt*"[6] (translated as "mind," CJ 151), for Adorno it is the moment of the transsensual (*Übersinnliche*) that counts. This direction is again strongly emphasized in the final lecture where Adorno returns to the concept of truth in the artwork. Truth is decidedly not defined in moral terms. In fact, Adorno questions the value of discursive concepts, defining instead the artwork as a different path to the truth. However, and this complicates his theory, he also underscores the complexity of the work of art, its mixture of truth and untruth. To be sure, the ambiguity of the artwork as such is not a radically new insight—much would depend on the specific use of this trope.

For Adorno the lectures of 1958/59 were a work in progress, the opportunity to clarify his fundamental concepts and their organization. While the lecture notes from 1961/62 are not yet available in print, we have of course the final version, now as a book published posthumously in 1970. Here we observe a significant shift in Adorno's treatment of the philosophical tradition. Now the distance toward Kant, i.e. the ultimate rejection of Kant's approach, is much less pronounced. On the other hand, the commitment to a form of aesthetic theory represented by Hegel, which was emphasized in 1958/59, is less in evidence. In fact, more than once Adorno objects to the consequences of Hegel's emphasis on the content of the artwork. In *Aesthetic Theory* we can observe a new balance between Kant and Hegel, which gives Kant more weight than a decade before. This shift calls for a closer analysis of Adorno's renewed engagement with Kant's writings. Clearly, the enhanced prominence of Kant has little to do with a deeper commitment to Kantian orthodoxy, for instance the theory of aesthetic judgment. In fact, these elements play an even smaller role than in 1958/59. Dogmatic and normative aspects are no longer decisive for the enduring appreciation of Kant. In terms of a total assessment of Kant's *Critique of Judgment* Adorno would not hesitate to call the approach and the specific elements of the argument outdated and no longer binding for the contemporary discussion, which, however, does not imply that Kant's thoughts are no longer relevant. This distinction is especially important for *Aesthetic Theory,* where the discussion of Kant is very much integrated into Adorno's own discourse with an emphasis on the concept of form.

Still, the positive assessment of Kant is never without reservations. A good example of this resistance can be found in the first section, entitled "Art, Society, Aesthetics," where Adorno compares Freud's approach to art with Kant's theory. While he confirms Kant's major advancement, i.e. the radical claim that the aesthetic sphere must be free of external interests, he is critical of Kant's abstract manner that pays no attention to the psychological aspects explored in Freudian theory. As Adorno notes, "The dynamic character of the artistic is much more fully grasped by Freud's theory of sublimation" (AT 10–11). What makes the Kantian theory ultimately superior for Adorno is its insight into the spiritual essence (*geistige Wesen*)[7] of art, which results from the distinction between the practical and the aesthetic habitus (*Verhalten*), while in Freud's theory artworks, at least according to Adorno, are ultimately no more than sublimated representations of sensual interests. As it turns out, even in this comparison, which is basically decided in favor of Kant, Adorno remains ambiguous. Not only does he acknowledge Kant's blindness to the psychological mechanism of sublimation (in this reference the fact that the autonomy of the aesthetic sphere is the result of forceful sublimation), he also objects to Kant's moral theory, specifically the connection between the artwork and the moral sphere. "The idea of something beautiful, which possesses or has acquired some degree of autonomy in the face of the sovereign I, would, given the tenor of his philosophy, be disparaged as wandering off into intelligible realms" (AT 11). In short, Kant's concept of the transcendental subject blocks the full unfolding of the artwork and its reception. Harshly enough, Adorno speaks of a "castrated hedonism, desire without desire" (AT 11). The more the long paragraph unfolds, the more the praise of Kant's notion of a satisfaction without interest is questioned as a shortcut that misses the deeper meaning of artistic labor and aesthetic reception. Ultimately Adorno argues that both Kant and Freud miss the core of the artwork, either because of a formalist appreciation or a psychological reduction.

At the same time, it becomes apparent that Adorno's critique of Kant prepares the ground, although not systematically, for his own theory. Two elements come into the foreground: the utopian aspect, the invocation of the artwork as a "dream image of a better life, unconcerned with the misery from which this image is wrested" (AT 12); and second, the extreme distance between the idea of happiness and the definition of moral obligations. Adorno writes: "The measure of the chasm separating praxis from happiness is taken by the force of negativity in the artwork" (AT 12). Implicitly Kant's theory of the beautiful as a symbol of the ethical (*das Sittliche*) is firmly rejected. Thus the integration of Kant's theory finds its limits where the larger stakes are being discussed. In particular Kant's attempt to reconnect the aesthetic sphere with the moral sphere is resisted, if not excluded from Adorno's conception.

The search for affinities, on the other hand, brings us back to those areas that already dominated the lectures of 1958/59, namely natural beauty and the sublime, two aspects of Kant's thought that are almost identical for Adorno. A whole chapter of *Aesthetic Theory* is devoted to natural beauty, a chapter in which Kant makes a prominent appearance. He takes on the role of a defender of the importance of nature against the claim, assigned by Adorno to Hegel, that only artworks as products of man deserve serious aesthetic attention. Against post-Kantian aesthetic theory Adorno quotes with emphasis from §42 of *The Critique of Judgment,* where Kant praises the superiority of natural beauty compared with the lesser quality of man-made objects. Adorno's commentary is worth noting:

> But they [Hegel and other philosophers] thereby missed the experience
> that is still expressed unreservedly by Kant in the bourgeois revolutionary
> spirit that held the humanly made for fallible and that, because the humanly

made was never thought fully to become second nature, guarded the image of first nature. (AT 64)

The contrast underscores the turning point in the history of aesthetic theory, the loss of the concept of natural beauty at the moment when the successful bourgeois revolution is completed, while Kant at its beginning still realizes the artificial nature of social arrangements, including those in the sphere of culture. Connected to this logic, in Adorno's mind, is the moment of recapturing nature, of overcoming the element of reification. Obviously, Kant's theory is given a meaning that its author was unaware of.

What could already be noticed in the lectures of 1958/59 has become more pronounced in *Aesthetic Theory:* Adorno selects concepts and themes as he finds them in Kant's Third Critique, in order to integrate them into his own theory, which means that he is less interested in Kant's system than in specific elements that can be used in support of his own argument. Part of this strategy consists of emphasizing aspects of Kant's text that transcend the intent of the author. In his assessment of natural beauty, for instance, Kant's theoretical position becomes the springboard for Adorno's broader and historically more differentiated understanding. Far from accepting Kant's a priori deduction of the beautiful, Adorno emphasizes the changing relationship between nature and human observer, i.e. the cultural mediation that speaks against an abstract definition of natural beauty in the first place. As Adorno asserts: "Whoever wishes to define the conceptual invariants of natural beauty would make himself as ridiculous as Husserl did when he reports that while ambulating he perceived the green freshness of the lawn" (AT 70). For Adorno Kant's systematic and abstract approach remains blind to the mediated nature of aesthetic evaluation, to the way it responds to and is part of specific constellations in which the observer is no less affected than the objects that are judged as beautiful. Obviously this assessment is theoretically no longer Kantian, since it has shifted the concept of the beautiful from the subject to the object. Adorno's assertion that "natural beauty is suspended history, a moment of becoming at a standstill" (AT 71) makes this clear. The priority of the object vis-à-vis its experience is strictly maintained.

The explicit emphasis on the objective side suggests a greater proximity to Hegel than Kant. This was certainly the case in the lectures. In *Aesthetic Theory* the constellation has become considerably more complex insofar as Hegel's theory comes under severe criticism, a polemic that, at least in part, uses Kant. Although Adorno is in agreement with Hegel's critique of Kant's formalism, he objects to Hegel's rationalism that means to deduce art "rationalistically enough, strangely ignoring its historical genesis, from the insufficiency of nature" (AT 75). Specifically, he objects to Hegel's repression of the *Naturschöne* that disappears in the transition from reality to art. Adorno's emphatic insistence on the significance of the *Naturschöne* as a (fleeting) moment of reconciliation finds in Kant at least a strong and sustained appreciation of the *Naturschöne* that is completely missing in Hegel. This critique of Hegel's aesthetic takes a more radical turn when Adorno asserts that Hegel fails to understand the beautiful:

> Hegel's philosophy fails vis-à-vis beauty: Because he equates reason and the real through the quintessence of their mediations, he hypostatizes the subjective preformation of the existing as the absolute; thus for him the non-identical only figures as a restraint on subjectivity rather than that he determines the experience of the non-identical as the telos and emancipation of the aesthetic subject. (AT 76–77)

In short, a truly dialectical aesthetics will have to critique Hegel as well. In this critique Kant's Third Critique sometimes functions as a counterweight to Hegel. In this context contradictions that Adorno means to discover in Kant do not at all decrease the significance and value of the Third Critique; rather, they demonstrate a moment of the aesthetic judgment that only a dialectical theory can truly unfold. Adorno notes the following contradictions:

> On the one hand, Kant treats the judgment of taste as a logical function and thus attributes this function to the aesthetic object to which the judgment would indeed need to be adequate; on the other hand, the artwork is said to present itself "without a concept", a mere intuition, as if it were extralogical. (AT 97)

Yet Adorno accepts this contradiction not as a failure of the author but, insofar as it actually exists within the artwork, as part of its spiritual and mimetic nature (AT 149, ÄT 223–224). Thus, for Adorno Kant's major contribution to aesthetic theory cannot be measured in terms of his success or failure to develop a philosophically coherent system free of contradictions but only in terms of his deep insights into the subject matter, some of which even transcend the author's own intentions.

In the section "Subject-Object" this complicated relationship receives additional attention when Adorno tries to position his own theory vis-à-vis Kant on the one hand and Hegel on the other. While Kant is criticized again for his subjective formalism (the attempt to ground aesthetic theory in the transcendental subject), Hegel is attacked for an objectivism that "overlooks the objective mediatedness of art by the subject" (AT 166). Against these problematic options Adorno asserts the centrality of the artwork as mediated through the subject (producing and receiving) and the material (as content). For this reason Adorno shows little interest in Kant's concept of the genius. Kant defines the genius as "the talent (natural gift) that gives the rule to art" (CJ §46, 186), and continues: "Genius is the inborn predisposition of the mind (*ingenium*) through which nature gives the rule to art" (CJ §46, 186). Here the emphasis is placed on the close connection between nature, artist, and rules that the artist may disregard. For Adorno this conception overestimates the degree of freedom given to the artist. The artist is, as he puts it succinctly, a tool for the production of the artwork: "The artist could be called the extension of a tool, a tool for the transition from potentiality to actuality" (AT 166). In this process the artist follows the requirements of the aesthetic material rather than personal ideas that he or she chooses to express.

In his own fairly brief discussion of the concept of genius (AT 170–172, ÄT 253–257) Adorno gives a rather critical account of its usefulness for the understanding of modern art. Seen in the context of the philosophy of history, Adorno contends, the concept brings together two diverging tendencies around 1800: the search for authenticity (against artificial products) and the assertion of freedom in the production of the artwork. As Adorno comments, "The concept of genius represents the attempt to unite the two with a wave of the wand; to bestow the individual within the limited sphere of art with the immediate power of overarching authenticity" (AT 170). Adorno's critique points to the problematic empowerment of the artist as a God-like creator who produces in competition with nature (AT 170, ÄT 255). In Adorno's eyes the glorification of creative power (*Schöpfertum*) is pure bourgeois ideology. Although this critique is primarily directed against later idealism (beginning with Schiller), Kant's theory is, at least in part, included. However, when Adorno offers a description of an artist or an artwork that could be truly called "genial," he is remarkably close to Kant again. He writes: "The genial is a dialectical knot: It is what has not been copied or repeated, it is free, yet at the same time bears the feeling of

necessity; it is art's paradoxical sleight of hand and one of its most depend-
able criteria" (AT 171). It was Kant after all who defined *schöne Kunst* as
more than imitation of conventions (tradition), who rethought the conception of aesthetic traditions as mediated through nature. The dialectic of
freedom and necessity, which is essential for Adorno's concept of artistic
production, owes much to Kant, actually more than Adorno is willing to
concede.

It is the fundamental reservation against Kant's philosophical approach,
against the transcendental subject as the source of theoretical, political, as
well as aesthetic analysis that sometimes makes it difficult for Adorno to
appreciate existing affinities. While on the whole *Aesthetic Theory* demonstrates a more positive attitude toward Kant than the earlier lectures,
the numerous references to Kant's work are by no means exclusively
affirmative. Adorno's proximity to Kant's *Critique of Judgment* can be
found especially in those areas where Kant describes the role of nature, for
instance the concept of the sublime. At the same time, we have to note that
Adorno is far from following Kant's position that reserves the sublime to
phenomena of nature. Instead, from the 1950s on Adorno explores the
transition from the sublime in nature to the sublime in the work of art as
the birthplace of modern art, as the moment when art reaches autonomy.
In other words, he follows Kant only in order to go beyond Kant's theory,
by resisting the Kantian understanding of the sublime. Adorno defines the
sublime as the moment when art emancipates itself from a more functional
role that it is given; as Adorno would have it, in Kant's aesthetic theory,
"Kant covertly considered art to be a servant. Art becomes human in the
instant in which it terminates this service" (AT 197). Hence for Adorno the
sublime, as a moment of the artwork, demarcates the difference between
true, authentic art and *Kunstgewerbe*. However, this "transplantation" of
the sublime into the sphere of art, as much as it marks the emancipation
of art, is not without its own dialectic. While the reflection of the observing subject increases the spiritual element of art (*Geist*), it also contains
an element of domination (AT 197; *Herrschaftliches,* ÄT 293) that underscores the emancipating force of the artwork as well as the hubris of art,
"the self-exaltation of art as the absolute" (AT 197). The concept of the
sublime receives Adorno's emphatic attention not because he means to
explicate and affirm Kant's theory. Rather, it becomes a decisive tool in
order to introduce, both historically and systematically, the much larger

claim of modern art to contain a truth content. For Adorno aesthetic seriousness (*ästhetischer Ernst*) is limited to the sublime. As Adorno notes,
"The sublime marks the immediate occupation of the artwork by theology" (AT 198), an enormous increase in meaning, but also a much greater
exposure to failure, namely ideology and illusion.

Compared with the Kant interpretation of *Dialectic of Enlightenment,*
Adorno's postwar return to the Königsberg philosopher is characterized
by a substantial increase in complexity and depth. Although a certain degree of suspicion and resistance regarding the Enlightenment also defines
Adorno's later writings, there is no attempt to reduce Kant's work to the
level of instrumental reason. In fact, Adorno's engagement with Kant's
epistemology, his practical philosophy, and his aesthetic theory demonstrates the need to return to Kant in order to examine the earlier verdict, which was too simplistic. In this process of a careful reexamination
between 1950 and 1969 Adorno did not turn into a Kantian or advocate a
return to the neo-Kantian philosophy of his teacher Cornelius; yet he was
clearly interested in restoring some of the authority that Kant's thought
once had in Germany. His lecture courses in particular offered Adorno the
opportunity to introduce his postwar students to the demanding philosophy of Kant. The purpose of his teaching was in all instances (whether the
object was the work of Kant or a systematic aspect of philosophy) the relevance of Kant for contemporary philosophy. However, this relevance was
shown to be historically mediated. Kant is seen as part of a larger philosophical context that extends from the seventeenth to the late twentieth
century. He is part of the historical dialectic of modernity, a major philosophical force that redefined central philosophical problems. It seems that
Adorno was ultimately least ready to accept Kant's authority in the arena
of aesthetics. As much as he used Kant's Third Critique to clarify fundamental aesthetic questions, he basically disagreed with Kant's system. He
is searching for a different type of aesthetic theory to which Kant's writings would make more specific thematic contributions through its discussion of the universal nature of the judgment of taste, natural beauty, and
the concept of the sublime. Adorno praises Kant for his steadfast assertion
of the autonomy of art, yet he is not, as we have seen, satisfied with Kant's
concept of art and his notion of aesthetic experience. Unlike the majority of theorists, he acknowledges the importance of *das Naturschöne* in the

wake of Kant, yet his explication of the concept amounts to a significant revision of Kant's theory. One could argue that the greatest affinity between the aesthetic theories of the two philosophers concerns the concept of the sublime. But even in this instance Adorno's interpretation reworks Kant's conception to such an extent, as we have seen, that it could not be called Kantian in a strict sense. Of course, Adorno was completely aware of these shifts, regarding them as inevitable and necessary in order to preserve the essence of Kant's philosophy, which in his eyes was not identical with the structure of the Kantian system. In fact, Kant's system had to be questioned and deconstructed for the purpose of contemporary philosophy. At the same time, Adorno insists that the contemporary philosophical discussion cannot succeed without Kant (and Hegel), that it depends on a continued critical appropriation which is not limited to a mere reproduction of Kant's argument, since this argument is always seen as part of a larger philosophical constellation.

Adorno's approach stands in sharp contrast to contemporary attempts, therefore, to rescue Kant's aesthetic theory by restoring its foundation and its argument. Part of this exercise would be the sharp distinction between aesthetic judgments and judgments concerning empirical objects (*Erkenntnisobjekte*) a distinction that Adorno plays down. Of equal importance is the differentiation between aesthetic judgments and mere expressions of a "private feeling." It becomes crucial to restore the claim that a judgment of taste, although merely subjective, mainly concerned with *Lust* or *Unlust* of the speaker, is universal. This means that the judgment cannot be empirical and contingent. Instead, the judgment based on a feeling of pleasure is structured in such a way that it can claim acceptance by all other members of the human community because Kant assumes an a priori in the reception of the sensuous data. The object pleases without concept, according to an a priori rule that allows the observing subject to recognize harmony within the object.

The result of this approach is a concept of the artwork that significantly differs from Adorno's notion. As Andrea Esser points out, we are not dealing with an object or a structure but with a process in which the subject generates aesthetic meaning.[8] In other words, the artwork as an aesthetic phenomenon is not given but subjectively constituted. The artwork becomes "objective" only through a process of communication shared by multiple subjects, i.e. it is, strictly speaking, intersubjective.

2

The Ephemeral and the Absolute

The Truth Content of Art

Aesthetic Theory was published in 1970, a year after Adorno's death. Initially dismissed or attacked, it has become his most widely and carefully read work. While critics still disagree about the interpretation of the text, there is more or less consensus on its significance as the culmination of Adorno's oeuvre and its importance for the contemporary aesthetic debate. More controversial, however, is the value assigned to Adorno's contribution to the contemporary discussion. The broadest, and also most orthodox, claim for *Aesthetic Theory* is that it provides a comprehensive framework for the assessment of art in general. A more modest claim would be that *Aesthetic Theory* forcefully and successfully explores the fate of modern art, including the avant-garde.

Among interpreters of Adorno three basic positions can be distinguished. First, there is still a core of more or less orthodox readers for whom Adorno's *Aesthetic Theory* represents the most advanced articulation of the aesthetic problematic.[1] For them competing theories are either theoretically inferior or historically less relevant. Therefore they deny the need for a reassessment of Adorno's theory in light of more recent experiences and theoretical developments. Next we find readers who acknowledge the significance and value of Adorno's writings but insist on analyzing them in the context of later theories, such as those of Habermas or Luhmann.[2] This position foregrounds the historical relevance of Adorno but also the task of going beyond Adorno's theory. For the third position the emphasis shifts from a positive historical assessment to a more critical or even negative one. Here Adorno's theory is perceived primarily as outdated and therefore in the way of new perspectives.[3] Some of the more familiar objections concern Adorno's resistance to popular art and his rigid emphasis on aesthetic autonomy defined in terms of the sovereignty of the artwork. Of course, the rejection of Adorno's understanding of art can be articulated in different theoretical terms ranging from a Foucauldian denial of aesthetic autonomy to a reconsideration of the aesthetic in Bourdieu and Luhmann.

The recent polemic against the Adorno orthodoxy has highlighted two moments of his theory. On the one hand, it has challenged Adorno's philosophical assessment of modern art, in particular his conception of the end of art and the impossibility of returning to a stable and unquestioned concept of art; on the other, it has foregrounded the narrow parameters of Adorno's theory, i.e. its Eurocentric nature and its failure vis-à-vis the contemporary global art scene. His more hostile critics focus on the failure of his most central claims and therefore call for no less than a replacement of Adorno's aesthetic theory. The problem with this type of critique is its theoretical foundation. It tends to share an unacknowledged common ground with more orthodox interpretations. That is, it is grounded in the very kind of interpretation that orthodox Adorno critics have put forward to defend his work. I suggest that it is time to reexamine this discourse, to review a set of notions and ideas that have guided the reading of *Aesthetic Theory* since 1970. They have defined the parameters of the discussion and thereby also the character and the limits of criticism. Those who later called for an overdue revision or an outright rejection of Adorno's theory operate on the basis of an assessment of Adorno's writings that claims the authority of the author. Hence they can speak in the name of the author whose self-representation they use for their own purposes. The purpose of this chapter is to break away from this approach whose historical legitimacy is by no means denied. Instead, I want to explore the possibility of an alternative understanding of *Aesthetic Theory,* one in which key concepts receive a different interpretation, thereby changing the configuration of the theory and by extension the dogma. The point of this exercise is not to engage in polemical confrontation but to open up a different perspective— one that will allow us to see Adorno's work in an unexpected light. While Adorno has served in the contemporary discourse mainly as the voice of aesthetic autonomy, I want to show that this interpretation has overlooked or downplayed those passages in *Aesthetic Theory* where the authority of the artwork is radically questioned and where the highly problematic status of art is foregrounded. Seen in this light, Adorno appears to undermine his own defense of art in a late-capitalist society.

In order to bring this perspective on Adorno to light, we have to take seriously the theological moment in Adorno's late writings—not as a defense of positive religion but rather as a way of defining the Absolute that determines the aesthetic realm.[4] Of course, this approach could easily lead to a romantic reading of Adorno in which the religious and the aesthetic spheres are ultimately merged. This, however, is not the route Adorno meant to take. His insistence that art can be understood in terms of a truth content does not mean that it can be treated as a stable object. The truly radical element of Adorno's theory comes to the fore in his emphasis on the enigmatic nature of the artwork and its fleeting character that is threatened by failure and ultimate *Überflüssigkeit*. In *Aesthetic Theory* these radical elements are balanced by more familiar moments; namely, the philosophical sublation of art—i.e. the process that enables the artwork to be rescued through its philosophical interpretation, which is admittedly both necessary and violent insofar as it is fixated on the use of concepts.

Critics have tended to emphasize a precarious balance in Adorno's late work between the enigmatic nature of art and its philosophical interpretation. For instance, J. M. Bernstein, arguing that Adorno's concept of the artwork can be integrated into philosophical discourse, has written that "in Critical Theory [including Adorno], philosophical aesthetics is about reason and only about reason."[5] By drawing a strong line from Marx to the first generation of Critical Theory, Bernstein emphasizes both the rational and the critical intent of the project in which the aesthetic finds its appropriate place. On the one hand, Bernstein points to the critique of instrumental reason in the work of the Frankfurt School; on the other, he defines aesthetic theory as a specific philosophical discourse concerned with traditional categories of aesthetic experience, but now "as reformed

in the light of the practices and experience of artistic modernism."⁶
For Bernstein, it is the historical configuration (modernism) that rede-
fines the discourse, i.e. the way traditional concepts such as the beautiful
and the sublime or style, genre, form can be used. The rigid division between the sensible and the rational realm, clearly stated by Kant, is reinter-
preted as the result of disenchantment and repression. In this constellation,
Bernstein argues, art preserves what is lost in the sphere of reason. Hence
aesthetic theory must be about reason or, to be more precise, about the
fate of reason in modernism. This claim has two consequences. First, it
reinstates the priority of philosophical discourse (as a critical intervention)
vis-à-vis the artwork; second, it provides a mode of functional integration for art into the larger social context (modernity and advanced capitalism). The discussion of a social context, however, raises the question of the
autonomy of art. The idea of autonomy is indispensable for Bernstein's
reading, since it allows him to both separate and connect the aesthetic and
the realm of reason. On the one hand, the artwork is acknowledged as
different from rational discourse; on the other, it can be understood as
part of a larger sociocultural constellation in which it takes over a critical
function. In short, "the double character of art entails that the affirmative
and negative aspects of art's autonomy mutually refer to one another, and
that hence, generally, for all aesthetic phenomena there will be a purely
aesthetic or internal way of regarding them and an external, social characterization."⁷ By highlighting the double character of art, Bernstein stresses
a specific moment of Adorno's concept of autonomy; namely, the hiatus
between the aesthetic and the social, the resistance of the artwork to its social context, but at the same time also the link and thereby negative social
function defined as the "return of the repressed."⁸

On the basis of this interpretation of the concept of autonomy in *Aesthetic Theory,* Bernstein develops a reading around four themes. He emphasizes the dialectic of form and content, specifically the negativity of
the artwork vis-à-vis its social context. Second, he focuses on the peculiar
status of the artwork in the economy—i.e. its commodity status, which it
articulates through its own fetishism of form against the fetishism of the
commodity. Third, he underlines the possibility of artistic progress in the
world of commodities as the radical pursuit of form leading to an abstractness that is analogous to the abstractness of the social structure. And fourth,
he points to the aporetic moments of Adorno's concept of autonomy and

emphasizes the vulnerability of the artwork, quoting Adorno's statement, "The shadow of art's autarchic radicalism is its harmlessness."[9] Yet even this crucial moment is read as a consequence of the social dialectic in which the vulnerability of the artwork is due to the threat of a commodity-driven society. In his ensuing discussion of the concept of truth content, Bernstein returns to his main theme, i.e. the centrality of reason for aesthetic theory, by contrasting instrumental reason ("the villain of the piece") and art.[10] In this binary opposition the truth of art is determined by its resistance to the process of rationalization that has characterized human history. In other words, Bernstein proposes to read *Aesthetic Theory* as a continuation of *Dialectic of Enlightenment,* which means that aesthetic theory becomes a historically inflected theory of rationality applied to art. In this constellation the concept of autonomy is the crucial bridge between aesthetic production and social construction.

Toward the end of the essay Bernstein suggests that the truth content of the artwork as a philosophical construct negates the work of art, quoting Adorno's statement that "each artwork, as a structure, perishes in its truth content" (AT 131–132). Worth noting is his conclusion that neither a communicative nor a pragmatic notion of truth would support Adorno's theory. This is one of the few places where the essay steps outside of Adorno's theory and at least suggests the possibility of another approach to the question of reason and, by extension, to the question of art. Yet this move remains without consequences, for Bernstein decides to remain strictly within Adorno's thought. Since for him Adorno's philosophy and his understanding of art are identical, one cannot escape from the rigor of the system. Had he decided to give greater prominence to the structure of Adorno's late work, specifically to the moments of antisystematic thought, the understanding of the aesthetic sphere and the place of the artwork in it might have been different.

In contrast to Bernstein, I want to suggest that in *Aesthetic Theory* Adorno follows two separate tendencies: on the one hand, he presses the ultimate importance of art in light of the failure of philosophy; on the other, he emphasizes the problematic nature of art to such a degree that its autonomy is in danger of vanishing. The result is a theological perspective that is absent from Adorno's earlier work. This moment comes to the fore especially in the discussion of the ultimate failure of aesthetic reconciliation (*Versöhnung*). Insofar as Adorno, possibly as an implied critique of Heidegger, rejects the notion of an ultimate mediation of metaphysical meaning (*Sinnvermittlung*), he opens up a space beyond the aesthetic—although, as we will see, this space cannot be entered or controlled by means of philosophical discourse.

Hegel's claim that in the work of art aesthetic appearance transcends the sphere of the sensuous, that it offers a *Durchscheinen der Idee,* is certainly present in *Aesthetic Theory,* but its claim is under duress. Not only has the relationship between the work of art and its truth content become considerably more complex and ambiguous, it seems that, in the final analysis, Adorno is no longer prepared to rescue the artwork, to give it the prominent place that both German idealism and European modernism assigned to it. As a critic, of course, Adorno himself was part of European modernism and a passionate interpreter of avant-garde music, defending the significance of modern art; his cautious hesitation, therefore, deserves special attention. In the posthumous text those elements that undermine the trajectory of a modernist defense of art come to the fore. They stand side by side with more familiar arguments—for instance, in the long section on society and art (AT 225–261), not to mention the old introduction, which Adorno later discarded as no longer adequate. These sections continue to argue for a social dialectic of art in which the meaning of the artwork is established through its determined negation, as Adorno had already argued in his essay "Lyric Poetry and Society." This approach then goes hand in hand with a theory of the artwork that emphasizes the concepts of material, technique, and process. These parts affirm the philosophical relevance of the advanced artwork (as opposed to the production of the culture industry) precisely by denying its positive function. Yet its significance as a critical intervention in a totally administered society is upheld. For this reason Bernstein can sustain his interpretation of *Aesthetic Theory* by referring to these parts of the text, paying due respect to the complexity of Adorno's argument. When we turn to different sections of the text, however, this reading is more difficult to uphold, because at times Adorno seems to push the limits of his theory and thereby undermine the more familiar negative dialectic.[11] The result is the abandonment of art as a critical counterpoint.

Adorno uses the example of the firework to demonstrate the extreme vulnerability of the artwork. Its brief appearance as a form of mere entertainment offers a completely different perspective, since its obvious lack of deeper and lasting meaning problematizes the search for significance or relevance. He writes, "They [artworks] appear empirically yet are liberated from the burden of the empirical, which is the obligation of duration; they are a sign from heaven yet artifactual, an ominous warning, a script that flashes up, vanishes, and indeed cannot be read for its meaning" (AT 81). It is telling that the example is taken from the sphere of entertainment, yet is a form that cannot be mass-produced, that remains unique in its fleeting appearance. It is also worth noting that Adorno reads the phenomenon as a form of writing asking to be decoded and thereby to receive meaning (*Bedeutung*). Yet the apparition does not give an answer, not because the answer is hidden or esoteric but because there is no meaning. The autonomy of the aesthetic sphere, its "afunctionality" (AT 81), claimed by idealism, is taken out of its familiar context. By using the firework as a model for entertaining art he deliberately undercuts the synthesis of form and content (*Gehalt*) and forcefully reduces the artwork to the moment of "apparition" and expression that cannot be stabilized. This move, however, is not to be taken as a denial of the spiritual element of the artwork, which Adorno later asserts; rather, it must be seen as a form of questioning meaning as a secure property of the artwork, as an element that can be rescued in a larger cultural context. Following the tradition of modernist aesthetic, Adorno calls attention to the moment of transformation of the empirical material, but he refuses to define this moment in terms of significant meaning. Transformation remains open-ended: "In each genuine artwork something appears that does not exist" (AT 82). Art promises, Adorno suggests, something it cannot deliver. Hence he distances himself from aesthetic idealism: "Idealist aesthetics fails by its inability to do justice to art's *promesse du bonheur*" (AT 82). Romantic theory attempted to apprehend this moment by underlining the *Unendlichkeit* of the artistic process, which still proposes a notion of truth in the form of *Ahnung*. By contrast, now looking back at the practice of artistic modernism, Adorno faces the negative moment with greater clarity: "Even radical art is a lie insofar as it fails to create the possible to which it gives rise as semblance" (AT 83). There is no guarantee that artworks will actually keep their promises, that the act of transformation will lead to a new and qualitatively different lifeworld.

If even radical art cannot be trusted, if it cannot be assumed to contain, even in mediated form, a moment of truth beyond its mere appearance,

what can be hoped for? Is there a path that leads to a recognition of significance and importance? As we might expect, Adorno's response is highly
ambiguous. In one respect, he holds on to an understanding that takes seriously the *promesse du bonheur,* i.e. the possibility of reconciliation, even
if this moment remains presently unfulfilled. As Adorno states: "For artworks it is incumbent to grasp the universal—which dictates the nexus of
the existing and is hidden by the existing—in the particular" (AT 84). By
evoking a universal Adorno suggests that there could be meaning in the
emphatic sense of the term. But this claim is almost immediately taken
back, modified, and restricted. According to Adorno, recent art, especially
radical works of art, move in the opposite direction. They create shocks
by exploding their own aesthetic form. "Art today is scarcely conceivable
except as a form of reaction that anticipates the apocalypse" (AT 85). It
is not accidental that Adorno invokes an apocalyptic scenario, the notion
of an end that swallows prior promises of history and human progress.
"Equilibrium" (AT 85) has become impossible; instead we are confronted
with loss of meaning (explosion). For this reason Adorno opposes the notion of mythical images as grounding forces proposed by Klages and Jung.
Instead, he emphasizes the moment of artistic illusion at the level of both
Erscheinung (appearance) and cultural significance.

Given the radical questioning of the aesthetic sphere and the artwork,
can the notion of aesthetic truth be mentioned at all? Put differently, can
Adorno still make use of the Hegelian tradition that claims a strong link
between the idea and the artwork? Adorno's answer is ambiguous. While
he acknowledges the importance of Hegel's philosophy as a major step
beyond Kant's formalism, a step that allows us to consider the truth content of art, he is highly critical of locating the truth content in the idea.
First of all, there is the criticism that philosophical discourse by its very
nature misunderstands the artwork: "Even idealism's emphatic concept of
the idea relegates artworks to examples of the idea as instances of what is
ever-the-same" (AT 128). Philosophical discourse is unable to articulate
the specificity of the artwork. Yet Adorno's critique seems to go further.
The very notion of a truth content, a notion that is at the heart of Adorno's
theory, comes under investigation, since it appears to clash with Adorno's
radical concept of the artwork. Hence Adorno continues: "The content
[*Gehalt*] of art does not reduce without remainder into the idea, rather, this
content is the extrapolation of what is irreducible" (AT 128). The crucial
term is "extrapolation" as a way of dealing with the relationship between the

artwork and truth content. Adorno suggests in this formulation that the elements that defy *Auflösung* (unbinding or dissolution) block the transition from the work of art (its structure) to the realm of the philosophical idea. As it turns out, the blockage is more than a methodological question; rather, it points to the deeply enigmatic character of the artwork. Hence only by closely examining Adorno's understanding of the enigma of art can we comprehend his unexpected radical departure from the philosophical tradition.

Adorno's concept of the enigma challenges traditional hermeneutics, which operate with the assumption of possible disclosure of meaning. What appears strange to the uninitiated reader becomes apparent and meaningful in the process of interpretation. Adorno holds against this process a more fundamental recognition of the artistic enigma: "The better an artwork is understood and the more it is unpuzzled on one level, and the more obscure its constitutive enigmaticalness becomes" (AT 121, translation modified). This means: the enigmatic nature of the artwork is part of its constitution rather than a specific element of its structure that the hermeneutic process can dissolve. For this reason, Adorno is confident that the hermeneutic process will always fail in the end. He uses the metaphor of the *Vexierbild* (picture puzzle) to explicate this fundamental difficulty: "Every artwork is a picture puzzle, a puzzle to be solved, but this puzzle is constituted in such a fashion that it remains a vexation, the preestablished routing of its observer" (AT 121). Of course, it is possible to establish through a process of reading the formal structure as well as the thematic configuration of the individual artwork, but this process, Adorno points out, misses the fundamental hiatus between the work and the act of reading. The failure of understanding at the level of the constitution of art (as opposed to the level of the structure of artworks) is caused by a disregard of the nature of aesthetic experience, its fleeting character that Adorno finds in the image of the rainbow. Any attempt to get close to the phenomenon in order to grasp it destroys the phenomenon. Under these conditions the question of truth in the artwork becomes not only difficult to answer but problematic in the sense that possibly there may not be an answer. As Adorno explains: "Ultimately, artworks are enigmatic in terms not of their composition but of their truth content" (AT 127). The search for the truth content as the ultimate exploration challenges the artwork as much as the enigmatic artwork challenges and potentially defeats the quest for the truth content. Nonetheless, Adorno tries to rescue the idea of a truth content as a solution to the enigma. This sudden and unexpected reversal deserves special attention. He notes: "The truth content of artworks is the objective solution of the enigma posed by each and every one" (AT 127). The enigma previously seen as insurmountable for aesthetic theory is now perceived as open to a solution (*Auflösung*). How is this revision possible? How can thought overcome the extreme hiatus?

A sufficient and appropriate answer requires a more extensive discussion of the enigmatic nature of art and, second, a closer examination of the conception of the truth content, specifically its relationship to the artwork. When Adorno claims the convergence of philosophy and art through the truth content he states the official program of *Aesthetic Theory*: "The progressive self-unfolding truth of the artwork is none other than the truth of the philosophical concept" (AT 130). This line of argument remains obviously rather close to German idealism (for instance, to Schelling's theory), something Adorno readily admits. Yet the way he develops the thought places the emphasis more on the failure of idealist systems than the nature of artworks. These are, as it were, compromised by the overstatement of idealism. Hence Adorno concludes that the search for meaning in the artwork legitimized by idealism has to be suspended and ultimately replaced by a different and more radical understanding of truth outside the concept of meaning. But this step is actually not developed in the following passage, which leads to a tentative but crucial definition of the truth content. Adorno writes: "The truth content of artworks is not what they mean but rather what decides whether the work in itself is true or false, and only this truth of the work in-itself is commensurable to philosophical interpretation and coincides—with regard to the idea, in any case—with the idea of philosophical truth" (AT 130). It is worth noting that Adorno shifts the question of truth from the consideration of meaning (*Bedeutung*) to the assessment of a more fundamental issue, namely the question whether a work of art is true or not. The compatibility of art and philosophy is measured in terms of a truth that is intrinsic to art (unlike an idea imposed from the outside). There can be no doubt that in this passage Adorno insists on the possibility of a philosophical explication of the artwork by emphasizing the transformation of aesthetic experience into philosophical thought ("Aesthetic experience is not genuine experience unless it becomes philosophy," AT 131). For this reason he asserts the moment of universality (*Allgemeinheit*) as a link between art and philosophy, a universal element that is, by the way, conceived as collective. But we have to remind ourselves that Adorno has not explicated what he understands by the truth of art. Does he refer to a specifically aesthetic truth (defined in terms of form and structure) or does he mean the truthfulness of the expression?

At this point we have to return to the enigmatic nature of art and the denial of reconciliation. In the section on the enigmatic character of art Adorno radically questions the status of art and foregrounds its unreliability and ambiguity. Artworks are relatively safe only in the context of an established cultural tradition in which radical doubt is not permitted. The value of art, Adorno suggests, always depends on the cultural presupposition that art should be assigned value. Yet when this taboo is broken, art remains without protection and is potentially exposed to complete devaluation. Moreover, since artworks are nondiscursive, they are unable to defend themselves, a task that is assigned to philosophy, but the procedure of philosophy is extrinsic to art. And, on the other hand, as we have seen, the intrinsic approach by way of hermeneutics likewise fails. As mere apparition the value of the artwork is seriously in doubt. Therefore the convergence of art and philosophy stipulated by Adorno seems to be an impossible task, since the universal element, supposedly contained by both must not be imposed on art by philosophy. In other words, the redemption of the artwork has to come from the inside. The radical doubt must be overcome with the help of the very fragility that characterizes the artwork. This is the task that Adorno pursues energetically, and by doing so he is forced to revise both the concept of art and the idea of the truth content (not to mention their relationship). In a nutshell, the path that Adorno follows leads him to the concept of spiritualization (*Vergeistigung*) at the expense of the artwork, which has to be sacrificed. As Adorno writes, "Artworks stand in the most extreme tension to their truth content. Although this truth content, conceptless, appears nowhere else than in what is made, it negates the made. Each artwork, as a structure, perishes in its truth content; through it the artwork sinks into irrelevance, something that is granted exclusively to the greatest artworks" (AT 131). Hence the transformation of the artwork to the level of its (immanent) truth content is the ultimate telos of art. Again, we have to remember that for Adorno the truth content through which the artwork can be redeemed must not be confused with ideas. Rather, the authenticity of the artwork is enclosed and articulated within the sphere of semblance (*Schein*); yet, at the same time, semblance points beyond itself, suggesting through its formal organization that there is truth. But Adorno does not assign a content to this concept of truth; there is only the moment of negation of empirical (social) reality and the element of *Sehnsucht,* the suggestion of the "possibility of the possible" (AT 132).

If one follows these reflections, one is led to familiar Adornian territory—the utopian aspect of art through rigorous negation. By foregrounding the category of negation Adorno arrives at a critical function of art in which the refusal of thematic engagement and the radical formal organization of the work of art are the only legitimate avenues for critique. In this context the radical notion of the sacrifice of the artwork is toned down while the compatibility of the aesthetic and the critical philosophical discourse are more strongly emphasized. Along these lines, Adorno notes: "Whereas art opposes society, it is nevertheless unable to take up a position beyond it; it achieves opposition only through identification with that against which it remonstrates" (AT 133). The specification of art as social opposition returns to a functionalist-dialectical understanding of art and moves away from the radical split between the enigma of art and the rational discourse of philosophy. However, in those parts of *Aesthetic Theory* where Adorno takes this hiatus most seriously, where he stresses the fundamental deficiency of the artwork, he is contemplating a different outcome, one in which the moment of spiritualization plays a central role. To this, the notion of the *Vergänglichkeit* of the artwork provides the logical contrast: "This was not contested until art began to experience itself as transient" (AT 179).

Adorno's concept of spirit (*Geist*) in the context of the definition of art must be kept separate from general notions of spirit in German idealism. In Adorno's discussion spirit appears as a supplement. He writes: "What appears in artworks and is neither to be separated from their appearance nor to be held simply identical with it—the nonfactual in their facticity—is their spirit" (AT 86). This definition underlines the paradox of the concept. While the spirit cannot be separated from (aesthetic) appearance, it is at the same time distinct from appearance. Again and again, Adorno points to the blindness of the artwork, which relates to its status as a thing in the world. This blindness is overcome through the spirit, which provides, to extend the metaphor, the eyes that allow the artwork to see. But it is important for Adorno that spirit is not imposed on the artwork from without. Instead, the spirit is a self-produced moment of the artwork, responsible for the animation (*Beseelung*) of the work as well as the interior force of objectivation. Hence Adorno defines the spirit of artworks as an immanent mediation between the work as thing and the work as expression of truth. It is the moment of transformation that Adorno wants to address and contrast to an approach that derives the truth of the artwork from the realm of ideas. While Adorno readily acknowledges the decisive advance of Hegel's aesthetic theory over older models (including Kant), he clearly and firmly differentiates his understanding of spirit. He criticizes Hegel for his "apology for immediacy as something meaningful" (AT 90), and suggests that radical spiritualization is its opposite. The phrase that Adorno chooses to articulate his own understanding is anything but self-evident: Spirit is "the mimetic impulse fixated as totality" (AT 90). Spiritualization can be achieved neither by mimesis (*Abbildung, Nachahmung*) nor by the mere use of the material (colors, stone, tones, etc.). For Adorno it seems to be the process leading to an organization of the material that becomes the basis for spiritualization. He uses the term "configurations" (AT 91) in order to describe the outcome of the process, yet he is obviously less interested in the outcome than the process itself ("something in a process of development and formation," AT 91).

As much as Adorno distances himself from Hegel, he follows the latter in historicizing the concept of spirit and its use in the history of art. Not unlike Hegel, Adorno conceives the emphasis on spiritualization as a specifically modern aspect of art. With modernism the pressure on the artwork to transform itself spiritually has become inescapable: "Only radically spiritualized art is still possible, all other art is childish" (AT 92). This verdict creates a narrow path for artistic production, a path that not only enhances the significance of the artwork as a bearer of spirit but also its constitutive problems. Adorno discusses them as the danger of abstractness, the separation of spirit from the sensual side, which becomes mere material, and a delight in barbarism as an unreflected gesture of refusal. On the whole, however, Adorno sees the process of increasing spiritualization since 1850 as a positive moment, as a necessary form of intellectual opposition against a lifeworld that has become almost uninhabitable (*verhärtete Welt*). Again, we note that the turn to a historical discussion, i.e. the examination of the link between the spiritualization of art, on the one hand, and the process of increasing reification of the social world, on the other, encourages Adorno to emphasize the legitimacy of the artwork and art in general, although he is aware of the pitfalls of this development. By the same token, he avoids the more radical question that he posed in his discussion of the enigmatic and fleeting nature of the artwork, an examination that subverts the very ground of art. Yet the radical articulation of spirit in the modern artwork, especially its abstract character for which the concept of the symbol is inadequate, creates an internal tension that threatens to destroy the artwork, not only because of the deprivation of the material but also because of the abstractness of the spirit, which turns into a mere rational concept. As Adorno reminds us: "the work itself does not make judgments" (AT 99). While the work may contain rational judgments, it remains itself outside a rational discourse.

As we have seen, Adorno's historical analysis, with its focus on modernism, provides a conditional form of legitimization for the artwork, but it keeps open and undecided the question of whether the artwork can be redeemed in absolute terms. But this question implies another more fundamental question, namely the quest for an absolute that can provide meaning to our lives. Adorno's attitude toward the theological dimension is highly ambivalent. On the one hand, he fully acknowledges the process of secularization that has weakened an older theologically defined metaphysical world order. The emancipation of the modern subject, he suggests, has undermined the legitimacy of this order but also, he adds, any notion of a positive frame of meaning (AT 152). On the other hand, he retains the notion of a meaningful absolute that also informs the definition of art. In his discussion of *Jugendstil* (art nouveau) this moment comes unexpectedly to the fore when Adorno asserts that the aesthetic principle of form implies meaning, even when the content of the work opposes the idea of meaning. Therefore "to this extent, whatever it wills or states, art remains theology" (AT 271). This sentence from the *Paralipomena* must be read together with a passage from the chapter "Towards a Theory of the Artwork," where Adorno establishes a link between the concept of the sublime and theology: "The sublime marks the immediate occupation of the artwork by theology" (AT 198). For Adorno it is the sublime artwork—he may think of Beethoven—that not only changes the limits of the aesthetic experience but also the degree of (spiritual) meaning that artworks are able to articulate. Adorno refers deliberately in this passage to Kant's concept of the sublime, which is restricted by Kant to the perception of nature. While Adorno does not accept this limit, he acknowledges Kant's motivation;

namely, the intent to keep art within the realm of beauty. Yet it is precisely this attempt to set borders that blocks the connection between art and the absolute. The following formulation highlights Adorno's insistence on this connection as well as his skepticism with regard to the substitution of religion by art: "Even the hubris of art as a religion [*Kunstreligion*], the self-exaltation of art as the absolute, has its truth content in the allergy against what is not sublime in art, against that play that is satisfied with the sovereignty of spirit" (AT 197). Still, the absolute outside the aesthetic sphere, which theology would examine, is by no means dismissed out of hand. Rather, it is retained as a figure of alterity, the other to which the advanced artwork strives without ever reaching it. As we have noted, the artwork stands on the side of *Vergänglichkeit* just as human beings are seen as marked by the "fragility of the empirical individual" (AT 198), which starkly contrasts with the eternity of the spirit.

The inevitable question, then, is: How serious is Adorno in his pursuit of a theological grounding of art and where would it lead him?[12] Clearly, Adorno would reject a line of reasoning that places art in the service of religion. The central concept of aesthetic autonomy forbids a dogmatic religious legitimation of art. Although he recognizes the religious function of premodern art and thereby its link to mythology, he stresses the moment of autonomy even in very early examples of artistic production (the example of Paleolithic art). Adorno's theological interest enters *Aesthetic Theory,* as it were, through the backdoor. First of all, there is the distinction between theology and myth, a distinction that contrasts spirit as a force of emancipation and nature as a form of unfreedom. But moreover, the theological element provides a sphere of radical transcendence against which the aesthetic sphere can be judged. Adorno argues in favor of a metaphysics of art as radically separate from religion (AT 138) as a form of *methexis* (participation) of the artwork. The artwork can articulate truth, although it is and remains blind. Yet it is necessary to grasp that the moment of participation is paid for by death: "Their own life preys on death" (AT 133). Through its death or dissolution the artwork shares the fate of "an autonomous entity" (AT 1), *das Seiende,* its *Vergänglichkeit.*

Within the Marxian tradition the contrast to Georg Lukács's aesthetic theory could not have been expressed in stronger terms. Where Lukács understands art as the representation of a reality that is on its way to a historical telos, Adorno discovers only glimpses of hope in a radical spiritualization of art that leaves both the social reality and its aesthetic representation behind. Occasionally this outlook has been called the fundamental pessimism of the first generation of the Frankfurt School, a pessimism that according to this reading was primarily motivated by the lessons of World War II. Yet this assessment, I believe, does not do justice to the theoretical configuration as such, for it overlooks the basic motivation of Adorno's thought, in particular the theological aspect, which has remained a largely unacknowledged element. As long as Adorno's aesthetic theory is read as part of his social theory, as long as the concept of critique has been foregrounded, the theological aspect has been hidden.[13] Put differently, the process of secularization, which plays such an important role in Adorno's diagnosis of the modern world, has also deeply impacted his own thought. Unlike Bloch or Benjamin, Adorno's thought remains committed to the demands of rigorous conceptual work. This commitment, however, especially in his late work, resists political practice and interprets thought as a form of political resistance in a world that has completely hardened (is totally administered). In part, *Aesthetic Theory* formulates a response to this condition in which the artwork takes up a central place as a locus of resistance. Art's lack of conceptual rigor (compared with philosophy) comes across as an advantage since it can point to a truth content beyond the realm of rational discourse. But the articulation of the truth content goes hand in hand with the sacrifice of the artwork. In order to highlight the moment of transcendence Adorno also emphasizes the *Vergänglichkeit* of the artwork, the fact that it is part of the world. This structure seems to exclude reconciliation. The hope that the world can be redeemed through art is denied. Unlike Herbert Marcuse, who holds on to the revolutionary potential of the aesthetic program of German classicism, Adorno rejects this solution and presents a strict dualism. Already in the *Philosophy of Modern Music,* this structure is clearly prefigured when Adorno writes, "The shocks of incomprehension...undergo a sudden change. They illuminate the meaningless world. Modern music sacrifices itself to this effort. It has taken upon itself all the darkness and guilt of the world."[14] Michael Pauen is correct when he notes that Adorno is attracted by eschatological ideas. The Other to which art refers (without being it) cannot be contained in the concept of a "historical reconciliation of world-immanent contradictions."[15] The absolute, while not present in the artwork, is invoked. Accordingly, Adorno differentiates between "epiphanies" (AT 103) and the expectation of the presence of the absolute in the artwork. This means that the aesthetic sphere, although not equal to a religious epiphany, evokes the absolute as a necessary but hidden dimension of art.

For the attuned and focused recipient, therefore, the approach to art not only demands attention and concentration but also a moment of ex-stasis (*Betroffenheit*), loss of control and opening up. The affinity to Gnostic thought is noticeable. The ecstatic experience turns into a moment of liberation, a moment of leaving behind the hardened social world. "What connects [Adorno] with Gnostic thought is the insistence on the difference between aesthetic experiences and sensual elements; therefore there is not only the characteristic reservation towards the sensual but also the notion that the sensual realm is linked to the powers of evil."[16] When Pauen concludes that Adorno, in close affinity to Gnostic thought (there is never the question of influence), strives for a moment of redemption he overstates his case, since, as we have seen, the aesthetic experience, insofar as it remains necessarily connected to the sensual realm, can only point to the truth content, which stands outside the work of art. However, cognition of the truth content through the process of rigorous interpretation, offers a perspective to liberation. Yet the destination of liberation cannot be articulated in positive terms, for the absolute is accessible neither to rational discourse nor to the artwork. Epistemologically the artwork has an advantage compared with philosophy: through the truth content it can transcend itself and at least move toward the absolute. This advantage is paid for by its own epistemological blindness, which can be compensated only by the intervention of philosophy. The act of comprehending the complete alterity of the absolute (in contrast to organized religion, which defines the absolute as god and the path to redemption in terms of god's intervention) describes the ultimate limit of human intervention. The pessimism that Adorno's critics have noted more than once is epistemologically grounded in the structure of his thought and specifically in his theory of art, which follows a tension-ridden double trajectory. On the one hand, it strongly emphasizes the exceptional status of art, its autonomy vis-à-vis social reality; on the other, it contrasts the value of art with the unknown and hidden absolute, stressing art's vulnerability and *Vergänglichkeit*. This means that reconciliation cannot be found in the artwork itself. At best, it can be hoped for in an intense aesthetic experience.

Historical analysis and theological (Gnostic) thought patterns enter into a complex relationship in *Aesthetic Theory* that is not free of contradictions. They converge in a radically negative position toward empirical history and its contemporary outcome. If one takes the theological figure seriously, and not only as a metaphor for an immanent process, one has to come to terms with the status of the absolute and, more specifically, with the relationship between the absolute and history. It would be difficult to read Adorno's theory as an extension of Hegel's phenomenology of the spirit. In contrast to Hegel, Adorno's theory of history recognizes its dialectic (in the wake of Marx) but does not acknowledge its positive outcome. Therefore, the concept of progress takes on a highly problematic meaning. In *Aesthetic Theory* it can be rescued only as a moment of the immanent process of the development of art. Progress is linked to the historically inflected organization of the artistic material in the artwork, representing the most advanced and most differentiated procedures. Aesthetically the concept of progress operates through negation: it involves "a negative canon, a set of prohibitions against what the modern has disavowed in experience and technique" (AT 34). Applied to social history, the concept has become, as Adorno reminds us again and again, part of a technocratic ideology. Hence the invocation of an absolute cannot arrest the historical process but it redirects our attention. It creates a counterpoint that enables Adorno to demarcate the boundaries of art, specifically its fundamental limitations as man-produced and part of the temporal realm. The theological figure therefore functions critically as a way of distancing Adorno's aesthetic theory from the *Kunstreligion* of the nineteenth century, that is to say, from a celebration of the aesthetic as a form of immanent reconciliation. Hence *Aesthetic Theory* is not, as some critics of Adorno have claimed, characterized by an overemphasis on the importance of art. While Adorno insists on the need for radical spiritualization when he discusses modern art, the concept of spirit is, as we have seen, part of the temporal sphere, although it is clearly distinct from the sensual. As a counterpoint, the absolute remains pure transcendence.

Where does this leave us? The emphasis on the theological moment in *Aesthetic Theory* could well be used as a basis for criticism. In his final assessment of Adorno's Gnosticism Michael Pauen, for instance, makes the theological trope responsible for Adorno's increasing pessimism vis-à-vis the postwar development. Since the Gnostic sees the temporal world in terms of enduring catastrophe, there is no room for political change.[17] More generally, the hiatus between theory (knowledge) and empirical world cannot be overcome, which means for Pauen that Adorno's theory, left to its own devices, becomes ultimately self-absorbed and blind.[18] It is worth noting that Pauen's criticism, which echoes that of a number of previous critics, is primarily focused on Adorno's social theory without much attention to Adorno's philosophy of art. Would the theological figure have the same disabling consequences in *Aesthetic Theory?* Recently critics have asked this question with greater rigor, emphatically rejecting a more historicist approach to Adorno's thought, demanding instead a response inflected by the contemporary problematic. These charges can be summarized in the following way: first, Adorno's theory remains locked in negativity based on a self-grinding dialectical reflection. Second, Adorno overrates the force of art and the aesthetic and thereby overburdens contemporary art. Third, Adorno's rigid opposition to questions of practice is no longer reasonable (if it ever was). Fourth, his critique of capitalism, while well-intentioned, is out of touch with the globalization of capitalism. Fifth, Adorno's dialectical method has to be replaced by a form of praxis-oriented pragmatism. The test for a new aesthetic theory is its usefulness rather than its complexity. Unlike Pauen's objections, this critique connects a general negative assessment of Adorno with a sharp criticism of his aesthetic theory, which comes across as outmoded and solipsistic. Yet closer scrutiny of the five points reveals that this characterization of Adorno is not without problems. The charge of overemphasis on the aesthetic sphere makes an interesting point in the context of the debate about mass culture, but fails to grasp Adorno's intent to limit the importance and value of art through the theological figure. If we understand this criticism as a refusal to buy into a reading of *Aesthetic Theory* that focuses on art as social criticism through aesthetic negation, the charge of overloading the artwork might be more plausible. In the end, the claim that *Aesthetic Theory* is outdated both in terms of method (dialectics) and content (understanding of art) is most difficult to handle, since it is historically obviously true but theoretically by all means an open question that cannot be foreclosed by an abstract and extrinsic claim of outdatedness. In this regard it is worth noting that Frederic Jameson turned the tables around and argued for the relevance of Adorno's thought precisely because it was "outdated" and therefore still contained a critical edge that later theory lost.[19] The fact that *Aesthetic Theory* was written in the 1960s and first discussed in the early 1970s in the context of the politics of the New Left has left its marks on the text, but does not necessarily exhaust the meaning and the truth content.

The call for a "return" to Adorno of the 1990s, in part an implied critique of the later Frankfurt School and in particular of Habermas, was least successful as an attempt to restore the work as a dogma or a plan to defend Adorno's position of the 1960s. Instead, what is significant and important for the present can be revealed only in a process of reading that takes note of the tensions and contradictions of the text. For this reason, I focused on the theological figure that the mainstream of the interpretations dealing with *Aesthetic Theory* have considered as marginal. This deliberate one-sidedness brought to the fore the serious skepticism of Adorno's theory with regard to the status of art and his strong resistance to any form of *Kunstreligion,* i.e. any attempt to assign art the place once occupied by religion. While Adorno openly acknowledges a metaphysical framework, he clearly rejects a form of aestheticism that brushes aside ethical concerns. One might even argue that he puts the advanced work of art, by way of its formal organization, in the service of ethical concerns, filtered through the concept of authenticity. In a radical formulation he calls for the end of art after Auschwitz. In his most famous verdict Adorno questions the justification of aesthetic production in light of the ethical demands of the Holocaust. This call is clearly not meant as, and should not be confused with, a judgment on the intrinsic fate of modern art, namely its ultimate self-negation, its wish to come to an end.[20] This fate only radicalizes the status of art in general. It is therefore not altogether surprising that, seen against the absolute, the otherwise sharply marked opposition between genuine art and the culture industry breaks down. The logic of critical resistance through the artwork, which dominates much of *Aesthetic Theory,* is superseded by the theological figure. In this light art and mass culture are allowed to show their similarities, the latter as the parody of the former, a parody that throws its shadow over the presumed purity of the artwork.

The Holocaust seems to pull art into its force field. The horror of suffering and the weight of the dead have created a caesura that cannot be eliminated or dialectically sublated. Hence the actual survival of art, the continuation of aesthetic production after World War II must be understood as an act of *Gedankenlosigkeit,* a lack of reflection that violates ethical obligations. To be sure, Adorno was correct to point out that these obligations would not be addressed by an authoritarian order but have to find their immanent response. As Adorno notes: "Radical art today is synonymous with dark art; its primary color is black" (AT 39). Adorno's rejection of cheerful art is closely connected with the weight of the dead. "The

injustice committed by all cheerful art, especially by entertainment, is probably an injustice to the dead; to accumulated, speechless pain" (AT 40).
The continuation of this sentence deserves our full attention, since Adorno
gives his radical assessment an unexpected turn: "Still, black art bears features that would, if they were definitive, set their seal on historical despair,
to the extent that change is always still possible they too may be ephemeral"
(AT 40). Adorno suggests a logic of historical despair articulated in "black
art," yet this logic is suspended in view of the mere possibility of change.
We have to note that the German phrase "es immer noch anders werden
kann" is even more indecisive than Robert Hullot-Kentor's translation
"that change is always still possible." This weak indication of something
different affects the artwork insofar as it alters the rigorous seriousness, its
blackness, and gives it an ephemeral aspect. Thus the ethical demand leads
to a paradoxical situation. The very intention of the artwork to include the
horror of mass death in its structure, the intention of absolute seriousness,
leads away from absolute seriousness to an ephemeral act of artistic production based on pleasure, i.e. on a sensual moment that is fundamentally
inadequate to the suffering of humankind. The paradox is the appearance
of happiness emanating from the artwork in the context of complete darkness. Put differently, art is by its constitution unable to live up to rigorous ethical demands, yet this very inability, the fact that it is bound to the
sensual, provides the happiness that is at least the *Vorschein* of redemption.
The ethics of the artwork becomes (or always was) "the capacity of standing firm" (AT 40) in a situation where standing firm is the most unlikely
response.

Given the problematic nature of art, its critical negativity (opposition)
on the one hand and its ephemeral character on the other, the status of
the theological figure becomes imperative, since both aesthetic and ethical concerns are determined by this question. Undoubtedly Adorno (and
Horkheimer) never contemplated a return to religion as a system of dogmas supported by a social institution. His critique of Christianity as a regression to forms of magic in *Dialectic of Enlightenment* makes that quite
clear.[21] Yet even the concept of a negative theology might still be too closely
linked to notions of a religious return. What we have to explore and grasp
is Adorno's translation of religious language for purposes that are analogous to but not identical with religion.

In the last thought image of *Minima Moralia,* entitled "Zum Ende," Adorno
reflects on the fate of philosophy in the face of despair (*Verzweiflung*).[22]

The figure of redemption, taken either from messianic Judaism or Christianity, provides Adorno with a structure to contemplate the future of thought when institutional philosophy has demonstrated its failure to make sense of the world and "exhausts itself in reconstruction and remains a piece of technique."[23] The alternative would be, Adorno suggests, a philosophy that contemplates things "the way they would present themselves from the standpoint of redemption."[24] While the perspective of redemption is suggested as the only one left, Adorno also undermines any expectation of a certain delivery. It is not the vision of the new philosophy that is difficult to grasp—in fact, Adorno calls this "the easiest of all because the condition irrefutably calls for such cognition"[25]—but the actual practice, anticipating redemption as a way of thinking. The actual practice, Adorno reminds the reader, remains captured by the very conditions it wants to escape. Philosophy's intention to reach the absolute (*Unbedingte*) through abstract consciousness must fail precisely because it is unconsciously part of the world it wants to escape. Thus the figure of redemption offers an alternative perspective but no certainty. As Gerhard Richter correctly observes, Adorno gives the impression of evoking the hope of redemption and simultaneously withdraws this promise.[26] The possibility of redemption depends on the insight that it is actually impossible. But for Adorno the recognition of this paradox does not result in intensified despair. Instead, the passage concludes with the statement that the question of whether redemption is real or not (the decisive moment in theology) is almost unimportant. In view of the demand (*Forderung*) the philosopher faces, we have to note that the actual fulfillment of the promise is unimportant. Philosophy persists by accepting its own impossibility as the challenge of its uncertain future. However, this prolongation also contains a break: it must open itself to a theological perspective without affirming an actual content.

As we have come to realize, the theological figure, while clearly not to be taken literally, is decisive for Adorno's thought. It provides both the perspective (which is not to be confused with a goal) and the task. Aesthetic theory stands under this sign as well. Thinking about artworks as linked to an undefined absolute spells out the ultimate stakes: the need to take them seriously as a form of condensed mirror writing (*Spiegelschrift*) that through its negation points to the unattainable other and the impossibility to take them seriously, since they are part of the temporal world in which they lack ethical responsibility.

3

Aesthetic Violence

The Concepts of the Ugly and Primitive

The concept of the beautiful occupies a central place in Adorno's theory, and therefore it is not surprising that commentators have focused much attention on it, specifically stressing the link between classical aesthetic theory and the theory of the modern artwork, which stands at the center of Adorno's endeavor.[1] In such accounts, the important issue is Adorno's attempt to reconnect the theory of modern art with Kant's and Hegel's reflections on art.[2] It needs to be remembered, however, that Adorno's *Aesthetic Theory* explicitly emphasizes the importance of the ugly in art. And yet the critical response to the concept of the ugly in Adorno's theory has been modest.[3]

That commentators have focused on Adorno's attempt to reconnect modern art theory with Kant's and Hegel's reflections on art is, of course, supported by Adorno's extensive treatment of the *Naturschöne*, which nineteenth-century aesthetic theory, in the wake of Hegel, had eliminated from its agenda. From this perspective, Adorno's treatment of the ugly in art fades into the background. Its significance becomes limited to its oppositional function in modern art. As important as this function is for Adorno, it by no means exhausts the meaning of the ugly. Adorno's presentation of the material has possibly made it more difficult to recognize the larger meaning of the category for his theory, since the section devoted to the ugly seems to be less worked out than other parts of the posthumous work. I think it unlikely that the author would have published the section in its present form, because its various and heterogeneous elements have not been fully synthesized. Differently put, the section's dialectical nature has to be reconstructed by looking at other parts of the text. As we will see, the concept of the ugly functions on multiple levels and can be traced through different sections of *Aesthetic Theory*. The task of this chapter will be not only to separate the multiple strands of Adorno's treatment of the ugly but also to consider the significance of the whole complex in Adorno's thought. The fact that Adorno discusses the ugly before he turns to the beautiful must be taken seriously—as an index of the importance he ascribed to this concept.

The obvious level, especially in *Aesthetic Theory,* is the role assigned to the ugly in German aesthetics, beginning with Schiller and Friedrich Schlegel and culminating in Karl Rosenkranz's *Ästhetik des Häßlichen* (1853), to which Adorno explicitly refers. In the architecture of *Aesthetic Theory* this element plays an important role insofar as it underscores a larger theme in Adorno's thought that is concerned with the important but precarious connection between classical aesthetics with its emphasis on the autonomy of the artwork and the theory of modernism and the avant-garde.[4] In this context the category of the ugly receives increasing attention during the course of the nineteenth century but remains in a secondary position as the negative of the beautiful. Yet it is precisely this order that Adorno means to challenge. Within the academic tradition that he invokes, this is a difficult task, because nineteenth-century aesthetics resisted the foregrounding of the ugly as a threat to the autonomy of art, and Adorno is not prepared to relinquish aesthetic autonomy. He must argue, therefore, that the ugly is compatible with the autonomy of art. For this purpose, Adorno introduces a second line of argument, namely the relevance of the ugly for modern art, and for the avant-garde in particular. In the context of modernist aesthetics the reversal between the beautiful and the ugly becomes necessary for a defense of the artwork against the impact of the culture industry and its commercialization of the beautiful. Adorno mentions *Jugendstil* as a primary example for this process. The autonomy of the artwork depends on its oppositional force, a quality that is enhanced by the ugly. It is precisely the violation of the traditional aesthetic code that separates the advanced artwork from the threat of the culture industry.

The two strands mentioned above, however, do not exhaust the significance of the ugly in Adorno's thought. In fact, they do not get to the root of Adorno's interest in the ugly. The third, and I believe most important, aspect is the link to the primitive and archaic. It is this nexus that raises the most fundamental and far-reaching questions, questions about the origins of art, its relation to myth and religion, and its changing function in human history. The relevance of these questions is, of course, by no means limited to *Aesthetic Theory;* rather, they also play an important role in *The Philosophy of Modern Music* and *Dialectic of Enlightenment.* Thomas Mann's novel *Dr. Faustus,* a work for which the young Adorno served as a musical consultant, would be another site for the examination of these fundamental problems, for Mann was especially interested in the connection between the primitive and the avant-garde artwork.

In *Aesthetic Theory* Adorno introduces this complex configuration in various parts of the text, but most prominently in the section on the ugly. What is more difficult to recognize is the intrinsic connection with the other strands of the argument. In the text that Adorno left us they appear as heterogeneous elements, each of them having its own distinct function. Neither the connections nor the broader context are worked out with the same rigor that we find in other sections of *Aesthetic Theory.* For this reason our analysis has to examine the elements as well as the not-fully-articulated whole.

While the section on the ugly in *Aesthetic Theory* opens with a reference to the German aesthetic tradition, thereby placing Adorno's treatment of the concept in the context of German idealism and its philosophy of art, in Adorno's work the problem of aesthetic violence through the ugly goes back to the 1930s, especially to *The Philosophy of Modern Music.*[5] Adorno's interpretation of Schoenberg and Stravinsky (in the second part, written later) discusses the ugly as a specific element of post-romantic music, a moment that characterizes the modernist artwork as a radical opposition to the conventions of romantic music. The ugly appears first and foremost as a formal moment, the result of techniques that refuse the final return from dissonance to consonance. In the case of Schoenberg, there is no question about the legitimacy of this radical move. As Adorno argues, the emancipation of the dissonance in the work of Schoenberg follows the historical logic of the material. Adorno speaks of the necessity of art with respect to its immanent development: "Under the constraint of its own objective logic, music has critically canceled the idea of the consummate artwork and severed its tie with the public (*kollektiver Wirkungszusammenhang*)."[6] Not only does the rejection of the traditional masterpiece deserve attention but also the loss of the collective grounding of art. This loss isolates the advanced artwork as a radical subjective expression of the individual artist, a process that increases the distance between advanced music and the general public. To the general public the radical work that strictly follows the logic (*Zwang*) of the material appears ugly. Yet for Adorno it is not the misapprehension of the audience that brings about the foregrounding of the ugly; rather, it is the work itself that violates traditional compositional solutions (*Harmonik*) and its corresponding aesthetic values (the beautiful). Hence Adorno can invoke "a canon of prohibitions" (PMM 32) as the guiding principle for the modern artist, the refusal to return to older solutions of technical problems. In this argument the opposition between the beautiful and the ugly receives new meaning. While the idealist philosophy of art insisted on the priority of the beautiful and treated the ugly as a negative second term, the transition to modern music unhinges this opposition from its conventional place and reverses the priority. Together with the rounded artwork, the beautiful as the aesthetic ideal has to be given up, since its preservation would be false. For Adorno the notion of the correct (i.e. the historically appropriate technical solution) has replaced the appreciation of the beautiful. Therefore in a note he stresses the contingency of specific accords, for example the "octave doublings" (PMM 176). They can be correct or incorrect depending on the "state of the material" (PMM 176). The state of material must be the primary concern of the composer—without regard to conventional aesthetic values.

The concept of the ugly becomes part of the discussion of modern music by way of the negation of the convention (style) and its connection with the concept of the beautiful. Yet this process contains more than the exhaustion of the beautiful; it raises the ugly as a new aesthetic quality linked to the advanced technique that presses the state of material. In this context the concept of the ugly has a purely formal character based on the immanent analysis of the history of modern music. In strictly technical terms—that is, in the correct or incorrect use of techniques—the category could be replaced with the term "radical dissonance." As Adorno explains with reference to Schoenberg's atonal works, "The first atonal works are depositions, in the sense of psychoanalytical dream depositions" (PMM 35). This character cancels the notion of aesthetic appreciation, which moderate modernism still wants to preserve. In other words, Adorno underscores the impossibility of an assessment based on given aesthetic concepts—unless their meaning can be detached from the tradition, allowing the ugly to become a positive term. However, we have to note that this reversal is consonant with the notion of progress in modern art, and specifically in modern music. Adorno does not mean to support a conscious return to older forms, to folklore or non-European art forms. His trajectory of modern music is tied to the development of European music and in particular to the fate of German music. This sets him apart, as we will see, from simultaneous trends in art criticism where the concept of the primitive plays a crucial role.

In Adorno's severe critique of Stravinsky in the second part of *The Philosophy of Modern Music,* this difference becomes quite clear. Based on the concept of immanent progress in music, he makes Stravinsky responsible for a turn in contemporary music toward a restoration of the tonal system. "Always at work in Stravinsky is the desire of the adolescent who wants to become a recognized, proven classic" (PMM 106). According to Adorno, the price that Stravinsky has to pay for this desire is a lack of rigor and consistency that becomes equivalent with regression. Yet the hidden classicism of Stravinsky, who appears to be part of the vanguard, is only one element that Adorno finds problematic. Of equal if not greater concern is Stravinsky's ambivalence toward the idea of culture, specifically his interest in folklore and the primitive. Stravinsky's rebellion against tradition invokes the barbaric and suspends the rules of musical culture. For Adorno, both tendencies—the lack of rigor and the flirtation with the primitive or folkloristic—demonstrate Stravinsky's compromise, his lack of persistence vis-à-vis the logic of the advanced musical material. "This tendency leads from domestic aesthetics—which adjust the soul to the status of a commodity—to the negation of the soul in protest against its commodity character; to sworn allegiance of music to the body, to music's reduction to appearance, which takes on objective meaning by disclaiming meaning" (PMM 109). Stravinsky's compromise brings him close to the very

culture industry that he means to reject. In this respect Adorno's critique
of Stravinsky is similar to his indictment of Wagner: a compromised rebellion results in technical regression, which thereby becomes part of a commercialized culture.[7]

Stravinsky's *Sacre du Printemps* in particular provokes Adorno's polemic, since this work, while musically the most advanced, openly embraces
the fashionable cult of the primitive. "This [*Sacre du Printemps*] belongs
to the years in which 'savages' were first called 'primitives,' to the world
of Sir James Frazer, Lucien Lévy-Bruhl, and Freud's *Totem and Taboo*"
(PMM 111). Adorno refuses to acknowledge the attempt to celebrate the
cultic sacrifice of primitive societies that the anthropologists have reconstructed, since for him it is nothing but an "anti-human sacrifice to the
collective" (PMM 111). While Adorno does not suggest that Stravinsky
seriously wants to reenact a mythic sacrifice, he opposes the uncritical celebration of a primitive past determined by the subjugation of the individual. The seemingly detached presentation of the sacrifice on the stage
remains, at least in Adorno's eyes, a regressive move: "When the avant-
garde avowed its attachment to African sculpture, the reactionary aim of
the movement was still entirely hidden: The gesture toward primeval history seemed to serve the emancipation of constricted art rather than its
regimentation" (PMM 112). Adorno is aware that Stravinsky's critique of
modern culture owes its impulse to the very liberalism it undermines, but
this subversion, he argues, ultimately affirms fascist violence.

The aesthetic celebration of the mythic sacrifice in Stravinsky's music
consciously violates the traditional aesthetic code in two ways. On the one
hand, it openly shows the barbaric act; on the other, it breaks away from
a romantic musical sensibility and embraces the primitive, also in musical
terms. Yet this confluence of theatrical content and music does not achieve
what Adorno demands, that is, musical progress. Rather, Stravinsky produces a compromised avant-garde in which the subversion of established
culture encourages the rise of social and political barbarism. This means
that Adorno rejects a form of the ugly that is incompatible with his concept
of artistic progress. While *The Philosophy of Modern Music* acknowledges
the legitimacy of the ugly in Schoenberg's music, in the case of Stravinsky
the verdict is negative because the ugly is linked to a form of regressive
primitivism. There can be little doubt that Adorno's harsh critique was
influenced by the increasing threat of the Third Reich in the late 1930s.

It becomes urgent for Adorno to carefully distinguish the aesthetic revolution of the European avant-garde and the political revolution of European fascism. The rather abrupt rejection of turn-of-the-century primitivism, for instance in the negative reference to African sculpture (*Negerplastik*), contains an unresolved tension between the aesthetic and the sociopolitical, a tension to which Adorno returns in *Aesthetic Theory*.

Adorno's critique of Stravinsky insists on the difference between the early European avant-garde around 1900 in Paris and its reassessment in the late 1930s. Now the cult of the primitive appears in a different light because the barbarism of the Nazis has become the literal application, the negation of high culture. Adorno's humanistic defense of a progressive, future-oriented concept of history represses those moments that would question the concept of progress itself. In the final analysis, however, the discussion about primitive culture around 1900 was a discussion about the liberal concept of progress. This is evident in the two works Adorno mentions, namely Freud's *Totem und Tabu* and Carl Einstein's study *Negerplastik*. Both challenge the notion of progress on which the liberal conception of history was built.

At this point, the analysis of Adorno's thought requires a detour, via a closer examination of Carl Einstein's work. A novelist and art critic, Einstein (1885–1940), who was closely connected to the German prewar avant-garde, believed that a serious reappraisal of African art was needed for two reasons. First, the contemporary interest in so-called primitive cultures (including African cultures) throws light on the aesthetic ideas of the European avant-garde. There are, Einstein suggests, significant parallels between the spatial configuration of cubism and traditional African sculptures. Second, these parallels are reason enough to question the conventional evaluation of African art as undeveloped and aesthetically unsophisticated. In other words, a serious and rigorous understanding of African art must challenge the conceptual apparatus of European art history. The critic has to remove layers of prejudices based on a Eurocentric conception of aesthetic development. "From the very beginning the negro is seen as the inferior part who has to be ruthlessly categorized; and what he has to offer is a priori judged as flawed. Fairly vague hypotheses of evolution were carelessly applied to him; for some critics he must submit to such procedures in order to fulfill a false concept of the primitive."[8] A methodologically rigorous engagement therefore requires a preliminary rejection of evolutionary theories and a distinct framework for the analysis of the material. In his methodological reflections Einstein underscores the dubious character of the term "primitive."[9] While it may serve as a positive term in a discourse that focuses on the elements of advanced civilizations, it also reinforces the contrast between European and African culture, thereby undercutting the very possibility of a meaningful comparative interpretation. While Einstein means to examine so-called primitive art, he does not want to emphasize its primitivism as a mere aesthetic stimulus for late European civilizations, the kind of stimulus Adorno criticized in his polemic against Stravinsky.

What are the requirements for this task? It will be necessary to distinguish between those elements that Einstein explicitly mentions and those that are part of his project but remain invisible in his argument. Although Einstein acknowledges the impact of modern art on the new assessment of African art, he warns against premature comparisons and calls for a distinct approach to African sculptures. At the same time, he has to concede that there is little empirical knowledge about African art history, both in terms of geographical regions (tribe culture) and in terms of historical development. Therefore he is left with the idea of a stylistic approach (*stilkritischer Aufbau*), an idea he rejects because of its problematic concept of development from simple to more complex forms. This leaves the critic with a highly heterogeneous collection of objects without a grasp of the totality. In this situation, Einstein decides in favor of a strictly phenomenological approach—a comparative analysis of the objects without regard to their background and their historical origin. According to Einstein, their striking features demonstrate the typical moments of African art.

It is worth noting that Einstein's method is as much the result of a lack of positive knowledge as one of an a priori preference for a formalist approach. One cannot argue therefore that Einstein rejects the concept of history and progress. What he rejects is the application of European history to non-European cultures. Einstein's warning against evolutionary thinking is meant to stop empty speculation in a field with very few secure markers. Given the lack of historical concreteness and depth, Einstein's formalist method searches for similarities and contrasts. He contrasts the African sculpture with the development of sculpture in Europe by setting up the opposition between *plastisch* and *malerisch,* and examines similarities between African and modern European art under the category of a cubic conception of space.[10] Above all, however, he emphasizes the religious nature of African sculpture, namely the fact that the figures are cult objects. Nonetheless, he does not draw the conclusion that, because of their religious nature, the sculptures are part of an earlier phase of culture, which European post-Renaissance art had left behind. In Einstein's study African culture stands apart, except in formal terms, namely in the configuration of space.

What does this mean for the assessment of the "primitive"? For Einstein it is important to remove from the evaluation of African sculpture the reproach of aesthetic deficiency, especially the lack of formal beauty. The formal qualities of the figures, he insists, have to be understood and evaluated in the context of African cult practices: "We will avoid the mistake of misunderstanding the art of the African people based on unconscious memories of some European art forms, because we approach African art in formal terms as an enclosed realm."[11] Einstein underscores the formal reasons for the particularity of African art. In other words, he treats the formal and the cultural aspect as codetermining the figure. The African artist is faced with a formal task that is different from that of the European artist and therefore, as Einstein suggests, also arrives at a different solution. Einstein emphasizes the cubic, three-dimensional character of the figures, but not as the result of a movement that suggests three-dimensionality; instead, three-dimensionality is instantly and completely realized in the form of the figure and can be comprehended as such by the viewer.[12] This formal structure is not to be confused with a naturalist rendering of the body. In his discussion of the representation of the body, Einstein makes this quite clear: "Frequently African sculptures are criticized for their so-called proportional flaws; but one has to understand that the optical discontinuity of space is transformed into purified form, i.e. into an order (since we are dealing with plastic form) in which the different parts are individually valued."[13] What appears to the untrained European eye as deformed and therefore ugly and barbaric reveals its formal consistency to a viewer who recognizes the cubic quality of the sculpture and the logic of its form. Proportions do not follow the requirements of a realistic representation; instead, "it depends to what extent the significant depth quotients, by which I mean the plastic resultant, are expected to express depth."[14] Einstein's analysis underscores the totality of the form rather than the aspect of representation. While he does not deny that the sculpture is meant to represent the god, he takes the religious meaning more or less for granted.

This conscious disregard for representation in the discussion of the cubic form draws attention to the unacknowledged tension of Einstein's approach. On the one hand, he means to establish the unique cultural context of African art by stressing the religious quality (cult practices); on the other, he wants to isolate the formal structure. While the religious emphasis would encourage the moment of representation (the god), the formal emphasis allows the comparison with European art. Unlike Adorno, Einstein sees a legitimate affinity between African art and European cubism. Cubism, he suggests, rediscovered spatial principles that African art had already established. In Einstein's mind, the comparison legitimizes both sides. The truth of modern European art supports the value of African art, while the authenticity of African art (rooted in religion) underscores the legitimacy of the European avant-garde. In Einstein's approach the problem of primitivism disappears, since the designation of African art as "primitive" is based on a European misconception. By introducing a separate logic for African art, Einstein can validate the influence of African art that Adorno acknowledges with suspicion. Yet we have to note that his African logic remains rather static and, as Einstein concedes, without historical depth. Therefore he contrasts European development with African being—in *Negerplastik* with a preference for the African side. At the same time, he remains attached to the concept of historical development when he discusses European art, as his later work *Die Kunst des 20. Jahrhunderts* (1926) makes quite clear. This raises the question, then, of how the impact of non-European art on European modernism around 1900 can be accounted for. The embrace of the barbaric, which for Adorno remains potentially a moment of regression, is for Einstein primarily a shift in the framework, a merging of two cultures, or, more precisely, a merging of formal structures.

Compared with Einstein's extensive analysis of African sculptures, Adorno's brief remarks about the problematic character of "primitivism" seem insufficient. His concept of artistic progress, derived from his interpretation of the new Vienna School, seems especially to confirm the dominance of the European development, possibly even a linear conception of history. Yet Adorno's question is different from Einstein's concerns. While the latter responds critically to cultural thought patterns, Adorno looks at the return of the repressed. For him the celebration of the primitive marks a problematic critique of modern European culture because it simply refuses to deal with the accumulated burden of human history. This will be, of course, the central theme of *Dialectic of Enlightenment,* written a few years later. Still, Einstein's book *Negerplastik* was a challenge that Adorno refused to take seriously when he wrote the second part of *The Philosophy of Modern Music,* presumably because of his concern with the fate of European history. One can see the traces of this rejection even in *Aesthetic Theory.* In different parts of the text he returns to the question of archaic art, when he examines the question of the origin of art.

A brief recapitulation of *Dialectic of Enlightenment* is inevitable in order to explicate the relevance of the archaic and primitive in Adorno's thought. The text ostensibly addresses the failure of the Enlightenment, the failure of progress in human history. More specifically, Horkheimer and Adorno argue that the overcoming of myth has remained incomplete. The result is a new kind of barbarism introduced and propagated by totalitarian regimes. At the philosophical level, the violence of the totalitarian state corresponds to the return of the mythic, which Adorno addresses in the Odysseus excursus. At the center of this discussion stands the concept of the sacrifice. The need to sacrifice a preselected member of the collective for the good of the same collective is described by Adorno as "a state of archaic deficiency, in which it is hardly possible to make any distinction between human sacrifice and cannibalism."[15] For Adorno magic thought, which legitimizes and rationalizes human sacrifice, is irrational in its support of nonfreedom. As Adorno writes, "The magic collective interpretation of sacrifice, which wholly denies its rationality, is its rationalization: but the neat enlightened assumption that, like ideology today, it could once have been the truth, is too naïve" (DE 52). The concept of progress, central to the Enlightenment, is always already compromised by myth, since reason rationalized the very structures it means to overcome. What stays in place, Adorno argues, is the pattern of exchange. Even the rational critique of sacrifice in the name of self-preservation holds on to the notion of exchange. The civilizing process itself, by means of rationality, is the source of mythic irrationality: "This very denial, the nucleus of all civilizing rationality, is the germ cell of a proliferating mythic irrationality" (DE 54). As Adorno points out, Odysseus's cunning, his superior rationality, can defeat the older mythic forces, but remains tied to the fundamental structure. He gains control over nature by subjecting himself to the laws of nature—it is self-preservation through adaptation.

The victory of the Enlightenment is based on the elimination of the irrational forces of myth. The price to be paid for this victory was the need to dominate nature and, even more important, human self-destruction, which means that mythic structures have not been truly overcome. "In the enlightened world mythology has entered into the profane. In its blank purity, the reality which has been cleansed of demons and their conceptual descendants assumes the numinous character which the ancient world attributed to demons" (DE 28). The return of mythic terror challenges the idea of progress that the Enlightenment defined as its goal; moreover, it challenges the notions of linear history and stages of evolution. Thus Horkheimer and Adorno's understanding of the dialectical process of history places the emphasis on the copresence of the old and the new, an alignment that defies the idea of progress. The ancient terror, they suggest, has not disappeared; it has only taken on a new form. In *Dialectic of Enlightenment* the relevance of their insight for aesthetic production, an aspect that would especially interest Adorno, is not closely examined, but the presence of the archaic or primitive in the modern world is acknowledged as a fundamental problem that cannot be brushed aside as a mere fashionable phenomenon. Therefore Adorno's brief treatment of the question in his critique of Stravinsky proves unsatisfactory.

Although Adorno's last work has been rightly defined as a theory of the modern work of art, there are a number of competing concerns that are either closely related to the central theme or surface only here and there. One of them is the origin of art and the nature of archaic art. A lengthy excursus is dedicated to questions of origin, which the editors offer as part of the Paralipomena.[16] It has the form of a critical assessment of the existing literature on this topic. By and large, Adorno remains unimpressed by the work that has been done in this field, since he is dissatisfied with the prevailing methods. Briefly put, Adorno is equally suspicious of an ontological approach (Heidegger) and the results of positivistic research. Still, he is also not satisfied with Croce's verdict that the question of the origin of art is aesthetically irrelevant, for he maintains, against Croce, that art cannot be categorized as "an invariant form of consciousness" (AT 326). Hence, the search for the origin of art is defined as the search for historical beginnings, more precisely for the moment when art separates itself from the oldest known cultic practices. Ultimately, Adorno is less interested in the distinction between the camp that underscores the naturalistic representation in the oldest works (Arnold Hauser, for example) and scholars who stress the symbolic meaning. When he speaks in his own voice, he foregrounds the beginnings of subjectivity as a crucial step for the production of art: "Although expression is seemingly an aspect of subjectivity, in it—externalization—there dwells just as much that is not the self, that probably is the collective. In that the subject, awakening to expression, seeks collective sanction, expression is already evidence of a fissure" (AT 328). Adorno focuses neither on representation nor on symbolic meaning; instead, he insists on the moment of expression as a decisive element. Here we have to consider that he defines expression as always already mediated by the Non-Ego, namely the collective. Therefore, as Adorno concludes, it is impossible to grasp the original unity of art. Such original unity (*Wesenseinheit*), as the philosophical point of departure, already presupposes a distinction within the work, on the one hand (material and form), and the social collective, on the other.

Following the direction of *Dialectic of Enlightenment,* Adorno's own understanding of early art emphasizes the moment of mimesis as the oldest, pre-aesthetic approach in which, as part of the magic practice, subject and object are not yet distinguished. In the earliest known artworks, however, this state is already surpassed, for instance in works such as the cave paintings. These paintings, according to Adorno, are characterized by "striking traces of autonomous elaboration" (AT 329)—i.e. by aesthetic qualities—without losing the magic quality of early mimesis. It is this second aspect that also marks later art as something that has not quite caught up with the process of civilization. Returning to the central theme of *Dialectic of Enlightenment,* Adorno writes, "But aesthetic comportment is not altogether rudimentary. An irrevocable necessity of art and preserved by it, aesthetic comportment contains what has been belligerently excised from civilization and repressed, as well as the human suffering under the loss, a suffering already expressed in the earliest forms of mimesis" (AT 330). While the original separation of mimetic impulse and aesthetic production can be determined only after it happened, the artwork, including the advanced work, cannot completely detach itself from the magic element. For Adorno, who looks back at the origins of art from the perspective of the modern work of art, these traces of mimesis are a significant moment, a form of regression in the eyes of scientific rationalization; yet it is a form of regression that remains essential for humanity as long as the concept of reason is tied to human self-destruction.

In one of the fragments of the Paralipomena Adorno attempts to define the relationship between aesthetic and pre-aesthetic moments in the artwork. He suggests that ancient art (*vergangene Kunst*) is not coincidental with its cultic function, but it cannot be described as the opposite; "Rather, art tore itself free from cult objects by a leap in which the cultic element was both transformed and preserved, and this structure is reproduced on an expanding scale at every level of its history" (AT 286). Put differently, the history of art preserves the cultic element in all its phases, including European modernism. It is not accidental that a closely related fragment examines the nature of the cultic or mimetic moment. Looking at modern art, in particular at the works of Picasso, Adorno notes the "marks of the frightening" (AT 287), i.e. the shock produced in the viewer by the deformation of the represented object. Unlike Einstein, Adorno does not interpret the deformation in cubism as an exclusively formal problem. Rather, he insists on the presence of older elements, a historically legitimate return of the horror in cultic figures. This means that, in Adorno's late thought, the ugly is not a purely formal question; rather, it is closely linked to the larger issue of the origin of art and the significance of the cultic element. As long as one looks at Adorno's understanding of the ugly exclusively or primarily in the context of the modern history of aesthetics, one will miss this crucial link. The organization of *Aesthetic Theory* suggests such an approach, since the question of the ugly is discussed in the traditional proximity to the beautiful. However, this proximity is deceptive, for Adorno, notwithstanding his high regard for Kant and Hegel, remains hostile to the idea of classicism.[17] Hence he insists not only on the historical priority of the ugly but also on its continued relevance in modern art.

As a critic of modern art (with an emphasis on music) Adorno realizes that the conventional definition of the ugly as a negation of the beautiful does little to explain the powerful presence of the ugly in modern art, because a formal definition can at best acknowledge the phenomena but not assess their origin and legitimacy. Yet it is precisely the legitimacy of the ugly that is at the center of his analysis. It determines both the content and the form of the artwork. The representations of social misery in naturalist plays and novels violate the conventional aesthetic code; even more explicitly the highly unpleasant and repulsive make their appearance in avant-garde poetry (i.e. in Baudelaire and Gottfried Benn). Adorno comments: "The repressed who sides with the revolution is, according to the standards of the beautiful life in an ugly society, uncouth and distorted by resentment, and he bears all the stigmas of degradation under the burden of unfree—moreover, manual—labor" (AT 48). It is the task of modern art to be on the side of those social phenomena that have been treated as taboo. Yet we have to note that Adorno does not speak out in favor of the aestheticization of the ugly; in fact, he explicitly problematizes the use of humor in poetic realism as a means to tone down and integrate the abject. The critical function of the modern artwork, specifically its opposition to the social status quo, Adorno tells us, is supported and enhanced by the presentation of the ugly.

For two reasons, however, Adorno's advocacy of the ugly should not be confused with a naive commitment to naturalism. First of all, Adorno resolutely rejects the poetic celebration of human suffering; second, he underscores the formal demands of the artwork. The transformation of the ugly into form results in the cruel. By opening itself to the cruel, the artwork resists its own tendency to strive for formal reconciliation. Adorno notes: "The subjective domination of the act of forming is not imposed on irrelevant materials but is read out of them; the cruelty of forming is mimesis of myth, with which it struggles" (AT 50). The radical formal experiment, which makes visible the cruel, repeats the moment of cruelty in myth, but it does not stop there. At the same time, Adorno suggests, the cruel contains a moment of critical self-reflection. Art "despairs over the claim to power that it fulfills in being reconciled" (AT 50).

While the representation of the ugly in the artwork as a form of social criticism is an important point in Adorno's inquiry, it by no means exhausts the significance of the ugly. Adorno's brief discussion of the cruel points to another, deeper level of his argument, namely the banished but ultimately not entirely subdued power of myth in the modern world. This is the place where the central theme of *Dialectic of Enlightenment* merges with the analysis of the origin of art in *Aesthetic Theory*. Adorno's resistance to the idea of formal reconciliation in German classicism, insofar as it denies or minimizes human suffering, leads him to the archaic and primitive, where aesthetic reconciliation has not yet occurred. Although he strongly emphasizes, as we have seen, the rupture between magic practices and art, he equally stresses the importance of the mythic ground. This, however, means that the ugly is prior to the beautiful: "If one originated in the other, it is beauty that originated in the ugly, and not the reverse" (AT 50).

This seemingly formal shift (the beautiful becomes the negation of the ugly) opens up a dimension of art that traditional aesthetic theory could not accommodate within its system. Following the strategy of *Dialectic of Enlightenment,* Adorno's own theory embraces the ugly in both the archaic and the modern work because they share, although in very different ways, the impact of mythic structures; that is to say, they are participating in as well as negating the power of myth. In the reversal suggested by Adorno, the beautiful takes on a new meaning. It becomes part of the historical process of a problematic human history. "In this principle [of order] the antithesis to the archaic is implicit as the play of forces of the beautiful single whole; the qualitative leap of art is a smallest transition. By virtue of this dialectic the image of the beautiful is metamorphosed into the movement of enlightenment as a whole" (AT 52). Briefly put, the concept of the beautiful is historically marked as the transition from the archaic and primitive to a later cultural stage. While this transition, according to Adorno, contains in itself a moment of progress, a stronger articulation of the aesthetic, it cannot completely escape the bond with the archaic. "The affinity of all beauty with death has its nexus in the idea of pure form that art imposes on the diversity of the living and that is extinguished in it" (AT 52). Where art succeeds in bringing about aesthetic reconciliation, it does so at a high price, namely the death of the nonaesthetic material. This brings us to a somewhat unexpected conclusion: the rigorous defense of the autonomy of art, a central theme of *Aesthetic Theory,* finds its limit in the concept of the ugly, which is a label for the primitive and archaic. Although the ugly is grounded in the archaic, i.e. in the sphere of nonfreedom, it also articulates the force of life against the death of the aesthetic form.

As a formal treatment of an aesthetic category, Adorno's section on the ugly comes across as heterogeneous and incomplete. The author appears to be unable to make up his mind about what exactly he wants to examine. The frequent shift in emphasis from the philosophical tradition to modern art, the role of the archaic, and the relationship between myth and art confuses a reader who is expecting the development of a linear argument. Obviously *Aesthetic Theory* refuses to honor this expectation and places the emphasis on the unfolding of the conceptual material. One has to find the right key in order to open the section. Although Adorno seems to call attention to the importance of the philosophical tradition by making it the point of departure for his discussion, it turns out not to be the key that opens the door to his deeper concerns. Instead, the significance of the ugly for the articulation of the modern artwork points us in the right direction. The subversive force of the advanced work of art violates conventional aesthetic norms by foregrounding the ugly and rejects the false reconciliation of the beautiful. The critical function of the ugly in modern art, however, is closely connected with Adorno's concept of history in *Dialectic of Enlightenment*. The dialectic of progress and regression resurfaces in *Aesthetic Theory* as the dialectic of the modern and the archaic. For this reason, the difference between magical practices and early art is of great importance for Adorno. This means that behind the question of the ugly lies the larger issue of the primitive and its meaning in modern, enlightened society. Of course, Adorno was not the first theorist to discover this problem. Nietzsche and Freud had offered decisive insights with which Adorno was familiar. As we have seen, in *The Philosophy of Modern Music* his response to Freud was brief and insufficient; the implicit engagement with Nietzsche in *Dialectic of Enlightenment,* on the other hand, was more serious. But it is not the question of influence that is of interest for the present discussion. Instead, in the final section I will focus on Adorno's place within the theoretical constellation of modernism.

When Freud, in his essay "Animism, Magic, and the Omnipotence of Thought," mentions in passing that there is an area in modern culture that has remained close to the stage of animism, namely art, the proximity to Adorno is hard to overlook. Freud writes, "Only in art does it still happen that a man who is consumed by desires performs something resembling the accomplishment of those desires and that what he does in play produces emotional effects—thanks to artistic illusion—just as though it were something real."[18] More specifically, Freud suggests that art was originally not a purely aesthetic phenomenon but served other purposes, among them magic functions. At the same time, one must note that this observation—which Adorno must have known—is part of a larger argument concerning the place of animism and magic in human development. Consequently, for Freud the proximity (if not the identity) of art and magic, and not the difference, is the significant insight. The essay develops an evolutionary model in which Freud calls attention to and then emphasizes the parallel between individual development and the evolution of the species. Primitive thought, i.e. animism, corresponds to narcissism in the same manner as the religious phase (the creation of gods) corresponds to the stage of object attachment outside the ego. In Freud's model there is no attempt to give a complete explanation of art or the aesthetic. The example he cites, namely the paintings in French caves, emphasizes an early stage of art when magic and aesthetic operated side by side. He assumes that the magic functions are today for the most part extinct. Still, it is important to note that Freud writes "for the most part" and does not thereby exclude the continued effect of older practices in art. In the area of art, the borderline between the primitive and the more developed form appears to be less clearly marked, which leaves art in an ambiguous position vis-à-vis the developmental scheme that Freud uses. Still, Freud leaves no doubt about the process of enlightenment and its goal. Human maturity is reached in the scientific, postreligious stage when all thoughts of omnipotence, which motivated primitive cultures to develop elaborate animistic thought structures, have been relinquished. For Freud, full enlightenment is not the equivalent of domination of nature but the resigned insight that human beings have, individually as well as collectively, only limited power. While Freud holds on to an evolutionary scheme to map human history, he also questions it by drawing attention to psychic pathology. In his comparison between neurotics and primitives, he alludes to the insight that the narratives of the Enlightenment (which Freud shared) must be regarded as failures, or, in a different reading, he points to the impossibility of the Enlightenment.

The overlap between Freud and Adorno is considerable. Both theorists underscore the ambiguity of art in the history of human culture. Both point to the proximity of magic and art, but they place the emphasis differently. Where Freud highlights the proximity of art and magic as a defining moment of primitive culture but thinks of modern art as mostly free of such elements, Adorno, as we have seen, emphasizes the initial difference, thereby focusing on the specificity of the aesthetic as a vital moment of its origin, but he allows for a greater presence of the magic in the modern artwork. In other words, by remaining attached to the primitive, for Adorno the advanced artwork resists the process of Enlightenment. Of course, there is considerably more emphasis on the legitimacy of this resistance in Adorno's thought than in Freud's theory. Still, Adorno recognizes the ambiguity of the modern artwork, its tendency to return to the logic of mimesis. For Adorno there is no longer a clear-cut distinction between modern and primitive culture, which Freud takes over from the anthropologists of his time (i.e. James George Frazer and E. B. Tyler), nor is there a firm belief in science. The radical critique of historical progress in *Dialectic of Enlightenment* would have shocked even the Freud of *Totem and Taboo*.

In this regard Nietzsche's critique of the Enlightenment resonates more strongly with Adorno's thought. Moreover, Nietzsche's emphatic reevaluation of the function of art in the process of culture results in a new approach to the primitive and, by the same token, to a different understanding of science. In *The Birth of Tragedy* the contrast between Apollo and Dionysus, between measured form and the eruptive forces of the primitive, creates a space for the rejuvenation of art in Nietzsche's own time, a renewal that Nietzsche hoped Wagner's opera would bring about. For the young Nietzsche, this is not merely an aesthetic question; it concerns the future of culture, since rationalism, embodied by Socrates and the dominant aspect of Western civilization, has damaged and diminished the forces of life. By examining Greek tragedy, Nietzsche rediscovers those elements of early culture that the philologists of his time, saturated with the ideals of modern classicism, were prone to overlook or failed to take seriously. In order to celebrate Greek culture as a culture of reconciliation, he must draw attention to its darker side, namely the Dionysian orgies. Dionysian culture is portrayed as the opposite of Dorian culture, and Nietzsche comments, "That repulsive witches' brew of sensuality and cruelty was powerless here; the only reminder of it...is to be found in the strange mixture and duality in the affects of the Dionysiac enthusiasts."[19] While Nietzsche acknowledges that the orgiastic cult of Dionysus came from the East, he also emphasizes the intrinsic quality of the darker side; it is the part that Apollonian Greek culture had repressed. Nietzsche's archaeology of Greek culture results in two discoveries. On the one hand, he uncovers the pre-Olympian world—in other words, the barbaric and cruel; on the other, he defines the world of the Olympian gods as an illusionary aesthetic reality. By turning these layers of culture into principles, Nietzsche can conceive of Greek tragedy as the mysterious marriage, the true synthesis of Greek culture. This shift from an archaeological to a systematic perspective will later enable Nietzsche to put forth Wagner's opera as the new cultural synthesis, a rebirth of ancient tragedy.

The recognition of the barbaric and ugly in archaic culture leads Nietzsche to a differentiation between literary genres. While the epic fulfills the requirements of the Apollonian and tragedy represents a synthesis of the

Dionysian and the Apollonian, poetry articulates the Dionysian element most succinctly. The poet "has become entirely at one with the primordial unity...and he produces a copy of this primordial unity as music" (BT 30). As Nietzsche reminds us, no aesthetic production can access the primordial unit (*Ur-Eine*) without mediation. The suffering is transformed into music, but this very process occurs under the impact of the Apollonian principle. The ultimate goal is therefore not the immediate articulation of suffering but the appearance of redemption. The rediscovery of the barbaric and ugly in *The Birth of Tragedy* should not be confused therefore with its unmitigated celebration. Rather, the purpose is the recognition of archaic horror as a vital and necessary element of culture that finds its appropriate expression in art. For the early Nietzsche, the aesthetic justification of life stands at the center of his project. Still, this project includes the continued efficacy of the archaic.

Nietzsche makes the loss of myth and the rise of Socratic rationalism responsible for the decline of Greek culture and therefore calls for a rebirth of myth. Toward the end of the essay, the Dionysian principle and myth seem to merge, although Nietzsche initially distinguished them. Greek myth comprises the narrative of the ancient Greek people. It is, in other words, already one step removed from the Dionysian principle. This means that the myth of tragedy "participates fully in the aim of all art, which is to effect a metaphysical transfiguration" (BT 113). This means that in Nietzsche's schema, myth and art are on the side of the transfiguration of unbearable suffering. In *Dialectic of Enlightenment* Adorno and Horkheimer, as we have seen, differ sharply from this analysis. Myth denotes the realm of bondage (*Unfreiheit*) that characterizes archaic and barbaric, and its return in totalitarian political systems does not hold a Nietzschean promise of aesthetic reconciliation. While Nietzsche's critique of the Enlightenment moves in the same direction as Adorno and Horkheimer, it finds its goal in aesthetic reconciliation, which implies an indirect legitimation of human suffering. The refusal of aesthetic reconciliation under the sign of the beautiful is one of the central considerations of Adorno's aesthetic theory. For this reason, he underscores not only the primacy of the ugly over the beautiful but also the crucial importance of the ugly and horrible in modern art. He emphasizes the negative moment as a force of opposition that classical philosophy of art keeps in a secondary position. This attitude throws also a different light on his critique of Stravinsky.

His attack on the celebration of the primitive is possibly also directed at the sublation of pain and horror in *The Birth of Tragedy,* since Nietzsche's understanding of music keeps it in the realm of aesthetic illusion.

To be sure, Nietzsche's commitment to Schopenhauer's metaphysics, which supported his early assessment of music, later vanished. Already in *Human, All Too Human,* his approach to music is driven by different concerns. Fragment 217 of the first volume analyzes the development of modern music in a manner that is rather close to the perspective of *The Philosophy of Modern Music.* Nietzsche describes the advent of modern music, by which he probably understood late romantic music including Wagner, as a process of intellectualization. Where older music emphasized the sensual, the new music underscores the abstract intellectual quality, which means that the listener has to focus on the meaning. But the increase in expressive power, Nietzsche suggests, corresponds to a loss in sensual refinement. The new music is not only louder but also coarser. The point Nietzsche wants to make is that both the structure and the reception of music have transcended the realm of the beautiful. Nietzsche notes, "Then, the ugly side of the world, the side originally hostile to the senses, has now been conquered for music; its sphere of power especially in the domain of the sublime, dreadful and mysterious has therewith increased astonishingly."[20] The process of intellectualization legitimizes the ugly, which classical music had either forbidden or kept on the margins, as a moment of musical expression. Nietzsche's response to this development is highly ambivalent. While he appreciates the increase in symbolic meaning, he also deplores the loss of sensuality and the rise of the ugly. Anticipating Adorno's concept of the culture industry, he comments on the split between advanced and popular music. In popular music the ugly makes its appearance without symbolic meaning. He points to "the enormous majority growing every year more and more incapable of comprehending the meaningful even in the form of the sensually ugly and therefore learning to seize with greater and greater contentment the ugly and disgusting in itself, that is to say the basely sensual, in music."[21] The distinction between the meaningful ugly in high art and the ugly in the low forms of mere sensuality allows Nietzsche to deal with the prohibitions of traditional music aesthetic against the ugly and the repulsive. It is important to note that the increase of the ugly is not treated as part of the return of the primitive; rather, it is the result of the new music's striving for symbolic meaning.

In short, it is conceived as an internal process in the history of nineteenth-century music. In his analysis of Schoenberg's music, Adorno arrives at a similar position. The greater importance of the ugly in modern music is the result of unresolved dissonances; briefly put, it is the result of the internal logic of the composition. There is no need to invoke the Dionysian to explain the embrace of radical dissonance.

As we have seen, in *Dialectic of Enlightenment* Adorno revised his position when he recognized the need to examine the archaic and primitive more carefully. The concept of myth, broadly defined, became the vehicle for this exploration. Myth, Adorno and Horkheimer argued, was not only the opposite of the Enlightenment (as the embodiment of oppression) but also part of the Enlightenment as a form of reason. Their intertwinement marks the fatal flaw of history. Hence a Nietzschean celebration of the Dionysian is completely missing in *Dialectic of Enlightenment.* This aspect does not change in *Aesthetic Theory.* The stronger recognition of the ugly as a defining element of both archaic and modern art is not related to Nietzsche's Dionysian primitivism; rather, it draws attention to the critical function of the work of art. While the early artworks struggle to reveal their distinct aesthetic character against the realm of magic, the modern work demonstrates its critical opposition to classical reconciliation by way of its refusal of the harmony of beauty. Whereas the later Nietzsche wavers between the celebration of classicism (Mozart) and the acknowledgment of decadent European modernism (Wagner), Adorno tends to equate classicism with problematic aesthetic solutions. In *Aesthetic Theory* he acknowledges the archaic and primitive as a crucial element of early art, but the perspective is the opposite of that of the early Nietzsche. Adorno focuses attention on the difference between art and magic. In short, he underscores the process of civilization, in which art partakes while it resists the notion of a rational evolution (science). Artworks need the moment of enchantment that science must resolutely refuse.

PART II

4

Reality, Realism, and Representation

The specter of realism haunts Adorno's theory. The concept is both used and rejected in his theory of the novel, which is available mostly in the form of isolated essays that focus on individual novelists. Adorno's resistance to the notion of realism is grounded in his concept of the artwork, in particular its emphatic distance from empirical reality.[1] This aspect is forcefully articulated in his understanding of poetry. In his seminal essay "On Lyric Poetry and Society" (1957; NL 1:37–54) Adorno attempts to persuade an audience of educated German listeners that poetry, while first and foremost determined by the formal organization of its language, is somehow also connected to the social conditions of its time.[2] Rhetorically, he uses the supposed suspicion of the audience that he might intend to impose on poetry a sociological approach from the outside, in order to argue for the possibility or even necessity of an intrinsic sociology of literature. While his listeners or readers might have granted the feasibility of a sociology of the novel, they would have most likely rejected a sociological approach to poetry because the content of poetry, it seems, does not lend itself easily to such a method.

The underlying assumption of this argument is that a sociology of literature is based on a comparison between the content of the artwork and the social phenomena surrounding it. In other words, the investigation seeks to uncover the reflection of the real world in the artwork. The fictional world of the novel, for instance, is supposed to mirror the historical conditions. By deliberately choosing poetry rather than the novel or the drama, Adorno makes his case more difficult to argue, but he also raises the stakes. If one can demonstrate that a connection between the poem and its social environment does exist, the legitimacy of a sociological approach becomes apparent and a broader use of the method can be considered. Adorno seeks to win his argument by laying out the conditions for a persuasive procedure. First of all, the relationship to the social has to be substantive, that is, explicating an essential element of the poem; second, the expressive moment of the poem must be connected to the universal (*das Allgemeine*). Yet Adorno immediately qualifies this statement by suggesting that the universal is not the same as the universality of the concept but a particular moment transposed to a higher level. Third, the procedure of reading must not look at the social position of the poem or its special social interests (for instance, speaking out for a revolutionary or conservative political cause).

How would a sociology of poetry operate and succeed if these conditions were met? Its point of departure would be formal analysis, exploring the language of the poem, because it is through the medium of language that both subjective expression and the objective articulation of the social problematic are generated. Yet this objective aspect cannot be defined in terms of reflection (mirror). Adorno is adamant that such a procedure would miss the essential meaning of the poem and degrade it to the level of ideology. In short, the sociological procedure is not about detecting parallels. Instead, Adorno underscores the moment of negation. Using the example of Goethe's poem "Wanderers Nachtlied," he notes: "The note of peacefulness [in the poem] attests to the fact that peace cannot be achieved without the dream disintegrating" (NL 1:41). According to Adorno, the empirical world impacts the poem, but not through imitation, which would create a positive similarity between the artwork and society. It is more appropriate, Adorno insists, to describe this impact as negative correspondence. Still, there is a form of objective correlation that an advanced sociology of poetry has to examine.

This correlation between the artwork and the outside world, quite apart from the specific requirements of a sociology of art, is central to Adorno's aesthetic theory. It can be found in different parts of his work and at different levels. In conceptual terms, it poses the question of the role of aesthetic representation, including its relationship to the notion of reflection and the specific features of realism.[3]

In this chapter I examine this question with the awareness that Adorno does not use the term "representation" or foreground the concept. The analysis will begin with the role of realism in Adorno's theory and move from there to more complex aspects of representation, including the concept of the monad as Adorno's model for the autonomous structure of the artwork. This part of the analysis will be primarily concerned with *Aesthetic Theory*. Finally, the inquiry will return once more to the question of representation in poetry as the theoretically most challenging aspect of representation.

Given Adorno's rather pronounced bias for the modern novel (Proust, Kafka, Thomas Mann, Beckett), one might expect him to avoid any proximity to authors such as Balzac and Dickens who so clearly represent realism. As it turns out, this is not the case. Adorno devoted three essays to the nineteenth-century European novel. Admittedly, their goal is not a full examination of the issue of realism, but, sometimes indirectly, they do engage this question and provide valuable insights into Adorno's theoretical position. Surprisingly enough, the essay "Reading Balzac" (1961; NL 1:121–136) opens with a sociological remark about social distance in early nineteenth-century France rather than an assessment of Balzac narratives and style. Looking at Balzac's novels, Adorno does not hesitate to see them in the light of the radical social changes during the early phase of high capitalism. In short, it is the content rather than the form that arouses Adorno's interest when reading Balzac. He mentions the rhythm and the dynamic of French society that Balzac's novels try to imitate (*nachahmen*). This looks like a rather conventional approach to Balzac until Adorno makes his decisive theoretical move by introducing the Marxian concept of alienation (*Entfremdung*) as a social category that throws light on the social relations depicted by Balzac. The essay dwells on this phenomenon in order to define the task of the novelist who is attempting to open up reality. Social reality is the point of departure in Adorno's assessment of Balzac's novels. At the same time, we have to keep in mind that this social reality is perceived as already determined by reification. "Reification is more terrifyingly radiant in the freshness of dawn and the glowing colors of new life than the critique of political economy at high noon" (NL 1:122). Although it is only Marx's theory that at a later historical stage develops the needed cognitive insights, Balzac's novels provide through their narratives the very images of the new social relations. What these novels accomplish, Adorno tells us, is the "sensory evidence" (NL 1:122) of the social totality as defined by Hegel and Marx. Even Balzac's tendency to overemphasize the lurid element of interpersonal links, the proximity to a melodramatic understanding of human affairs, serves as evidence of social truth in Balzac. Far from measuring his novels against the literary standards of later realism (for instance, Flaubert), Adorno validates Balzac's style as the appropriate form of representing the social totality of his time. Moreover, the fact that Balzac's characters do not show the psychological refinement of later realism is taken as evidence of a sharper penetration of the social structure. Their appearance as puppets rather than differentiated individuals proves for Adorno the power of reification. Balzac understands that human beings are no longer autonomous subjects.

It is hard to overlook that Adorno in his exploration of Balzac's novels relies on the category of representation, although the term is not used in the essay. Even the question of realism is mentioned, including an affirmative reference to Lukács's 1952 study *Balzac and French Realism*.[4] Adorno's decision to open the essay with an assessment of nineteenth-century French history leads to a comparison between this reality and its presentation in the fictional world of the novel. The question, then, becomes how this comparison is conceptually worked out. Here Adorno follows his own direction that is ultimately at odds with Lukács's theory of realism, for what he praises in Balzac's novels is not so much the faithful depiction of an existing social world but the utopian element, which he finds articulated in Balzac's proximity to German music. In short, the moment of representation that Adorno foregrounds is not identical with the depiction of appearances, because these social phenomena are already bewitched (*verhext*), they are part of a reified structure that does not become legible through conventional methods. Put differently, Adorno claims that only a method that transcends conventional depiction can do justice to the new reality. This means that the conventional narrative method of realism is unable to open up reality. Therefore he underscores the nonrealistic elements in Balzac, the strangeness of his representation, which becomes historically and aesthetically true precisely because it violates prudent, commonsense assessment. According to Adorno, the need to narrate the social totality, as Balzac perceived it, drives him to a method in which the total connectedness of all human relationships presents itself as paranoia. Nothing is left to chance; every moment of the plot and the characters is overdetermined. In other words, for Adorno Balzac's method accomplishes the disclosure of the social totality by making the deformation visible. Economic reality itself, while rational in its drive toward industrialization and complete market capitalism, becomes partly irrational in its social consequences, which is the very element that Balzac brings into the foreground. In this context, however, the concrete object has no longer the function it once had in the epic. Now it serves as incantation (*Beschwörung*) for a world that can no longer be represented as a total presence of concrete objects.

The modernity of Balzac's novels, Adorno tells us, is their ultimate lack of concrete experience, the moment of narrative construction that reveals the broken and contradictory nature of the imagined totality. As Adorno notes, "The realism with which even those who are idealistically inclined are preoccupied is not primary but derived: realism on the basis of a loss of reality" (NL 1:128). Thus examining plot and characters does not affirm Balzac's status as realist, at least not in any conventional sense. Instead, Adorno's references to individual figures and constellations—for instance the relationship of Nuncingen and Esther or Lucien Chardon and the actress Coralie—evoke the sense of a hyperreality that is more intense than bourgeois life. Against Engels, whose letter to Margret Harkness Adorno mentions,[5] and Lukács, Adorno asserts that the historical as well as aesthetic truth of Balzac's novels cannot be contained under the label of realism. On the other hand, Adorno also maintains that Balzac is able to grasp the social reality of his times in his novels because his prose does not "yield to realities but rather stares them in the face until they become transparent down to their horrors [*aufs Unwesen*]" (NL 1:132). Here Adorno uses a strong metaphor to mark the difference between Balzac's literary method and conventional realism. But what precisely does it mean? The remainder of Adorno's essay is an attempt to elucidate the image.

For Adorno the transparency of Balzac's novel is the result of a narrative strategy that uses force to make the totality visible. It creates a density of connections and personal relations that empirical reality cannot match. Thus the social world becomes truly legible because the author uses the detail to tell us more about the meaning of the whole. What Adorno understands as Balzac's violation of the code of realism (which, by the way, is never clearly defined in the essay), serves an essential function, i.e. the representation of social totality. In other words, the representation of social totality requires a literary method that must transcend realism. Realism therefore must not be used, Adorno argues, as an invariant transhistorical norm. "Invariants are incompatible with the spirit of the dialectic even if Hegelian classicism vindicates them" (NL 1:132). While it remains unclear whether this dictum is meant as a critique of Lukács, it underscores the dialectic of social reality and literary representation, which of course is also at the very center of Lukácsian theory. Adorno affirms Balzac's achievement as a novelist no less than Lukács, but he turns the argument around. Where Lukács in the wake of Engels sees the triumph of realism, Adorno discovers a literary method that follows its own logic in order to uncover the structure of social reality. This is probably meant as a critique of Lukács, although the essay avoids a polemical tone. At the same time, Adorno makes no serious attempt to explicate his critique in theoretical terms. Like Lukács, he invokes the difference between a given, though changing social reality and the literary reality in Balzac's novels, and similar to Lukács he places the emphasis on the disclosure of the social totality through literary means. In other words, he shares with Lukács, whether it is explicitly stated or not, the use of the concept of representation. He differs from the older critic in his assessment of Balzac's mode of representation by denying its realistic character, which is important to Lukács. This different emphasis allows him greater flexibility in his description and evaluation of Balzac's novels. Although when he discusses the literary context of these novels he points to their dated formal organization and style, he is prepared to rescue them from the fate of oblivion because of their somewhat crude freshness. But ultimately, even this freshness would not suffice to secure Balzac's place in literary history, which Adorno means to confirm. It is the historical movement itself, the extraordinary dynamic of bourgeois society, in spite of the individual suffering, which Balzac does not cover up, that in Adorno's mind reveals the "promise of justice on the part of the whole" (NL 1:134). It appears that Adorno reads Balzac with Hegel's understanding of history in mind, yet without the latter's aesthetic classicism.

Adorno's critique of literary realism, seen in this light, opens up the transition to the modern artwork, to the prose of Proust and Kafka— that is, precisely to those novelists whom Lukács wants to remove from his normative understanding of realism.[6] This tendency is most delicately suggested in a small piece on a passage in *Lost Illusions* in which Adorno interprets Lucien's review of a Boulevard comedy, written specifically to praise the leading actress without much regard for the literary quality of the play. For Adorno this is the occasion to demonstrate at least three things at the same time: the function of the review in the novel as the turning point in the career of the young writer; the analysis of Lucien's small piece, now seen as an early example of the new critical form of the feuilleton in the Paris press; and finally, quite self-consciously, his own essay as a feuilleton, written without the conceptual apparatus of his more serious essays. The piece, titled "On an Imaginary Feuilleton" (NL 2:32–39), denies its own intellectual labor just as Lucien's review denies or sells out the moment of critique that is expected in a theater review. In other words, Adorno plays with the moment of corruption that he both uncovers and celebrates in Lucien's review. The corruption of the press is not only Balzac's favorite topic but also that of Karl Kraus and his admirer Adorno. By inventing this new form Lucien loses his virginity as a poet and becomes worldly, exposing himself to the critique of his true friends as well as that of the narrator. Yet Balzac uses this opportunity to demonstrate through the concrete literary form (and Adorno underscores this) the actual fall from grace and simultaneously the representation of a different segment of society, namely journalists. For Adorno this double move is proof of Balzac's power of realism in the radical cognitive sense of opening up the social world of his time. Still, it is worth noting that Adorno's praise of Balzac's literary craftsmanship focuses on elements of the content rather than the formal organization of the novel, since in this constellation the form of the feuilleton is itself meaningful content. Without calling attention to it, Adorno's essay on the fictional feuilleton underlines the importance of literary representation and the underlying belief in an objective reality to which the novel can refer. Furthermore, Adorno does not question that the truth of literary representation can be measured, at least in part, against this outside world.

By downplaying the "realistic" features of Balzac's novel, Adorno, whether intentionally or not, opens up a path to the modern novel. His essays on Kafka, Proust, and the position of the narrator in the modern novel were written obviously in defense of the modern novel against the Stalinist verdict on the one hand and conservative attacks on the other. By now, to be sure, this aspect has lost its urgency, striking today's readers as outdated. Even Adorno's intervention against the popular existentialist interpretations of Kafka as a problematic interpretative assimilation of the literary texts that misses their authentic nature by imposing an abstract philosophical apparatus has lost most of its original force. Nonetheless, in both instances one can detect traces of a representation model in Adorno's analysis. While they are fairly obvious in the case of Proust because of the explicit social dimension of *À la recherche du temps perdu,* they are more difficult to find when he reads Kafka, since here the opponent is the philosophical or theological rather than the orthodox Marxist critic. In more general terms, as Adorno asserts in "The Position of the Narrator," the realist impulse of the novel has to overcome realism: "If the novel wants to remain true to its realistic heritage and tell how things really are, it must abandon a realism that only aids the facade in its work of camouflage by reproducing it" (NL 1:32). As long as this indictment of realism is taken also as an indictment of representation, Adorno's stance seems to be contradictory and his emphatic embrace of the modern European novel appears as a narrow defense of formalism. But Adorno implicitly distinguishes between realism and representation. The concept of representation turns out to be the larger and overriding one; it is a concept that is ultimately compatible with the form of the modern novel.

While the impetus of the Proust essay follows the Hegelian dialectic of the concrete and the universal and places the emphasis on Proust's deliberate efforts to build his narrative world out of numerous, carefully described and annotated objects and persons, the thematic aspect is kept in the background. It is more implicit than explicit, yet understood as indispensable when Adorno looks at Proust's achievement as an analyst of the French society of the late nineteenth century. Explicitly, Adorno calls Proust a social critic, although, as he himself notes, Proust does not disagree with the norms of the society he portrays. His critique, Adorno asserts, results from the narrative procedure itself. "As a novelist, however, he suspended its system of categories and thereby pierced its claim to self-evidence, the illusion that it is a part of nature" (NL 1:176). Yet it is important to realize that this critique, while remaining immanent to the world of the novel, presupposes a social reality that is juxtaposed to and represented in the novel without being imitated in a literal and rigid sense. Thus, for Adorno the truth of Proust's novel has also to do with its engagement with the social world, specifically with its ability to articulate the moment of reification through narrative strategies that counter the false appearance of a natural reality that can simply be portrayed. Furthermore, Adorno extends this reading to an analysis of his own experience in a postliberal twentieth-century society. "The people who are decisive in our lives appear in them as though appointed and dispensed by an unknown author, as though we had awaited them in this very place and no other;...perhaps divided up into several figures, they cross our paths again and again" (NL 1:176). In brief, through its narrative construction, including its complex constellation of characters, Proust's novel offers a truthful paradigm for understanding social relations, which means that for Adorno social and aesthetic truth cannot be separated.

So far one might argue that Adorno's approach to Balzac and Proust is rather similar. In both instances, while acknowledging the period difference, he upholds the moment of representation as essential for the truth content of their novels. Then the question arises: What makes *À la recherche du temps perdu* a modern novel? As Adorno suggests, there is a surprising proximity to surrealism. Instead of psychological differentiation, Proust develops mythic images, in order to disclose social and psychological meaning. It is the disenchantment of the world caused by reification that Proust's mythic images capture. The narrative methods of bourgeois realism would fail to make these moments legible. Thus for Adorno the transition from a liberal bourgeois society to later capitalism requires a new and different literary strategy to remain truthful. But the task of literary representation does not disappear; rather, it takes new formal means to accomplish the same end. It is not accidental that Adorno in this context invokes Lukács's *Theory of the Novel* as a model for understanding the dialectic of sociohistorical and literary-structural change, since the early Lukács conceptualizes the novel (as distinct from the epic) as a literary process of disclosing simultaneously the state of the (isolated) subject and the (reified) world. Lukács's category of the contingent in particular turns out to be helpful for the interpretation of Proust, insofar as it brings out the meaningless detail in the novel out of which the whole has to be negatively constructed. Yet this construction, Adorno underscores, must give up on the hope of discovering a positive meaningful totality. While the struggle for reconciliation is attested to Proust, there is no possibility of ever reaching it in permanence.

In Adorno's readings of Kafka this precise moment is carried even further. For Adorno Kafka remains the quintessential modernist, but a modernist who is mostly misunderstood by his interpreters because they assign a metaphysical meaning to his novels when precisely this kind of meaning must be questioned. Its rejection very much colors Adorno's engagement with Kafka in his essay "Notes on Kafka" (1953; Pr 243–271), which remains the more substantial intervention.[7] Since the proper rediscovery of Kafka's novels emphasizes not only the crucial importance of the concrete detail but also their unusual and striking narrative strategy, which forbids contemplative distance, the question of their truth value takes on an urgency that neither Balzac nor Proust can claim. Thus Kafka's literary "method" must become the center and cornerstone of the essay, thereby relegating the moment of representation to the background. Adorno's reading explores various formal elements, among them language and style, configuration of characters, the use of names and metaphors by citing examples, which gives his own essay the character of an enumeration of discrete examples held together by commentary. When approaching the semantic side, Adorno refuses to offer an all-embracing meaning, choosing instead to elucidate the text by referring to Freud's interpretation of early human history (for instance, the killing of the father by the members of the *Urhorde*). Again, he underscores the proximity to surrealism and its method of shock. At the same time, the question of meaning, which has always haunted Kafka scholarship,[8] does not disappear. Neither does the aspect of representation. Both of them are ultimately connected, yet in an unusual way. While in the novels of Balzac the representation of a social reality generates meaning, in the case of Kafka it is meaning that generates representation. Hence Adorno notes: "He does not directly outline the image of the society to come, ... but rather creates it as a montage composed of waste-products which the new order, in the process of forming itself, extracts from the perishing present" (Pr 251–252, translation modified). Surprisingly, Adorno invokes the principle of montage in order to capture Kafka's method of representation in which the single moment, the devastated material (*Stoff,*) is assembled to create meaning, although this meaning is the opposite of a meaningful totality. Thus it is difficult to define what this mode of representation actually consists of and what its ultimate goal might be. In Adorno's eyes the radical nature of Kafka's narratives is reflected in his extreme reduction of the human fate, his determined dismantling (*Abbau*) of all those differentiated psychological and social configurations that define an advanced modern society, leading to a déjà vu of general availability (*Verfügbarkeit*) and collectivization. Thus the images, out of which representation is generated, are the opposite of the themes and motifs that affirm the structure of a meaningful social world. They are aggressive and destructive; they are "hermetic memoranda [containing] the social genesis of schizophrenia" (Pr 255), understood as the collective state of mind reached in the phase of late capitalism and fascism.

The reversal of meaning and representation stated above allows Adorno to link the fictional world of Kafka to the economic and political conditions in central Europe during the 1930s. Although Kafka's novels obviously were written before 1933 and in no way offer a realistic depiction of life under the conditions of fascism, Adorno seeks to detect unexpected structural parallels, though not at the level of visual similarity. Rather, for Adorno they become legible through the mediation of shared meaning. The moment of general regression that defines Kafka's alien world, its neglected and even retarded character, seen from the perspective of an advanced liberal society, is the equivalence of the fascist reorganization of social and political relations. For example, Adorno notes: "In the *Castle* the officials wear a special uniform, as the SS did—one which any pariah can make himself if need be" (Pr 259). Thus Adorno's reading becomes allegorical by focusing on the concrete textual detail and assigning it a meaning that is not contained in the plot or the human figures as they are described. It is only at the conceptual level that the parallel between fascist society and Kafka's world becomes legible. This conceptual level owes its force to a Marxist theory of late capitalism that mediates between actual history and the hermetic world of Kafka's novels. Its special feature is the emphasis on decay and regression. It allows the reader to decode this strange and hermetic world without reducing its threatening character, which Adorno wants to preserve against any interpretation that simply converts the literary text into theoretical meaning, as do, for instance, theological readings.

For Adorno, then, Kafka's literary achievement consists of recognizing and articulating through fictional narratives the social tendencies of his period. That this formulation has a Lukácsian ring should not surprise us, since both theorists share a commitment to the concept of representation. But while in the work of the mature Lukács this concept is closely connected to the concept of realism and therefore distant from modernism, in the work of Adorno the modernist novel, despite its rejection of realistic narrative devices, is perceived as a representation of a theoretical model rather than a reflection of the sensible world. The potential danger of this approach is the repetition of the theory itself, reformulated as a disclosure of aesthetic meaning. An example can be found in the following statement: "The hermetic principle [of Kafka] is that of completely estranged subjectivity" (Pr 261), for this statement could also be applied to numerous other modern novels. This problem cannot be completely avoided because the theoretical level functions as the mediating link between the literary text and the outside world. Each of them, approached without the conceptual tools of theory, remains blind.

One would seriously misunderstand Adorno's intention if one read his interpretation of Kafka as a description of the empirical features of the Third Reich. The goal of his essay is considerably more radical. Through a reading of Kafka's texts he seeks to open up a deeper level of reality, a level that conventional history would miss because it clings to the facts. Instead, with the help of the literary text, Adorno means to throw light on the hidden, dark side of history and disclose its essence. History itself, conceptualized as a forward-moving process, is under scrutiny. This is the moment for Adorno where the strange and eccentric character of Kafka's stories brings to light the damaged nature of the historical process, the failure to keep up with the promise of the enlightenment. In obvious proximity to *Dialectic of Enlightenment,* Adorno underlines the return of the archaic and the force of myth as decisive elements in Kafka. The possibility of human freedom is denied, since "the boundary between what is human and the world of things becomes blurred" (Pr 262). Yet what Kafka discloses is more than the confirmation of Adorno's theory (which of course is the case); it creates a concrete representation of the theory, a representation that is far more shocking than the theory itself. The concept of depersonalization that Adorno introduces to capture the nature of the fictional figures and their relations cannot capture, as Adorno realizes and underscores, the sensual moment of this process. This leads to the conclusion that the truthfulness of Kafka's representation lies not in the similarity between the empirical facts and their configuration, on the one hand, and the phenomena of the narrated world of the novels, on the other. Rather, it lies in their structural affinities generated and articulated by theory (of late capitalism), with the important caveat, however, that the semblance of the artwork is assigned a higher degree of spiritual energy.

This remains the paradox of Adorno's approach: while Kafka's novel is treated as a closed construct without insight into the conditions of its production and meaning, it contains a depth of meaning (*Sinn*) that is waiting for disclosure. This methodological feature also explains Adorno's low interest in narratology—in, for instance, an analysis of Kafka's plot structures or his treatment of time. What fascinates Adorno when he reads Kafka are the concrete images of persons and places, of particular moments within the plot. Thus his reading tends to be iconographic and focused on the detail, thereby favoring allegorical signification, which then becomes the basis for the construction of representation by way of theory. Adorno's engagement with Kafka in particular makes clear that representation is by no means identical or even similar to realism. Any formal construct in modern art can serve as a means of representation as long as there is something like an empirical reality out there, which matters in spite of its serious, and possibly hopeless, imperfection because of its relentless impact on the individual subject. In his polemic against Lukács Adorno explains why he so vigorously resists realism in modern art: it presupposes reconciliation between the subject and the world at a time when this reconciliation is not possible in the social reality we inhabit today.

A closer look at this polemic on the occasion of Lukács's study *Realism in Our Time* (1958) will enable us to clarify Adorno's concept of representation as part of his own aesthetic theory by way of a comparison with the Lukácsian position.[9] In this context the polemic itself is of secondary interest, since much of it was part of a confrontation determined by the conditions of the Cold War in which Adorno decided to play the part of the defender of the West, including Western modern art. The more interesting and certainly more relevant aspect of Adorno's essay "Extorted Reconciliation" (1958) is the desire on Adorno's part to counter the orthodox Marxist theory of realism, to which Lukács largely though not completely adhered, with a position that allows him to understand modern literature as a legitimate extension of nineteenth-century realism in its encounter with historical and social reality. Nothing angers Adorno more than the charge of solipsism against the avant-garde because it denies the desire to grasp and account for the world, a moment crucial for Adorno's own theory.

At face value the polemic is about the charge of the distortion of reality in modern art.[10] The fact that Adorno accepts this charge at all implies a moment of objectivism in his own theory, which must be explained and sharpened in his fierce attack on Lukács. A brief summary of the polemical side of the essay must suffice to prepare the examination of the theoretical stakes of the encounter. These stakes, as we will see, force Adorno to rethink the dialectic of art and reality and more specifically the relationship of the formal organization of the artwork and the structure of the historical world. While the polemic tends to simplify Lukács's theory of realism in order to demonstrate its utterly deficient character, there is enough theoretical resistance to demand a fuller exploration on Adorno's part. However, in the essay Adorno responds to this implied demand only up to a point, leaving unresolved some important elements of his own theory, elements to which he will return later in *Aesthetic Theory*.

The thrust of the polemic can be summarized under four aspects, namely (1) the inability to understand the critical importance of form in general and the formal organization of modern art in particular; (2) a dogmatic adherence to the norm of realism; (3) the misconception of contemporary reality in socialist countries; and (4) the loss of the dialectical method, which the early Lukács had mastered so well. In short, Adorno's verdict is that the work of the late Lukács is an example of theoretical regression symptomatic for the state of philosophy and aesthetics in the Soviet bloc. There are occasional moments when Adorno recognizes important insights on Lukács's part, but they remain marginal for the meaning of the whole argument.

Repeatedly Adorno charges Lukács with disrespect for the significance of aesthetic form. He is especially upset about the claim that modern art is characterized by distortions of reality, which are the result of a misconception of reality on the part of the artist. He disapproves of the tendency to define the comparison of empirical reality and the artwork in terms of content (*Stoff*), and specifically the attempt to measure the construct of the artwork by transferring the elements of empirical reality into the artwork, for instance the modern novel, without mediation. In other words, he opposes a form of aesthetic criticism that begins its work with the uncritical acceptance of the outside world and uses this world as the norm for the evaluation of the artwork. When he explains the correct approach he emphasizes the priority of the artwork and the analysis of its construction before its relationship to the outside world can be considered. The dogmatic adherence to realism, and by extension to social realism, is, as Adorno correctly observes, the result of Lukács's uncritical infatuation with reality. By accepting social reality as the base for aesthetic production, Lukács is forced into a theory of imitation or reflection in which the proximity of the content of the artwork to reality becomes the measure of its aesthetic success.[11]

It should be noted that Adorno, in his desire to downgrade reflection theory, does not make a serious attempt to explore its more complicated structure. The obvious point for Adorno is the insight that this theory is rather helpless when confronted with modern art. But we will have to revisit this point since it covers up Adorno's own involvement with the problem of reflection, for which he has to find a better solution. While Adorno by all means recognizes the importance of bourgeois realism and even defends it against Lukács's narrow and dogmatic appreciation, he completely dismisses socialist realism as a deeply flawed construct that precisely distorts the (miserable) reality of socialist countries by depicting their world as harmonious and reconciled. This polemic moves from the arena of literary criticism to the field of social critique, arguing against the success of the socialist revolution in the Eastern bloc. Adorno charges that these countries are in fact characterized by regressive instead of progressive tendencies. They have not reached the Western standard. In the manner of Cold War exchanges this criticism is asserted rather than theoretically developed or empirically demonstrated. In theoretical terms, however, this deficit does not matter very much because the negative verdict remains outside of Adorno's own theoretical response to Lukács. For Adorno only the most advanced capitalist societies matter when we are concerned with the fate of modern art.

Ultimately, Adorno's attack is motivated by what he conceives as the loss of dialectic thought in the work of the late Lukács, his capitulation vis-à-vis the Stalinist authorities that have turned Marxist dialectics into an abstract schema that mostly serves the needs of the power elite. This regression, Adorno argues, has affected his assessment not only of the present social and political world at large but also of the central aesthetic issues. It is the lack of mediation between the artwork and empirical reality in particular that is responsible in Adorno's eyes for the shortcomings of reflection theory. Reflection theory remains at the level of a comparison favoring the notion of art as a realistic imitation of reality. But the charge does not stop there. In addition, Adorno holds against Lukács a positive resolution of the historical dialectic in state socialism. His polemic focuses on the moment of a false reconciliation between the socialist goal and the economic and intellectual poverty of state socialist societies. This defense of the West carries its own forced momentum by remaining mostly silent about the very reification that Adornian theory typically puts at the center of the analysis of modern capitalist societies. Which means that the precarious state of the avant-garde, of which Adorno is quite aware, remains outside of his engagement.

The polemical intervention, as we have seen, falls short of a thorough theoretical assessment of Lukács. Such a critique remains hidden under the brush of aggressive rhetorical firework. In order to bring the critical response to the foreground, we have to examine specific passages of the essay more carefully by putting pressure on Adorno's assertions. Adorno points to consensus between Lukács and himself when he asserts that art is a form of knowledge, but then holds against Lukács that he misunderstands art as more or less identical with science (*Wissenschaft*):

> Lukács simplifies the dialectical unity of art and science so that it becomes a pure identity, as though works of art merely anticipated something perspectively which the social sciences then diligently confirmed. What essentially distinguishes the work of art as knowledge *sui generis* from scientific or scholarly work is that nothing empirical remains unaltered, that the contents become objectively meaningful only when fused with subjective intentions. Although Lukács differentiates his realism from naturalism, he fails to take into account that if the distinction is intended seriously, realism will necessarily be amalgamated with the subjective intentions he would like to banish from it. (NL 1:227)

For Lukács the separation of realism and naturalism is a crucial move because it allows him to differentiate an aesthetically successful representation from a mechanical, merely imitative one. According to Lukács, realism entails more than imitation of empirical reality in the manner of photography. Through the use of specific formal means realism can grasp the essential structural moments of reality that remain hidden underneath the surface. It is worth noting that Adorno turns this argument against Lukács by shifting the emphasis from the distinction between depth and surface (which he himself uses in his argument against realism as reflection) to the difference between a dialectical and a nondialectical understanding of aesthetic production. The artwork transcends the labor of the social sciences by transforming the empirical elements (*Stoff*) into something in which the subjective intention of the artist is expressed. Adorno uses the German word *verschmelzen* (melt) to indicate the aesthetic dialectic. Thus it becomes apparent that he is not really interested in the Lukácsian problematic of defining realism. While he is equally concerned with the cognition of social reality and the formal organization of this cognition in the artwork, he places the emphasis on the transformation of the empirical material as it occurs in the moment of aesthetic production through the intervention of the artist. Hence for him there is a significant but no fundamental difference between a realistic and a modern novel in their respective modes of representation. The modern novel is simply more radical in the use of formal means to transform empirical reality. This radicalization itself, however, is not accidental; rather, it is caused by the structural transformation of social reality. Here Adorno is in full agreement with Brecht. The formal means of aesthetic production have to be adjusted to the structure of social reality. From Adorno's perspective, therefore, Lukács fails to grasp the dialectic of form and reality by insisting on a normative realistic mode of representation.

Obviously, Adorno seeks to rescue the modern artwork from the negative verdict of distortion, which poses the question of its truthfulness. He approaches this question by distinguishing between the logic of science and philosophy on the one hand and the logic of the artwork on the other. Thus he writes: "Its [the artwork's] logicity is not that of a statement with subject and predicate but that of immanent coherence: only in and through that coherence, through the relationship in which it places its elements, does it take a stance....It passes no judgments; it becomes a judgment when taken as a whole" (NL 1:232). The advantage of the artwork compared with the scientific argument is its synthetic nature. Although less precise in its formal judgments, it gains, Adorno tells us, through its greater balance vis-à-vis the whole of the world. Put differently, its cognitive advantage is its ability to articulate social totality.

Using the Benjaminian distinction between the material content (*Sachgehalt*) and the truth content of an artwork (whether his use is correct or not is not our concern in this context), Adorno offers a different approach to the problem of representation. He suggests that Lukács's theory of realism remains tied to the *Sachgehalt* (the level of material), while his own theory seeks to capture the truth content of the artwork by underscoring the difference between aesthetic reflection and the needed expression of those elements of experience that negate the imitation of the empirical. Yet this attempt does not substantially improve his own understanding of representation beyond the level he reached in earlier parts of the essay, since his polemical intent limits the scope of his own argument. Focused primarily on rejecting Lukácsian reflection theory, Adorno does not fully articulate his own concept of representation.

Is there a more elaborate and successful engagement in *Aesthetic Theory?* Within the larger section on art and society the question of representation is broached in different ways without being the central theme. While Adorno repeats and also modifies the arguments presented in his essays, there are moments when he, now motivated by the larger context of the chapter, offers formulations that somewhat clarify his theoretical position. In part, his continued critique of realism throws more light on his own understanding of the relationship between art and society. It goes without saying that mere imitation of social reality is dismissed out of hand, and that the fixation of the artist on the empirical phenomena (naturalism) is considered the lowest form of mediation. Since mediation is treated as the articulation of the negation of reality in the artwork, it becomes necessary to determine the precise nature of this negation in the formal organization of the artwork. Is there room for representation? In those passages where Adorno discusses the problem of realism it becomes clear that he tacitly relies on a notion of representation without stating this explicitly. By asserting that art and society are converging in the content (*Gehalt*) rather than the exterior material, Adorno reframes his implicit notion of representation by freeing it from the concept of reflection. What are required, however, are both an objective and a subjective element in the connection. While the subjective moment refers back to the intent of the artistic production, the objective moment underscores the fact that the artwork does open up and unfold the social without imitating its phenomena. Hence the style of an author can be recognized as an element of representation, as in the case of Kafka when Adorno claims: "Kafka's epic style is, in its archaism, mimesis of reification" (AT 230).[12] Similar is the suggestion that twentieth-century constructivism is closer to the modern social world than an attempt to engage the same reality with the means of realism. Thus in his examples Adorno tries to demonstrate that the method of realism can at best be seen as a historically limited approach and not a general aesthetic norm to engage social reality. This assessment implies the strict theoretical separation of realism and representation.[13]

Yet the analysis has to go a step further to show the theoretical relevance of the notion of representation in Adorno's late theory. One path to explore this question is a closer examination of the role of the novel in Adorno's late theory; the other leads to the concept of the artwork itself, that is, to the core of *Aesthetic Theory*. For Adorno, as he notes in his Balzac essays, the novel is the modern genre par excellence because of its proximity to the capitalist market and the experience of a modern mass society. It is not surprising therefore that the passages where Adorno refers to or discusses the novel are marked by a certain degree of suspicion against the aesthetic quality of the novel. It is precisely its involvement with the crude elements of daily life that makes the genre dubious in Adorno's eyes. At the same time, he recognizes its importance for the evolution of modern art, the trajectory from the early English novel, in which the contingent elements of daily life are barely integrated, to the novels of Beckett, where the moment of representation of the social world is reduced to the bare minimum.[14] Looking at the novel from the perspective of its aesthetic potential, Adorno is mostly concerned with the problem of integration. The outside reality is typically referred to as the "other" that becomes an aesthetic problem because its elements are organized in a way that does not follow the requirements of aesthetic form. While Homeric epic could effortlessly integrate factual information of different areas, the modern novel, Adorno suggests in the wake of the early Lukács, is sensitive to its crude material elements because they resist meaning (*Sinn*). Therefore the question of meaning becomes particularly relevant when, as in the case of Beckett, the description of the outside world has been reduced to a minimum. Thus the problem of representation takes on special urgency in the novel of the avant-garde, where its form is confronted with the abstractness of social reality. "New art is as abstract as social relations have in truth become" (AT 31). Nonetheless, Adorno insists that this abstractness is presented in the artwork itself. In the case of modern painting, Adorno uses the distinction between image and copy (*Bild* and *Abbild,* ÄT 53) to mark the specificity of representation, underlining again the rejection of imitation as central to the artwork.[15]

Most clearly, however, Adorno's understanding of representation in the context of the novel form comes to the fore in a passage where he briefly discusses the evolution of the novel. At the center of this passage we find the tension between the mere facts of life and their meaning in the novel. How can the novel transform crude material into meaningful form? For Adorno this is not primarily a question of plot structure and character development. These elements, while necessary for the organization of the narrative, are not by themselves a guarantee of meaning (*Sinn*). He assigns meaning to a novel only when it transcends the level of the contingent description of life. Hence the concept of meaning in this passage is closely linked to the concept of truth in an emphatic sense. In Adorno's eyes, it defines the history of the novel that it moves from crude forms that barely go beyond the reflection of life to an organization where the outside world is artistically fully integrated (Flaubert, Proust) and thereby meaning is guaranteed, to a modernist mode where integration and meaning have become problematic (Beckett). In this context it becomes apparent that the category of representation is tied to the concept of truth, more specifically to its function in Adorno's philosophy of history. In brief then, representation in the artwork defines its historical truth in aesthetic terms. Adorno's concept of the artwork, although seemingly hostile to any notion of representation, ultimately bears this out. If the artwork is conceived as a monad, that is, as an entity without windows and completely closed vis-à-vis the outside world, the search for a moment of representation seems to be fruitless. However, while the model of the monad does not allow for imitation or reflection, it does permit representation. As Adorno notes in the draft introduction of 1959: "In the problem nexus of each and every artwork, what is external to the monad, and that whereby it is constituted, is sedimented in it" (AT 358). This somewhat opaque sentence becomes legible in the context of Adorno's aim to define the function of the individual artwork against the background of a genre or a class of artworks. He suggests that the individual artwork constitutes a problem nexus (*Problemzusam-menhang*), by which he means a link not only to other works but also to the social environment that through its aesthetic form it denies as the other. What Adorno calls the problem nexus describes its ability to take in history and thereby transcend its particularity. "It is in the dimension [*Zone*] of history that the individual aesthetic object and its concept communicate. History is inherent to aesthetic theory" (AT 358–359). This, however, suggests that representation within the monad is not only possible but also necessary to disclose meaning (*Sinn*). At the same time, it remains true that the artwork cannot simply leap beyond (*herausspringen,* ÄT 385) the confines of the monad without losing its aesthetic authenticity, although, as Adorno underscores, it must be aware of its own social mediation. Yet a valid theoretical insight in itself remains aesthetically extrinsic. Put differently, the artwork cannot simply dismiss its semblance.

In his more extensive discussion of the monadic character of the artwork in the segment "Toward a Theory of the Artwork" the Adornian conception of representation is even more forcefully explicated. Although admittedly treated as problematic, the model of the monad discloses the tension between the intrinsic and the extrinsic nature of the artwork. While artworks are perceived as isolated monads, they are simultaneously part of a larger historical context. Here Adorno's formulation deserves our full attention: "Artworks are closed to one another, blind, and yet in their hermeticism they represent [*vorstellen*] what is external" (AT 179). Adorno uses the German word "*vorstellen*" to mark the relationship between the inside and the outside of the monad, but he clearly avoids the terminology of reflection and imitation. The significance of this move reveals itself only later in the segment when Adorno turns to the dialectic between the particular and the universal. The question is: How do artworks participate in the sphere of universal ideas, which in the philosophical tradition denote truth? Adorno's answer, formulated as a critique of Hegel, is that the artwork as a monad leads from its "own principle of particularization to the universal" (AT 181). In brief, the truth content of the artwork cannot be separated from the notion of representation.

As we have seen, Adorno's conception of the artwork is determined by a dualistic structure. The artwork is constituted as separate from the outside world. In the case of modern art, this relationship is perceived even as distant and hostile. Yet it is precisely this distance, as Adorno points out, that through the moment of negation constitutes representation. Here we have to remind ourselves that this structure remains close to Lukács's *Theory of the Novel,* where the history of the novel is equally defined by the stark opposition between the artwork and modern society. Focusing on the hero as an individual subject, Lukács develops a number of narrative models (among them the novel of disillusion and the bildungsroman) to capture different aesthetic solutions to the basic conflict between the homeless subject and a hostile social reality, which means that the fictional world of the novel, presented through the means of narration, takes on the mode of representation, without turning into a mere reflection of the outside. Even in his polemic against Lukács in 1958 Adorno expressed his continued appreciation of this approach. In light of this consensus, the later differences between Adorno and Lukács, which first and foremost centered around the concepts of realism and reflection, deserve a second look. Adorno's essays on the novel and individual novelists rest on the theory of the early Lukács, but augmented by *History and Class Consciousness. The concept of reification taken over from this work becomes very much part of Adorno's understanding of modern art, including the modern novel.* Adorno, like Lukács, treats the novel as the objective correlative of modern history. In the wake of Lukács, he emphasizes the philosophical meaning of the novel. Its abstract organization, compared with the organic form of the epic, underlined in *Theory of the Novel,* is taken over by Adorno as an argument against the theory of realism in the later Lukács. But the formal abstractness, now seen through the lenses of Marxist theory, becomes the objective correlative of reification in the social world. In short, Adorno could mine the early Lukács for his critique of the latter's later work. There is nothing in the *Theory of the Novel* that would block the appreciation of the modern novel and modernism in general. To the contrary, the profound alienation already detected in the hero of the novel of disillusion (Flaubert) would become only more extreme in the modern novel.

   The Adornian theory of the culture industry based on the notion of radical commoditization of cultural production in general is heavily indebted to the theory of universal reification in *History and Class Consciousness.* Once this theory is extended to literary criticism, it underscores the need for vigilant resistance to the debasement of literary forms, including the novel. Thus in his essays on the nineteenth-century novel Adorno stresses the modern elements and plays down the moment of realism that is important for Lukács in *Realism in Our Time* as an indication of correct reflection. Therefore realism, when found in twentieth-century novels, is treated in Adorno as a sign of the growing impact of the culture industry. In other words, realism becomes an index of mere entertainment and the loss of truth.

Lukács's condemnation of the modern novel, on the other hand, is based on a similar theory, namely the claim that aesthetic production in advanced capitalist society, unless corrected by the critical author, leads to the distortion of literary forms and genres. Thus the modern novel, because of its (subjective) narrative method and style, appears as a false representation of social reality. But it is important to note that this contrast points to an underlying identical theoretical structure marked by the dualism of social reality and artwork and the existence of an objective correlation between the two. Neither Lukács nor Adorno can discuss the truth or value of the novel without recourse to this structure, a point that has to be carefully considered when adjudicating their differences.

Looking more closely at Adorno's actual use of the category of representation, it turns out that it functions on different levels.[16] As a reader of realistic fiction (Balzac, Dickens) Adorno uses the concept to distance himself from the conventional notion that the fictional world of realistic novels reflects or depicts empirical reality, i.e. the notion that they offer an actual portrait of existing social conditions. Therefore he emphasizes the nonrealistic elements in Balzac. At the same time, he strongly insists on the representational character of Balzac's novels; they are supposed to disclose not only a relationship between the fictional and the nonfictional world but also an objective correlative. This correlation operates at a deeper structural level and is not (always) revealed in terms of plausible characters and probable plot structures. Literary representation is given greater freedom than the work of the historian or sociologist. Yet for Adorno this higher degree of freedom is not random. Rather, he interprets it as an aesthetic process by which the inherent meaning of the outside world can be uncovered. This argument becomes especially important in the case of the narrative strategies of the modern novel that intentionally violate conventional notions of realism. For Adorno these strategies enhance the possibility of exposing the intrinsic structure of the modern world. Still, in either case the concept of representation functions at the level of equivalence. The careful reader of the realistic and modern novel realizes that they contain, although by way of different narrative strategies, an objective interpretation of social totality.

There is, however, in Adorno's theory another level where the concept of representation functions in a highly abstract manner. It can be extended therefore to literary forms and genres that are typically not mentioned in connection with the concept of representation. The concept of the artwork as a monad, as completely separated from the outside world, suggests, at least prima facie, a lack of representation; but at second sight, the artwork reveals a more abstract process of representation, since the idea of a monad requires the presence of the outside in the inside of the monad, that is, a link, although it is a negative link. By focusing exclusively on its own formal organization and attending to the structure of its content (*Gehalt*), the artwork, Adorno contends, also represents the outside world, its other. While Adorno in his discussion of the novel allows for a moment of reflection in the use of representation, in his theory of the artwork in *Aesthetic Theory* this tendency is mostly absent. Here the concept of representation has the function of establishing the meaning (*Sinn*) of the artwork beyond its aesthetic form. Thus Adorno seeks to establish a connection between the particularity of the individual artwork and the orbit of ideas. However, the concept of representation, as it is suggested in this argument, cannot be conceived in positive terms, which would turn the artwork into a mere repetition of abstract ideas. Rather, representation functions through determinate negation: "The more total society becomes, the more completely it contracts to a unanimous system, and all the more do the artworks in which this experience is sedimented become the other of this society" (AT 31). Modern art in particular, as Adorno points out, is left with the task of articulating that element which cannot be expressed (*das Unaussprechliche*) through absolute negativity. Yet even in this extreme situation the correlation of inside and outside is not given up, since Adorno is not satisfied with the moment of radical expression, as important as it is for his theory.

Our analysis arrives at an unexpected conclusion: the concept of representation, at first sight only a minor element in Adorno's theory in connection with the assessment of the novel, has broader implications. For Adorno, one of them, surprisingly enough, is the interpretation of poetry. For this reason we have to return, at least briefly, to the essay "On Lyric Poetry and Society" with its claim that an intrinsic sociology of literature is possible. As a method it engages the outside world by engaging the language of the poem. Adorno gives two examples to demonstrate his claim; the first one is Mörike's poem "Auf einer Wanderung," the other one Stefan George's "Im windes-weben." His commentary explains how the correlation should be understood. In the case of the Mörike poem Adorno underscores simultaneously the formal aspect and the significance of the content. In short, for Adorno the extraordinary achievement of the poem consists of rendering a specific social experience (that of the enchantment of the small German town) and articulating a specific poetic style, namely the proximity to Greek meters, creating a unique historical synthesis. But how can this reading disclose a social meaning? Adorno proceeds in two steps. First, he reflects on the self-consciousness of German classicism, its neo-humanist ideals; and, second, he connects the particular Mörike poem to the utterly precarious concept of classicism. In this way he seeks to open up the specific state of historical experience (*geschichtliche Erfahrungsstand*). But the difficulty is that this state is not identical with the concept of classicism. One cannot therefore simply subsume the poem under this category. Rather, Adorno has to find the precise mediation between the style of the poem and the typical expectations of the period. The poem's aesthetic achievement, which is identical with its historical achievement, consists, Adorno suggests, of merging the modern private experience of the lyrical subject with the classical language that Mörike inherited from an earlier generation. Adorno calls it a "utopia of what is close" (NL 1:48, *Utopie des Nächsten*), a brief moment of reconciliation in a historical process that does not move toward reconciliation. In sum, in Adorno's reading of Mörike the category of representation has two complementary aspects. There is the suggestion of phenomenal similarity through reflection (the visual image of the small town) and the construction of negation, namely the contrast between the utopian moment of the poem and the reality of modern alienation caused by industrial capitalism, which Mörike does not admit to his aesthetic orbit.

In the case of the George poem Adorno makes a similar argument, but there is also a significant difference. The aspect of reflection, still present in Mörike's poem, has dissolved. George's poem, as a modern poem, no longer has a topic (content). Therefore the sociologist must focus exclusively on the use of language. The social dialectic articulates itself through the forceful negation of modern reality. Yet this dynamic of aesthetic distance, Adorno suggests, does not remove the poem from its own time (which

George as a neo-romantic would like to do). The mode of representation is a purely negative correspondence, "ascetic omission" (NL 1:52, *aske-tisches Aussparen*), as Adorno calls it. The mediation between the poem and its environment, which is the mature phase of industrialization in Germany, is established exclusively through its formal construction. The following formulation makes this clear:

> In the age of its decline George sees in language the idea that the course of history has denied it and constructs lines that sound as though they were not written by him but had been there from the beginning of time and would remain as they were forever. (NL 1:53)

Obviously, such a reading does not render the material details of the early twentieth century when the poem was composed. Its sociological relevance is of a different kind. It defines in philosophical terms the sociohistorical meaning of the poem. Without philosophy of history the concept of representation could not develop its power. This is not only true for the interpretation of the George poem; it defines the theoretical underpinnings of Adorno's sociology of literature in general. Both the artwork and empirical reality become legible only on the basis of a philosophy of history.

5

A Precarious Balance

Rereading German Classicism

Among Theodor Adorno's contributions to literary criticism, his essay "On the Classicism of Goethe's *Iphigenia*" stands out as an intervention that provoked strong unintended reactions when it was delivered as a public lecture at the Free University in Berlin in 1967. It also stands out as a text that decisively articulated its author's position in the complex postwar discussion about the function and value of the German literary tradition. At stake here was the question of a German literary tradition *tout court*. Could, or should, contemporary German criticism appropriate its literary past? Was there a German canon that was worth holding on to after the Shoah?[1] Adorno himself had expressed his doubts on this matter when he questioned the validity of poetry after Auschwitz. The historical irony, however, was that those in the audience who shared Adorno's doubts—that is, the radical Free University students—denounced the Goethe lecture when they heard it delivered on June 7, 1967. What they were denouncing was Adorno's seemingly aesthetic posture, demanding a political response instead. The fact that Adorno criticized the celebration of German classicism and insisted on a very different reading of Goethe's famous play *Iphigenia in Tauris* did not satisfy them, for at that time they were preoccupied with the physical violence of the Berlin police, which had led to the death of one of their members in the context of the visit of the Persian shah on June 2.[2]

The divide between Adorno and the students in 1967 brings to the fore a dialectic that had been set in motion in the 1950s, when Adorno expressed his dissatisfaction with postwar literary criticism and demanded a form of critique that was both broader in scope and more substantial in its goals. By questioning the concept of culture, Adorno brought into view precisely those problems that mainstream literary criticism after 1945 had strenuously tried to keep out of sight. Of course, Adorno was not recommending the dissolution of the aesthetic in order to reach the political. Even in his late Goethe essay, he held on to the idea of a truth content of the literary work that could not be reduced to the question of political strategy. Adorno's critique of German classicism, which is severe and radical, sets out to rescue Goethe's drama by reading it as one would expect, against the grain. In the final analysis, Adorno even turns against Benjamin's critique of Goethe and defends an understanding of the poet and his role in the German tradition that was not only unfamiliar but also provocative: Goethe's *Iphigenia in Tauris* is presented as a radical play. In this respect, Adorno's interpretation of *Iphigenia* was deeply political, but it was not a guide for political action. Indeed, the logic of Adorno's reading undermined conventional assumptions about the solution of political conflicts. His complex defense of Goethe's humanism resisted the very idea of strategic political action. The confrontation with sedimented clichés of German literary history, and specifically that of Goethe's supposed classicism, enabled him to regain the true significance of the literary tradition, that is, its actual meaning for his own time.

When viewing Adorno's literary criticism as a body of texts, it becomes obvious that despite his doubts about the concept of a literary tradition, he was more convinced of the aesthetic relevance of past German literature than of contemporary works. With few exceptions (among them Samuel Beckett), Adorno demonstrated hardly any interest in discussing contemporary literature. In a lecture he gave at the Bayrischer Rundfunk in 1952, he offers some reasons for his unexpected reticence. In "On the Crisis of Literary Criticism" he argues that not only has literary criticism lost its former relevance but so has literature itself.[3] In fact, Adorno establishes a causal connection between these two crises. In part, the staleness of postwar criticism in Germany is grounded in a loss of substance in contemporary literary production. It should be noted that the conservative camp of post-war criticism shared this assessment. Friedrich Sieburg, the influential editor of the literary section of the *Frankfurter Allgemeine Zeitung,* and Ernst Robert Curtius, the well-known professor of Romance literature at the University of Bonn, were two notable examples of this outlook.[4] A rather different question is whether Adorno can be said to have shared with this group their understanding of the task of criticism, as some observers have suggested. His lament over the decay of literary criticism compared with the vigor of the 1920s could be read in this light. Adorno, however, is keenly aware of the human tendency to view the present as a dim shadow of the past, and therefore he acknowledges the structural problem. Anticipating Jürgen Habermas's later analysis of the public sphere, Adorno emphasizes the crucial importance of a liberal press for the strength and vitality of public literary criticism. The concept of critique depended on the authority, that is, the independence of the bourgeois press (*bürgerliche Presse*), which was completely destroyed by National Socialism in 1933. *Kunstbetrachtung* (art appreciation) replaced criticism. The historical specificity of the argument is important for Adorno's assessment of the postwar situation. The formal restoration of liberal democracy, he suggests, has not (yet) recovered the former spirit of the liberal press and the concept of critique. Looking at the history and present situation of the feuilleton, Adorno believes that public debate has not been fully reestablished: "Clearly, the element of productive negativity is largely absent in the generation currently practicing criticism in Germany" (*NL 2:306*). Because he does not mention names or newspapers and journals, it is not clear if this indictment of postwar criticism in Germany supports the dissatisfaction of conservatives such as Sieburg, Curtius, and Günter Blöcker, or if he perceives their work as proof of the decline of criticism. While this ambiguity cannot be resolved, Adorno's emphatic invocation of Karl Kraus as the model for public criticism suggests that he means to keep his distance from critics who believe in the longtime stability of the literary tradition. Adorno explicitly rejects the isolation of literary criticism when he notes: "Great criticism is conceivable only as an integral moment in intellectual currents: whether it contributes to them or opposes them, and such currents themselves draw their force from social tendencies" (NL 2:307). In other words, Adorno insists on the link between the literary sphere and the larger sociohistorical tendencies that define the condition of possibility of rigorous critical interventions—an unmistakable gesture against the routine of book reviewing. The names of Gotthold Ephraim Lessing, Heinrich Heine, Friedrich Nietzsche, and Kraus stand in for an idea of serious critique that means to determine more than the rating of individual writers.

Although Adorno does not explicitly distinguish between the critic and the reviewer, in the manner of American criticism, one can deduce from his essay on literary criticism that for him the task of criticism has little to do with book reviews in the literary section of newspapers. Instead, the task always includes the literary works of the past, at least those that are still relevant for the present. In fact, the mediation between the past and the present becomes Adorno's central interest when he begins to participate in literary discussion in postwar Germany. This emphasis is even stronger than in the work of Walter Benjamin, who saw himself very much as a facilitator of the contemporary European dialogue. Adorno's interventions are not only highly selective, mostly focused on individual authors and texts, but also emphatically engaged with the past. The reason for this emphasis has to do with what Adorno describes as the uncertainty of the literary tradition. The very concept has become questionable to him for several reasons.

Adorno's immediate concern with the German literary tradition, especially in the 1950s, is with its abuse under National Socialism. How can one trust authors whose works were used to support the ideological purposes of the regime, among them Goethe, Hölderlin, and Heinrich von Kleist? Clearly, the German literary tradition was compromised by fascist criticism, and this impact did not, as Adorno knew, simply cease in 1945. His fierce polemic against Heidegger in the 1964 essay "Parataxis" is motivated by his horror of a "German" Hölderlin, and this reading of Hölderlin would continue to influence the reception of the poet into the 1950s. However, the broader theoretical concern is based on the tension between tradition and modernity. For Adorno, tradition is essentially a premodern concept grounded in a precapitalist economy. "The category of tradition is essentially feudal, as Sombart defined the feudal economy as traditional. Thus tradition and rationality contradict each other, although rationality developed within tradition."[5] This means: the notion of tradition is bound to a form of production carried out by craftsmen; the individual method of production can be handed down from generation to generation. Capitalist production, on the other hand, as Adorno notes, undermines both the sense of immediacy and continuity. The rationality of the market devalues the past (and its cultural works) as no longer up-to-date and cutting-edge. Enlightened pragmatic rationality refuses to acknowledge the value of the cultural past, insisting on the possibility of and the need for progress. Therefore the concept of tradition becomes irrational, standing outside the rationalizing force of the market; but it is still indispensable as a way of recuperating the past. Still, the authenticity it claims is always already doubtful, a mechanism invented to fill a gap between the market and the lifeworld. In short, for Adorno the concept of tradition is, as a construct, necessarily ideological and therefore in need of critique.

Adorno's critique makes use of the false moment of tradition by turning it against itself. The modern artwork, he argues, is defined in terms of its refusal to make use of traditional aesthetic means. "After the disintegration of tradition the artist experiences its force as the resistance that the traditional puts up" (OL 33). Differently put, what appears to be firm and stable in the notion of tradition is actually neither firm nor stable. Rather, the semblance of continuity in the history of art and literature covers up the actual rupture and discontinuity caused by the organization of the literary market, the gap between the older work and the later one that seemingly uses the former as its point of departure. While modern artists find themselves caught in the dialectic of a critical production that denies the return to the old, the critic must both recognize and reconstruct the historical development of art and question the impression of a continuous stream that links the works to each other. This means that the critic must acknowledge as well as question what is offered as tradition, especially when it comes with the claim of being a secure cultural possession. The aim of the small essay "On Tradition" is therefore by no means the eradication of the literary past combined with an emphasis on the contemporary scene. It calls for a critical analysis of the past in which the very categories of understanding literary history as a given tradition are open to rigorous examination. In this respect, Adorno takes up a position that carefully scrutinizes the attempts of postwar academic criticism to restore a sense of belonging through a semblance of stability and continuity. While we do not know to what extent he was familiar with the then-popular literary histories of Fritz Martini and Gerhard Fricke, mostly written for university students—works that aimed at producing a narrative that would satisfy the expectations of the new political regime—he was aware of the fervent efforts of postwar academic criticism to restore the literary tradition. The only prior interpretation of Goethe's *Iphigenia in Tauris* he cites in his own essay, namely the article of Arthur Henkel, was published in one of the collections of interpretations prepared and published for the purpose of training students at the university. The inclusion of Goethe's play was a clear index of its normative status, that of an outstanding example of the German literary canon.

Adorno's critique aims at an unreflective and thereby ideological concept of tradition, but does not argue against the idea of preserving the literary works of the past. In fact, in view of the enormous cultural destruction carried out by the National Socialists in the name of a new vision of Germanness, the task of recuperation becomes crucial. As Adorno explains, a critical relationship to the tradition is not restricted to the recuperation of past artworks but extends to contemporary literary production. Using the example of Samuel Beckett's plays, he wants to demonstrate the extent to which past styles and models are present in these plays through determinate negation. The loss of subjectivity in Beckett's characters points to the centrality of the subject in classical drama, for instance, Goethe's plays of the 1790s.

The labor of critical recuperation that Adorno postulated after his return to Germany touches on and competes with the simultaneous project of cultural restoration undertaken by academic criticism, with a strong emphasis on the age of Goethe (classicism and romanticism). Scholars such as Emil Staiger, Ernst Beutler, Benno von Wiese, and Gerhard Storz focused their attention on Goethe and Schiller, frequently combining a biographical and a stylistic or rhetorical approach, but unmistakably with the intent of rebuilding a strong sense of the national canon. One of the early occasions for this project was the public celebration of Goethe's two-hundredth birthday in 1949 in close proximity to the foundation of the Federal Republic.[6] The celebration of Goethe's life and work served, as one would expect, multiple functions, among them that of legitimizing the new political regime. Not surprisingly, the East German state made similar use of the poet by claiming him for the working class. Adorno's critical interventions during the 1950s and 1960s have to be read against the background of the conservative project of *Bildung* through the reappropriation of the literary tradition with a marked emphasis on German classicism. The unmistakable normative element in the idea of German *Klassik* had a double function. On the one hand, it organized the conception of German modern literary history as a process from relatively modest beginnings in the sixteenth century to its climax around 1800, followed by a relative decline in the nineteenth century. On the other, it contained forceful value judgments about the importance of Weimar for a German project of individual and collective *Bildung*. The major poets and the figures around them such as Wilhelm von Humboldt and Johann Gottfried Herder were reexamined to legitimize the fragile German identity of the postwar era.

As an academic teacher at the University of Frankfurt, Adorno was in close proximity to these efforts. Essays such as "In Memory of Eichendorff" (1953) and "On Lyric Poetry and Society" (1957) document his complex engagement with the project of restoration, its effort to regain literary and aesthetic standards, as well as its blindness vis-à-vis the larger social forces that were driving it. The essay on Goethe's play *Iphigenia in Tauris,* written a decade later (i.e., at a time when the cultural restoration of the Federal Republic had been completed and was already coming under critical scrutiny), continues the earlier efforts by examining the concept of classicism that German scholarship used to frame the interpretation of Goethe's middle period (1785–1805): a period supposedly marked by the overcoming of the cult of genius in the Storm and Stress period, the integration of poetic production into public service at the court of Weimar, and the turn to ancient Greek culture, especially in Goethe's stay in Italy (1786–1787). Part of this process was the rewriting of the *Iphigenia* play, which was first performed in 1779 at the Weimar court, a performance in which Goethe played the role of Orestes.

In Adorno's essay the difficult genesis of the drama receives no attention; the early prose version of 1779 is not even mentioned, since Adorno, following the critical and scholarly tradition, places the emphasis on the final version, which allows him to praise the extraordinary quality of Goethe's verses. By choosing the classical version of the play as the authentic form of the artwork, Adorno seems to affirm the conventional notion of classicism that academic criticism celebrated in its efforts to appropriate the play for the literary tradition. This affirmation is carried further in the explicit distinction between Goethe's early period, defined in terms of excess, and a later process of restraint and growing soberness. These elements, of course, raise questions about Adorno's position. How close is his reading to the mainstream of Goethe criticism and the notion of maturation mentioned before? Adorno makes no effort to establish his position in the context of previous scholarship—with one exception. He mentions affirmatively the essay of Arthur Henkel, a former student of Max Kommerell, published in Benno von Wiese's collection of drama interpretations in 1964.[7] He invokes Henkel as the exception to the conventional approach, which he paraphrases in the following manner: "The prevailing view still sees Goethe's development in terms of the cliché of a maturation process. After the *Sturm und Drang* period, according to this schema, the poet learned self-discipline" (NL 2:153). He goes on to explain how in this view, especially, the influence of classical antiquity resulted in a process of self-clarification that allowed Goethe to fully appreciate the need for pure art.

Against this mainstream of Goethe scholarship, Adorno stresses two related moments in Goethe's later work: the difference between a supposed process of maturation and the actual authenticity of the classical work as an aesthetic phenomenon; and, second, "the force of the negative" (NL 2:153) as an element that does not simply disappear. Specifically, Adorno credits Henkel with foregrounding the importance of myth and the mythic in Goethe's play. At the same time, he invokes Walter Benjamin's essay on Goethe's *Elective Affinities* as a model for a deeper understanding of myth. In this way he forcefully distances his own interpretation from what he perceives as the conservative mainstream of Goethe criticism. The divide is marked in terms of recognizing the centrality of myth and history against a reading that underscores the importance of transcendent eternal ideas. Where convention sees a *Bildungsdrama,* Adorno discovers a *Zivilisationsdrama* in which the process of civilization in its painful dialectic is articulated. By emphasizing the content of the play in these terms Adorno prepares a double move: he opens up a deeper level of understanding of the play and at the same time defines its place in the historical dialectic of the eighteenth century. Almost unexpectedly, the problem of the transition from the Storm and Stress to classicism, previously discussed as a false convention, returns as the problematic contrast between nature and civilization in the philosophy of Rousseau and its impact on German literature in the 1770s. The concept of maturation, however, is replaced by the need for the artist to recognize the dialectic of aesthetic form. As Adorno notes, "Goethe had to see in it [the Storm and Stress movement] the futility of the gesture of immediacy in a state of affairs characterized by universal mediation" (NL 2:156). Form is always negotiated within the process of civilization.

How, then, does Adorno define Goethe's classicism? Contrary to the scholarly tradition, he neither speaks of a return to ancient Greek culture nor does he use the terms of pure form, especially formal perfection. In fact, he explicitly rejects formal perfection in the wake of Bertel Thorvaldsen or even of Schiller's Kantian aesthetics as inadequate because of its lack of substance. Rather, he stresses the moments of content and history, more specifically the level of archaic barbarism. For Adorno the material of the drama, i.e. the mythological narrative, is the determining moment, much more than the aesthetic reworking of Euripides or Jean Racine. In other words, there is a notable emphasis on the literal meaning of the mythic material for the truth content of the play. Therefore Adorno asserts: "Goethean Classicism is to be deduced from its content" (NL 2:157, translation modified). This emphasis corrects the conventional reading of the play as a plea for *Humanität* (humanness). As Adorno underscores against the critical tradition, *Humanität* is by all means the theme of the play but not its truth content. While Adorno possibly simplified the critical reception of Goethe's drama after the war and overlooked more self-reflective readings, he ultimately presents an explication that stands in clear contrast to the mainstream of Goethe scholarship. But in this case, as in the case of his essay on the last scene of *Faust II,* the relationship between his own intervention and the scholarly tradition is more complex than the few references to previous interpretations suggest. This intricate relationship tells us more about Adorno's position than the rhetorical polemic against academic criticism at the beginning of the essay.

The critic who, although a conservative himself, is exempted from Adorno's negative verdict is Arthur Henkel, whose interpretation of the *Iphigenia* appeared as a chapter in the widely used 1964 *Das deutsche Drama,* edited by Benno von Wiese, one of the most influential Germanists of the postwar era. As we have seen, Henkel is credited with a deeper recognition of the mythological material of the play, although Henkel's reading of this material, as we will see, significantly differs from Adorno's approach. Moreover, Henkel's interpretation, intended for advanced students, makes clear that it stands on the shoulders of previous attempts listed in the extensive bibliography. He explicitly refers to the work of Emil Staiger, Kurt May, Oskar Seidlin, and Sigurd Burckhardt in his text. Among these, Staiger stands out as a highly acclaimed theorist and Goethe scholar whose writings had canonical status in the postwar period.[8] In keeping with older critical tradition, Staiger reads the play in the context of Goethe's biography, specifically the early years in Weimar, with his friendship with Duke Karl August and love of Frau von Stein in mind. Therefore, the Greek material, as it was known through Euripides, for instance, seems to serve a private and decidedly modern function, namely as the expression of Goethe's complex biography. At the same time, he evaluates Goethe's play by comparing it to Euripides, again with an emphasis on the modern qualities of Goethe's drama. Goethe, we are told, makes use of the Greek play without imitating it. Similarly, Staiger underlines the difference between Racine's and Goethe's intentions. Still, these comparative considerations remain at the level of intertextual themes and motives in literary history, without penetrating the function of myth in Goethe's play. It is only at a later point that Staiger calls attention to the Goethean use of the myth of Atreus and his family, especially in the lines of Orestes in act 3. It becomes clear that Staiger by all means understands the poetic force of Goethe's adaptation, precisely because the poet eradicates conventional rhetoric and thereby creates a more immediate impact. Staiger quotes the same lines spoken by Orestes from act 3 that Adorno will cite in his essay:

> Es stürze mein entseelter Leib vom Fels,
> Es rauche bis zum Meer hinab mein Blut
> Und bringe Fluch dem Ufer der Barbaren.
> (act 3, scene 1)

> Let life depart. My body plunge from cliffs,
> Into the seamy blood go reeking down
> To bring its curse on this barbarian shore.[9]

Staiger leaves no doubt about the seriousness of the mythological material and its very personal adaptation by Goethe. But he limits the full impact of his insight by arguing against a tragic solution of the play and stressing, following scholarly tradition, the possibility of overcoming the tragic constellation through the inherent possibility of human transcendence. While evil needs examination and explanation, "goodness goes without saying. This is the way man thinks for his own good [*zu seinem Heil*]."[10] This is the moment where Staiger claims *Iphigenia* for a humanist credo, pushing the negative moment enunciated in Orestes's outburst (and similar lines by Iphigenia) into the background. While Staiger is aware that the familiar "message" of Goethe's *Iphigenia* seems to be outdated—he refers to Nietzsche's philosophy of life as a critique of idealism—he simply insists on its contemporary relevance. Similarly, he will attack modern literature and praise the value of nineteenth-century literature in a public lecture in 1966, an intervention that became the origin of the so-called *Züricher Literaturstreit*. Given the attention this debate received in the Swiss and German media, Adorno must have been aware of Staiger's turn when he wrote his essay.

As we have shown, Staiger recognizes the power of myth for the meaning of Goethe's play and also acknowledges its exemplary nature without undue emphasis on its classical origin. At the same time, he follows critical convention when he places strong emphasis on *Humanität* as the ultimate meaning. When Henkel opens his own close reading with the observation: "Exactly this (the emphasis on pure *Humanität*) has empowered a long row of interpreters and orators to praise the drama as a religious festival of *Humanität*,"[11] he could have been thinking of Staiger's interpretation as well, not only in its attempt to rescue the notion of pure *Menschlichkeit* but also in his understanding of the play's focus, namely Iphigenia's efforts to overcome barbaric sacrificial rituals. However, little attention is paid to the fate of Thoas, although Staiger, more than Henkel and Adorno, compares Goethe's play with Euripides and thus notes the significant difference in the treatment of the king. As we will see, the truly notable shift in Adorno's reading is closely linked to a more intensive examination of the opposition of Greek civilization and barbarism in Tauris, an examination that Henkel's interpretation prepares for but does not carry out. Although Adorno rightly praises Henkel for a deeper realization of the importance of myth for Goethe's *Iphigenia,* Henkel remains in other respects closer to the mainstream than expected. At the same time, there can be no doubt about the intellectual rigor of his reading, which opens up perspectives that Staiger missed or left unexplored. His question vis-à-vis Goethe's play, "whether we can become a utopia" (IT 171), raises the stakes to a new level, since implicitly it contrasts the mythic element with the utopian moment, and by extension with the quest for emancipation from mythic bondage. Henkel's close reading follows this process in the development of the plot and the characters, placing the emphasis on Orestes and Iphigenia, especially her efforts to prevent violent regression. As he notes, "The modern Iphigenia does not understand herself as the battleground of divine, numinous powers; rather, she thinks of herself as a deferential and reasoning partner of the gods" (IT 186). While this formulation could be understood as a mere recapitulation of the conventional reception of the drama, Henkel's analysis of the fourth and fifth acts makes it clear that he discovers more than accustomed humanism. He rigorously examines not only Iphigenia's problematic efforts at self-defense and self-preservation, her use of ruse and lies, but also the existential aspect of her decision: "What is at stake here is more than a moral decision; it concerns her total possibility of being" (IT 189). Where the scholarly tradition saw a moral decision, Henkel uncovers an existential decision that risks everything.

Henkel's interpretation emphasized not only the modernity of Goethe's *Iphigenia* but also its radical nature and its relevance for a contemporary audience. These were the very aspects that Adorno could take up and carry further. His own polemic against convention could thus build on the insights of Henkel's analysis, which itself made use of previous interpretations. In short, the seemingly simple contrast between Adorno's critique of existing Goethe scholarship and his own inquiry turns out to be more complicated than assumed. In particular the claim that academic criticism had failed to grasp the seriousness of the mythic pattern is incorrect. However, by fundamentally altering the perspective of his approach, Adorno also changes the understanding of the function of the mythic in Goethe's play.

Unlike the articles of Staiger and Henkel, Adorno's essay is not limited to a close reading of *Iphigenia*. Rather, the question of Goethe's classicism is put into a larger context on a number of different levels, including that of German literary history and German culture. But most important, at each level Adorno reexamines the cultural tradition, using Goethe and his work as a crucial reference point. And it is no accident that Adorno chooses Goethe as his reference point. This particular author and this particular play matter to Adorno because they represent problems of great and ultimately universal importance. In other words, his approach is not that of the Goethe scholar or even that of the historian of German literary history, although he does some of both. For Adorno, it is the drama's claim to articulate and represent modern humanism that constitutes the challenge for his essay. He is concerned with the echoes of this claim in the late eighteenth century, before and after the French Revolution, and in the later twentieth century, after the horrors of World War II and especially the Holocaust. Raising these questions brings to the fore the political dimension of the play as well as its author, a dimension that academic criticism had either removed from the discussion or tightly controlled under the umbrella of *Humanität* as a timeless universal value. At the same time, as I will discuss later, this very move also contains its opposite, namely a warning against contemporary political and revolutionary action. Returning to Goethe's play and questioning its academic reception allows Adorno to focus attention on those aspects that destabilize its meaning. It is by no means only Adorno's reexamination of Greek myth that undermines conventional notions of modern, secular humanism, but also his forceful engagement of the concept of civilization within the play that significantly shifts the assessment of the literary work.

Adorno's reassessment uses familiar rhetorical strategies to move toward a fuller and more radical explication of the material. Through polemic he distances himself from conventional readings and the academic institutions that made these readings possible. As already noted, he is particularly scornful of biographical and historical clichés that have supposedly dominated the discourse of Goethe scholarship, among them the metaphor of maturation to explain Goethe's shift from his radical early work to the classicist self-control of the middle period. With equal force he rejects the historical concept of a development from the emotional outbursts of the Storm and Stress period (1770–1780) to the formal mastery in the works of the classicist period (1785–1805). However, this critique of older academic criticism does not lead to an exclusively aesthetic point of view. Adorno remains equally interested in the specific historical location of Goethe's authorship and the works of the classicist period. But he replaces the organicist model of maturation and purification with a dialectical concept of the transition from Storm and Stress to the period of classicism. This means that the demand for authentic expression (against the prevalent modes of sentimentalism and the rococo) in the 1770s returns sublated in the classicist style, which tells us that this transformation is neither a simple loss of truthfulness nor an unquestionable gain in civilized and formal restraint, but an immanent contradiction that becomes visible as a tension in the individual artwork.

Adorno's reading of *Iphigenia,* while attentive to the formal mastery of the drama, underscores the tension between the will to use the mythological material for a demonstration of modern humanism and the resistance of the material to this plan. For Adorno, this resistance can be located at more than one level. It is, first of all, embodied in Greek mythology, but also in the persistent affinities of the material with the radical social and aesthetic demands of Storm and Stress. The latter is more difficult to recognize, since it requires the concept of nature as mediating element. The more explicit moment of resistance in Adorno's essay is clearly the force of the myth of the house of Atreus, a force that Goethe skillfully employs as the dark background for the light of the civilizing process that the drama legitimizes. For Adorno, it is crucial to understand that this process is at the center of the play but is not to be confused with its truth content. To put it another way, Adorno carefully distinguishes between the official message of the play, namely the call for a humane society (*Humanität*), and the truth content (*Wahrheitsgehalt*), which discloses itself only through the tension between the civilizing process, as it is articulated through the interaction of the main characters, and the force of older mythical powers.

By stressing the significance of mythic patterns, Adorno returns to a theme that he first unfolded in the long excursus on Homer's *Odyssey* of the *Dialectic of Enlightenment* and again in a small essay on epic naïveté published in 1958. In sharp contrast to conventional appreciations of mythology, Adorno conceives of myth as a premodern force at the dawn of history that separates nature and civilization, bondage and freedom, the return of the same and the possibility of progress and emancipation. Hence Adorno underscores that "epos and mythos are two distinct concepts, and indicate two stages in a historical process which can still be discerned where the disparate elements of the *Odyssey* have been editorially reconciled."[12] At the same time, Adorno stresses the intertwinement of myth and epic in Homer, which is part of the dialectical process of enlightenment with which he is concerned. The interaction between the archaic mythic powers (for instance, Poseidon) and Odysseus is already defined in terms of rational planning and self-preservation. Still, these archaic powers are acknowledged as merely contained but by no means overcome. At the stage of the Homeric epic, the hero must use ruses and deception to preserve his or her life. The successful path is not, as Adorno points out, confrontation, but adjustment and mimesis. In short, in the Homeric epic, the struggle between rational and mythic forces is not yet firmly decided in favor of reason, while the ultimate outcome is already visible; therefore there is a tendency on Adorno's part to read the *Odyssey* as protobourgeois. What makes the epic stage important for the modern critic is the centrality of human sacrifice as an element of barbaric societies, a moment to which Adorno will return in his *Iphigenia* essay.

It is worth noting that the analysis of myth in *Dialectic of Enlightenment* places emphasis on the human response to myth, that is, on rational strategies to escape from and to control mythic forces. By comparison, the excursus does not fully explore the nature of the pre-epic, archaic level apart from citing the examples given in the Homeric epic (for instance, the Cyclops and Circe). Yet this much becomes clear: myth stands outside of historical time; it is marked by the repetition of the same fateful occurrences: "The world permeated by mana and even the world of Indian and Greek myth know no exits and are eternally the same" (DE 16). Therefore the threat to human self-preservation is not only the threat of annihilation but also the fate of unending suffering. The process of civilization, based on the use of reason, turns out to be a mere partial victory, since it cannot, as Adorno and Horkheimer claim, break the dialectic of reason and myth. The essay "On Epic Naïveté," written in 1943 but published only in 1958 (NL 1:24–29), remains close to the analysis of *Dialectic of Enlightenment,* underscoring the enduring character of myth as eternal repetition as well as the antimythological effort of the Homeric epic. Similarly, Adorno foregrounds the force of rational reflection as the element that undermines the naïveté of the epic narrator and anticipates thereby the modern novel. It is only in the late *Iphigenia* essay that the archaic and its violence receive full attention, surprisingly in a context that most interpreters have read as already determined by the superiority of civilization. Adorno refuses to take the victory of civilization for granted and returns energetically to those parts of the play that invoke the persistent violence of the mythic. At the center of this violence we find human sacrifice and its continuation in acts of violent revenge. The saga of the house of Atreus provides the proof for this interpretation.

To be sure, Adorno is not the first to discover the tension between the message of the play, which celebrates modern humanism, and its intricate structure, where the parts do not neatly fit together. However, he, more than his predecessors, links these tensions to the mythic ground of the play that shines through even in those moments when reconciliation seems to be achieved. As he remarks, "The masterpiece creaks, and by doing so indicts the concept of a masterpiece" (NL 2:166). Even the moment of complete reconciliation in Orestes's version of a peaceful community of his violent ancestors, a utopian moment, is revoked in the notion of fateful revenge. Adorno comments: "The deep dialectic of the drama, however, should be sought in the fact that through his harsh antithesis to myth Orestes threatens to fall prey to myth" (NL 2:168). For Adorno, Orestes, although he already stands outside myth and is able to confront its power without overcoming it, is threatened by regression to the level of myth. Explicitly, Adorno invokes the dialectic of enlightenment: "*Iphigenia* prophesies enlightenment's transformation into myth" (NL 2:168). Reconciliation therefore is ultimately not achieved, only the hope that it will become possible. Adorno's reading of act 5 points in the same direction. While it is true that a regress to the level of human sacrifice is avoided and a peaceful agreement is reached between the civilized Greeks and the barbarians, this agreement, as Adorno insists, is paid for by the barbarians. It is Thoas, not Iphigenia, who makes it possible and seals it with the final line "Fare well." This means that civilization has not transcended violence, but only refined it at the level of social intercourse.

At this point Adorno openly questions the construct of the drama, especially its resolution of the conflict. This requires a significant step beyond the horizon of the author. By changing the historical frame from the late eighteenth to the late nineteenth century, Adorno discloses the compromise of the very *Humanität* Goethe's drama wants to establish. The civilized conquest of the noncivilized part of the world under the umbrella of imperialism undermines the very idea of humanism. "There is no counterevidence that can fully allay the spontaneous reaction to *Iphigenia* that Thoas is being dealt with in an ugly way" (NL 2:164). By introducing an unexpected postcolonial perspective, Adorno turns the table against the idealist core of the play and deconstructs Goethe's efforts to claim the final victory of *Humanität*. Even Iphigenia's decision to disclose the ruse, a decision that exposes her brother and herself to violent death, is not taken as sufficient evidence for a successful reconciliation, since Thoas is not allowed to partake in the highest form of *Humanität*. In the play his fate remains to be its object, although it is he, as Adorno reminds us, who acts as the true agent of humanism.

Ultimately, Adorno's evaluation of Goethe's *Iphigenia* remains ambiguous. On the one hand, he forcefully recuperates the drama from its conventional reception by underscoring the importance of myth and the fragility of modern humanism. In other words, he emphasizes the anticlassicist elements of the play, arguing in favor of a critique of modernity. On the other hand, he affirms the centrality of *Iphigenia,* not only for Goethe's oeuvre, but also for the classical period of German literature. Goethe's classicism, especially the formal perfection of the play, is not in doubt. At the same time, this classicism becomes the target of Adorno's question: Does this ideal cover up a forced reconciliation? As we have seen, Adorno is in fact convinced that even Goethe's most subtle attempts to manipulate the structure of the plot cannot bring about a complete and untainted reconciliation. Yet it is also clear that Adorno does not fault the author for this failure. Rather, the historical moment itself fails to provide the condition of possibility for a solution in which *Humanität* is not the privilege of a social group or race. The historical moment at the time of the French Revolution allows for a new perspective where, at least for a brief time, *"das Mögliche"* (the possible) becomes visible. Adorno's cross-reference to Beethoven's Leonore aria and the first Alexey Razumovsky quartet toward the end of the essay invokes the same sense of hope that Adorno finds in *Iphigenia* (NL 2:169). As he notes, "Hope orders a halt to the making and producing without which it does not exist" (NL 2:169). In this reading Goethe's play becomes exemplary for the historical moment of its genesis, but is also endowed with the force to throw light on later periods when the hope that the drama celebrates has become less certain.

Adorno's interpretation of *Iphigenia* invokes Walter Benjamin's concept of myth in order to confront those critics who had treated the mythological material merely as a background for an essentially modern drama. Yet ultimately more is at stake than a critique of academic scholarship. No less than Benjamin, Adorno was faced with the role of Goethe in the German literary tradition and, ultimately, German high culture *tout court*.

He could not ignore that both Benjamin's essay on Goethe's *Elective Affinities* and his study of the German baroque drama express a serious, even severe and fundamental critique of Goethe.[13] In the 1920s, Benjamin had quite consciously forced this issue—for instance, in his critique of Max Kommerell's pathbreaking study, *Der Dichter als Führer in der deutschen Klassik* (1928). As Benjamin acknowledged, the study represented the claim of the George Circle to recuperate German high culture in a time of trivialized mass culture. There could be no doubt about the conservative character of this effort. Benjamin's 1930 review acknowledges not only the conservative aspirations of the book but also the powerful execution of the claim. Although Benjamin's praise of Kommerell is generous, it comes from a point of view that differs radically from that of the author. As he writes, "And in fact, with a radicalism unattained by any of its predecessors in the George Circle, this book constructs an esoteric history of German literature."[14] Specifically, Benjamin recognizes the stipulated affinities between Greek and German culture, as they are foregrounded by Kommerell, as the key to his esoteric reading of German culture. If German classicism is meant to be a *"Vorbild"* (normative example), then, as Benjamin reminds the reader, a number of questions must be answered, including what was the actual success of the leadership the German eighteenth-century poets offered, and the value *(Vorbildlichkeit)* of the struggle of these poets against their own time.

Notwithstanding his abundant praise for Kommerell's mastery of the historical material, Benjamin's disagreement with Kommerell is deep and irreconcilable. He refuses to accept the fundamental claim of Kommerell's study that it is possible or advisable to rescue German classicism. Why? The attempt must fail, Benjamin argues, because the German nation remained inadequate to the standards of Weimar. The new nationalism of the German Empire misunderstood the legacy of Weimar. But, as it turns out, this is not the only reason. Benjamin cannot conceal his doubts about the construction of the book and the notion of leadership with regard to poets. His remarks about Goethe in particular reject Goethe's claim as well as Kommerell's reconstruction. "But the impotence of that claim is as much a part of that picture as its title."[15] Kommerell's struggle to appoint the German classics as the founders of a new heroic era of the German people was doomed, since it mistook a literary constellation for a spiritual power that could actually change the world. We need to remind ourselves that Adorno was by all means aware of this verdict, a point to which we will have to return.

When Adorno was working on the two-volume edition of Benjamin's writings in the early 1950s, the edition that initiated the rediscovery of the almost-forgotten critic, the memory of his deceased friend and mentor was linked in a complicated manner to the memory of Max Kommerell, whom Adorno had known since the early 1930s.[16] As he pointed out in a letter to Benjamin, dated November 6, 1934, he had reasons to keep his distance from Kommerell, who had said that men like Adorno "should be put against the wall."[17] For this reason, he resented Benjamin's positive review of Kommerell's Jean Paul study (1933). While Adorno's negative response to the review could be explained as an understandable reaction to the unexpected praise of a right-wing critic, the political divide (in which Benjamin took a far more committed position than Adorno) does not ultimately hinder him from paying close attention to Kommerell's writings, just as his critique of Rudolf Borchardt in *Dialectic of Enlightenment* would not preclude a considerably more positive verdict on Borchardt's writing after World War II. For this reason, Kommerell's assessment of Goethe is, as Paul Fleming has demonstrated, relevant for Adorno's literary criticism. In the 1959 essay on the last scene of *Faust II,* Kommerell's essay on the same topic served as a subtext, although Kommerell is never mentioned. The central concern of Adorno's essay, namely the question of memory and forgetting, is clearly prefigured in Kommerell's. Yet the difference also has to be noted. "Kommerell... will cling fast to the transformative power of Lethe, of forgetfulness, while Adorno will ultimately distance himself from such blissful oblivion."[18] While Adorno's reading of the last scene of *Faust II* comes surprisingly close to Kommerell's interpretation by following the latter's argument about the radical transformation of Faust as the condition of his final redemption, a transformation that is defined in terms of forgetting, Adorno gives this reading a turn that sharply contrasts with Kommerell's intent. Where Kommerell's Faust forgets to transform, Adorno's Faust passes through oblivion to arrive at a new state of memory that is connected with the notion of hope as the return of what had been forgotten.

In the case of Adorno's *Iphigenia* essay, the intertextual situation turns out to be even more complex, first of all, since it is more difficult to establish a common referent, and second, because Adorno explicitly responds only to Kommerell's student Arthur Henkel. Only a few pages in Kommerell's *Der Dichter als Führer* are dedicated to Goethe's play, and they are, moreover, exclusively concerned with the prose version of 1779, which Adorno does not consider. Kommerell's approach is explicitly biographical with emphasis on the friendship between the young Duke Karl August and Goethe, a relationship rearticulated in the friendship between Orestes and Pylades. Kommerell's method of reading is exactly what Adorno denounces: the confusion between the life of the author and the literary text. In the fourth chapter of Kommerell's book, the interpretation of the play becomes part of the larger theme of spiritual leadership. In this reading of the German classics, Goethe takes on the role of the educator whose difficult task it becomes to shape the character of the young prince who is known for his willful and eccentric behavior. The theme of maturation and purification becomes the center of this narrative in which Goethe is involved as the court-appointed guide. According to Kommerell, Goethe himself, initially fully participating in the escapades of Karl August, leaves his youthful behavior behind and longs for distance and form.

Adorno's engagement with Goethe's drama seems to go in a rather different direction. The notion of poetic leadership, already criticized by Benjamin in 1930, finds no parallel in Adorno's essay. However, there are other elements that are rearticulated in Adorno's text, among them the tropes of the court (Weimar) and its importance for the poet, the poet's need for social integration in order to serve at the court, and, finally, the question of his self-centered subjectivity that is in need of transmutation. Adorno's unexpected praise of the small and relatively insignificant court of Weimar as a worldly center echoes Kommerell's evaluation: "Even the smallest court was allowed to experience the tremors of the world of great state powers; at least from afar,... through ethos, demeanor, and the way of expressing oneself Weimar participated in a global social form—in contrast to the attractions of Frankfurt, which were defined more in terms of locale and soil."[19] Goethe, Kommerell tells us, becomes part of this larger web. In short, Kommerell contrasts Frankfurt and Weimar, bourgeoisie and aristocracy, intensive and extensive expression. In a very similar vein, we note in Adorno's essay the clearly positive evaluation of Weimar's influence on Goethe: "The Weimar Goethe, who had sought out a link with high society and thereby with an international level of awareness, acted as an agent of the deprovincialization of the German spirit" (NL 2:156).

It is worth noting that Adorno, like Kommerell, mentions Weimar rather than Rome when discussing Goethe's growing understanding of the world. After all, the focus of his interpretation is the later version of the play. However, Adorno gives the topos of Weimar a different function. Where Kommerell stressed the process of maturation and Goethe's leadership role, Adorno points to the political function of Goethe's experience in Weimar, an experience that finds its highly mediated literary expression in *Iphigenia*. His interest in the fate of Orestes and Pylades therefore contrasts sharply with Kommerell's emphasis on friendship. For Adorno, the importance of German classicism, fragile and precarious as it may have been, could not be defined in terms of heroic leadership, as Kommerell and the George Circle would have it. Nonetheless, Adorno's essay returns to the notion of classicism as a historical category.

Adorno's critique of conventional academic literary history, which describes the transition from the literary scene of the 1770s, marked by radical formal experiments and thematic opposition to the social status quo, to the 1780s, defined by the efforts of a group of writers around Goethe in Weimar, as a process of calming down, repudiates the biological metaphors, but not the notion of historical development itself. Moreover, he accepts without much criticism the central role of Goethe in this schema. The comparison between Goethe and Jacob Michael Reinhold Lenz, for instance, is, as usual, decided in favor of Goethe: "The lack of power in the Storm and Stress period could not be attributed to a deficiency of talent in such highly gifted authors such as Lenz. Goethe had to see it in the futility of the immediacy in a state of affairs characterized by universal mediation" (NL 2:156). As a whole, the Storm and Stress movement is treated as inferior because of its specifically bourgeois character, which limits, as Adorno asserts, the force of its social critique. The literary opposition of the movement becomes merely rhetorical and thereby untrue to its original intent. It is not that Adorno disagrees with what he calls the radical nominalism of the Storm and Stress—that is, the striving for the concrete and particular—but he distances himself from its ultimate political ramifications, namely the French Revolution. The essay supports Goethe's negative attitude toward the revolution. "He was disgusted by the bourgeois who sets himself up as a hero; he had a sense of the dark secret of a revolution and an allegedly emancipated consciousness that, as in France around 1789, has to present itself through declamation because it is not completely true, because in it *Humanität* becomes repression and interferes with full humanness" (NL 2:161).

Adorno turns the critique of academic literary history into a political critique of Storm and Stress as the literary avant-garde of its time, because the movement fails to go beyond unmediated protest. But his critique does not stop there; its final target is the violence of the bourgeois revolution that promised freedom and *Humanität,* and possibly also an allusion to the verbal violence of the contemporary student movement. For Adorno, therefore, Goethe becomes the exception, not only in literary but also in social and political terms. He is able to transcend his early radicalism by aligning himself with the court of Weimar and by refashioning himself as a classical writer. Adorno explicitly denies the reactionary character of Goethe's alliance with court and aristocracy; it is for him the price that the new humanism had to pay. It is worth noting that Adorno extends this argument to its aesthetic aspect. Literary and aesthetic classicism, Adorno suggests, is the result of an antinomy that cannot be fully reconciled. Behind the insistence on formal control and the demand for aesthetic universality remains, Adorno tells us, the nominalism of Storm and Stress. This explains the fragility of classicism as a careful balancing act. As Adorno writes, "But the classicist solution is fragile because it is in fact prohibited by the nominalist antinomy, and it balances where no reconciliation is possible" (NL 2:160). Had Adorno been consistent, he would have extended this argument to the political realm as well. Goethe's alliance with the court did not restore the unquestioned former privilege of the aristocracy. In other words, Goethe's decision was equally fragile in social and political terms. In 1967 Adorno refuses to explore this moment more radically, possibly because he identified with Goethe's choice as the option that preserved *Humanität* against revolutionary radicalism. This is where he ultimately parts ways with Benjamin, for whom Goethe's choice expressed the lack of a true decision, a mere form of conformism that avoids confrontation with the demands of history. As much as Adorno invokes Benjamin's 1924 essay on Goethe's *Elective Affinities,* he does not share Benjamin's fundamental skepticism about Goethe's role as the central figure of the German literary canon. What Benjamin, in the wake of Kierkegaard, criticized as compromise, Adorno accepts as balance, which is not to be confused with reconciliation. However, Adorno remains silent about this difference, leaving the reader with the impression that his own interpretation is compatible with that of his friend.

What brings Benjamin's and Adorno's engagement with Goethe closer together again is the concept of crisis. And yet the cultural crisis of the Weimar Republic, to which Benjamin responded, was determined by the breakdown of the spiritual tradition that Goethe represented in the eyes of the educated middle class, whereas the crisis of the 1960s reflects the protest of the Left against the problematic restoration of this tradition in the 1950s, a situation that shows Adorno in a precarious position. Now, although in a highly mediated way, he defends a tradition that he had questioned in his youth. Obviously, 1924 and 1967 are very different moments in the history of Goethe's reception in Germany. The twelve years of National Socialism as well as the slow and difficult rebuilding of national cultural institutions after 1945 to which Adorno made decisive contributions divide these moments: while still critical of the uneven political and social development of the young Federal Republic, Adorno was clearly invested in the positive outcome of this process. The radical turn of the student movement in 1967, especially its use of verbal violence (at Adorno's lecture, for instance), questioned not only the social and political deficiencies of the Federal Republic but also Adorno's efforts and his numerous public interventions in the name of *Humanität*. Adorno's critical remarks about bourgeois violence and the destruction of *Humanität* by the very revolution that means to establish emancipation also address, at least indirectly, the political tensions of the mid-1960s and especially the strategy of the New Left. For Adorno, the left polemic recalled the aggression against the liberal public sphere in 1933. Therefore his own essay becomes a "precarious balance"; it is both critical and defensive, arguing against classicism and at the same time affirming Goethe's drama as a meaningful and truthful way of working through the problematic of human freedom and self-determination.

EPILOGUE

The decision to end this book with an epilogue rather than a conclusion is more than just a matter of nomenclature. A customary conclusion, one that offers a straightforward summary of the preceding chapters, must be resisted for it presupposes that Adorno's work can be systematically conceptualized without remainder, that it can be completely grasped by methodically reconstructing lines of argument. But Adorno's thought, as I have tried to show, eludes this approach, and this is so for a number of reasons.

First, the fundamentally essayistic nature of Adorno's writing, even when we are dealing with a major book like *Aesthetic Theory,* precludes the idea that it can be adequately appreciated with the help of a few key concepts that can somehow unlock the true meaning of the text. Any attempt to neatly summarize the essential teaching of Adorno, while tempting for pedagogical reasons, will therefore fail. Second, but related to the first point, is the fact that when considering Adorno's thought we are dealing with two fairly different kinds of writing—his theoretical

investigations and his literary criticism, the latter frequently in the form
of engaging individual literary texts—which are not necessarily in sync
with each other. There are subtle distinctions related to genre and occasion that cannot be simply relegated to the margins in order to arrive at a
unified message. The very notion of close attention to the text that guides
Adorno's literary criticism invalidates the traditional demand for conceptual consistency, and specifically the demand that a system of concepts can
fully and sufficiently explicate the artwork under consideration. Adorno
insists on the need for concepts, but we have to remember that his concepts are not conceived as fixed and static. They can do their exploratory
labor only when they are themselves in dialectical motion, a fact that affects both their content and their function. Third, while Adorno's mode
of thought does not change significantly over time, his outlook and position on specific questions and problems evolve, in some instances significantly. For instance, as I suggested in the first chapter, his understanding
of Kant's importance for contemporary aesthetic theory goes through a
number of phases. Similarly, his assessment of Lukács's later work, in the
mind of most of his readers definitively summed up in his essay "Extorted
Reconciliation," is considerably more complex and varies according to
the circumstances. Even within *Aesthetic Theory,* I would argue, Adorno's
thought is still evolving so that we find layers of ideas and arguments
within the text that resist systematic summary. Where such a summary
is attempted it may yield insight into Adorno's positions on specific issues
but it will inevitably fall short of capturing the complex and nonlinear
thought process behind those positions.

Rather than a traditional conclusion, therefore, I have elected to write
an epilogue, using this format as an opportunity to reflect on the goal and
purpose of this book. The preceding chapters are based on essays that
were written at different times and for different purposes during the last
decade. What they share, however, is the intent to do justice to Adorno's
theory and literary criticism by focusing on more specific problems, asking more detailed questions, and resisting established interpretations and
facile generalizations of Adorno's texts. Taken as a whole, the chapters
subvert the notion that Adorno's theoretical oeuvre can be safely located
within the sphere of philosophy; or, more precisely, that his music and literary criticism as well as his social criticism can be understood as mere
extensions of his philosophical thought. In this model the explication of

his philosophical position would necessarily ground and shape the reading of his literary and music criticism. The essays in this book follow a different path. They take seriously the interdisciplinary nature of Adorno's work, which means that it has to be seen as a configuration in which the different parts, representing individual disciplines, are not hierarchically organized with philosophy at the top. Instead, these parts, conventionally seen in the context of a specific discipline (for instance, musicology), support each other and feed on each other, resulting in an unusually complex intertwining of disciplinary methods and ideas. Therefore, the notion of an application of his aesthetic theory when we are referring to Adorno's literary criticism is misleading. It might be more helpful to think of his more abstract aesthetic theory as being grounded in the explication of artworks. This relationship is especially relevant for the role of Adorno's music criticism—for example, his understanding of the development of modern music—for the origin and organization of *Aesthetic Theory.* Moreover, Adorno explicitly reflects on the centrality of this relationship for the character of his theory. What distinguishes *Aesthetic Theory* from academic aesthetics, and even the great tradition of Kant and Hegel, is the strong presence of art criticism in the unfolding of the argument. Adorno's theory, in clear distinction from Kant's Third Critique, wants to be as close to the artwork as possible. As a consequence, the reader has to be aware of and pay close attention to the merging of disciplines and the fusing of methods. In *Aesthetic Theory* specifically art criticism, social theory, and philosophy come together in order to disclose not only the nature of art but ultimately the nature of the whole.

Adorno's serious doubts about the feasibility of aesthetics, already clearly expressed in the 1959 draft introduction of *Aesthetic Theory* and later reflected in the text itself, call into question the time-honored priority of philosophy as the most appropriate locus for aesthetic reflection. This is so for two reasons, the first of which has already been mentioned. It has to do with the limitations of the conceptual language of philosophy. Because of its abstract nature it cannot overcome the distance between itself and the artwork. The second reason has to do with the institutional place of philosophy. As an academic discipline, Adorno believes, philosophy has lost its privileged position as the final arbiter among the disciplines—a position it had enjoyed since the late eighteenth century, as Kant, for instance, forcefully claimed in *Der Streit der Fakultäten.* Its slow marginalization in a highly differentiated scientific order went hand in hand with its loss of public recognition. Philosophy's increasing lack of relevance outside the university has affected art criticism as well. Adorno's literary criticism, for example, was not written for the academy. The essays, sometimes based on radio talks, originally appeared in newspapers and journals. In short, they were part of the cultural public sphere of their time. In some cases they were explicit public and political interventions written with the stated intention to redirect public discourse. This context, although mostly forgotten today, must not be ignored. The institutional difference between Adorno's literary criticism and his aesthetic theory, which can criticize academic aesthetics but not escape the institutional home, establishes a notable tension between the two bodies of work, sometimes only subtle, but sometimes also very outspoken and jarring. Adorno's polemical essays, such as those against Lukács and Heidegger, have a very different register than *Aesthetic Theory*. As one would expect, their rhetoric underscores this contrast. In his polemical work Adorno is forceful but not always subtle. Therefore the intent to define the opponent in negative terms sometimes occludes the shared ground, as is the case in his attacks on Lukács and Heidegger.[1]

In briefest terms, the interpretation of Adorno's literary essays (and the same would apply to his essays on music) requires attention to the discourse of which they were a part. When Adorno turns his attention to Heinrich Heine, the reader has to keep in mind the resistance of German literary criticism of the 1950s to Heine because of his Jewish background. On the other hand, there is also the issue of Adorno's own doubts about Heine's poetry because of its supposed inauthenticity, an evaluation that Adorno took over from the famous Austrian critic Karl Kraus.[2] Similarly, Adorno's essay on Goethe's drama *Iphigenia in Tauris* invokes not only the uncertain status of Goethe's classicism after World War II but also Adorno's complex and difficult relationship with the academic criticism of his time. In short, the public character of these essays pulls them in a different direction than Adorno's meditations on natural beauty or the sublime. At the same time, it is essential to keep in mind that on a different level they also belong together, since they exchange insights and thought processes. In contrast to academic German aesthetics, Adorno insists on developing his theory in close proximity with the individual artwork. Yet the work is never simply an example to demonstrate a point.

Adorno's aesthetic theory is frequently categorized as quintessentially modernist—an observation that seems helpful at first in terms of framing the theory in historical terms. In light of the above discussion, however, such an observation is highly problematic in that it overlooks theoretical elements and thought practices typically found in postmodern thought, especially in Derrida's version of deconstruction. The similarities between Adorno and Derrida, among them the subversion of the Kantian subject, were acknowledged and subsequently became part of the philosophical discussion only in the 1980s and more generally in the 1990s. As I suggested in the introduction, these efforts have resulted in a systematic and historical reconfiguration of Adorno's work. Even in Germany, where the continuity of the Frankfurt School has typically been emphasized, the link between Adorno and Derrida has been foregrounded.[3] By focusing on the nexus between deconstruction and negative dialectics Adorno was moved out of his original place as the co-philosopher of Max Horkheimer and crucial member of the first generation of Critical Theory and into the realm of French theory. In geographical terms—at least for much of the international discussion—Adorno has been relocated from Frankfurt to Paris. As a consequence, the international postmodernist discussion about Adorno's present relevance has focused on the similarity of Adorno's theory and poststructuralist thought, notably Derrida's work. By the same token, the moment of continuity from the first to the second generation of Critical Theory has been deemphasized, if not ignored altogether, a move for which Habermas's severe critique of Adorno's position in *The Philosophical Discourse of Modernity* (1987) offered a convenient excuse. By placing Adorno in closer proximity to poststructuralism the insistence on his importance becomes more plausible under the conditions of postmodernity. The obvious gain of this configuration is the subversion of the modernist frame of reference, a frame that could point, at least implicitly, to the outdated nature of Adorno's theory. This gain, however, does not come without a price. In the new context the German theoretical tradition on which Adorno's writings are based becomes largely invisible.

Aesthetic Theory was written as a provocation to academic aesthetics; it presents itself as a subversive critique of the academic tradition of its own time, while simultaneously harking back to Kant and Hegel as points of orientation for the contemporary debate. This double move was not always understood and appreciated in 1970. The New Left especially, which demanded a strong political commitment, was impatient with Adorno's sustained dialogue with the philosophical tradition. Conservative and liberal critics, on the other hand, praised Adorno for this seeming attachment to the tradition but without granting the legitimacy of Adorno's radical critique of traditional aesthetics. Still, at the time of its first publication in 1970 one could objectively define the importance of Adorno's theory in terms of its sustained explication and self-critique of modern art. It would be difficult to claim the relevance of *Aesthetic Theory* in those terms today, since both the theoretical discussion and the development of art have changed in ways that Adorno could not have foreseen in the 1960s. While he had a sense of the "aging" of modern art and literature, as can be found in his reading of Beckett's *Endgame*,[4] the more recent return of philosophical aesthetics as an unquestioned academic discipline would have struck him as regressive. In particular, the return of foundational aesthetics would have been unappealing. In this respect Adorno's theory is clearly untimely today and only rarely mentioned in the mainstream of American philosophical discourse.

Ironically, this untimeliness may in fact be an advantage that ultimately contributes to a new significance for Adorno's theory today. The nature of that significance, however, has to be carefully considered. It would be a mistake, I believe, to insist on the unmediated relevance of Adorno's position, creating a neo-Adornian dogma that can be summarized for teaching purposes. For instance, the question as to whether *Aesthetic Theory* exhibits "actuality" or is merely a moment of the past is perhaps the wrong question. Instead, we have to consider its mediated presence in the contemporary debate, which possibly includes its untimeliness. Looking at the contemporary aesthetic discussion, it is obvious that the stakes were different in Adorno's time. The unresolved tension between his rigorous defense of modern art as not only autonomous but also sovereign and his subversive probing of the status of the artwork in absolute terms, thereby throwing doubt on the ultimate value of art, seems to be no longer present. The notion of a truth content of the artwork, central to Adorno's thought, seems to have lost its significance in the context of postmodernism, its artistic goals, and its theoretical self-reflection. While it is not too difficult to argue that poststructuralist thought picked up on Adorno's critique of the philosophical tradition, there are at the same time moments in his own thought that the next generation either ignored or failed to appreciate, for instance, the persistent commitment to the idea of reconciliation as the ultimate goal of the aesthetic process.

So how might a defense of Adorno be articulated today? In answering this question it is worth noting that Adorno himself provides a model for such a defense in his approach to Kant. He leaves no doubt that ultimately he does not share Kant's epistemology or, in the arena of aesthetic theory, Kant's understanding of the work of art. But this difference in no way diminishes his high appreciation of Kant. What he values in Kant's thought is its rigorous intellectual honesty, by which he means its refusal to cover up tensions and contradictions. Thus Adorno's reading of Kant underscores precisely these tensions as the result of his own radical questions. Indeed, as Adorno sees it, the real Kant is to be found not in the exposition of his ideas and arguments but rather in the reconstruction and exploration of his ultimately unanswered questions. This, I think, turns out to be a suitable model for approaching Adorno's aesthetic theory as well as his literary criticism today, since it avoids blind identification with Adorno. It acknowledges the historical distance that divides us from Adorno just as Adorno acknowledged the historical distance between himself and the period of Kant. In fact, Adorno's forceful recuperation of Kant after World War II stressed this distance as a way of recognizing the failure of the program of the Enlightenment in which Kant participated but which he also radically surpassed. Similarly, a sustained defense of Adorno today requires distance, it requires a new reading in which assumptions about Adorno's opinions and positions are suspended and exposed to critical scrutiny. Put differently, the point of such a reading would not be the preservation of by now familiar ideas and arguments or the improvement of Adorno's thought by creating a new dogma. Instead, such a reading would focus on Adorno's thought processes (i.e. his peculiar and unique form of dialectical thought that resolutely resists generalization) no matter what the implications might be for established dogmas regarding Adorno.

The chapters in this book are offered as a preliminary attempt to perform such a new reading, one that tries to remain as close as possible to the Adornian text and at the same time respects the historical distance that separates us today from Adorno. It follows Adorno's demand for immanence, while paying attention to the historical constellation of Adorno's thought, as it can be explored through intertextual and contextual reflections. The emphasis varies from chapter to chapter. While the Kant chapter and the chapter on the concept of the ugly required a considerable amount of intertextual labor in order to make legible the unique way in which Adorno explores specific aesthetic problems, the chapter on the absolute and the limits of the artwork focuses primarily on a particular segment of *Aesthetic Theory*. This procedure subverts the mainstream of Adorno criticism. The approach to Adorno's literary criticism follows yet another strategy by underscoring the public nature of his essays, which means that the rereading had to negotiate the tension between the literary work(s) under consideration, received opinions within the institution of criticism at the time of Adorno's critique, and Adorno's own intervention that draws on his theoretical insights. Hence the chapters look at Adorno's writings from different perspectives, using different methods, yet without the urge to systematize their findings. In other words, the interpretation makes no attempt to gloss over shifts and contradictions in the written record; indeed, it accepts and embraces them.

It is tempting to read Adorno's oeuvre within the framework of cultural and political pessimism that defined especially the late Weimar Republic, focusing on the disintegration of the political structure with the fatal rise of the radical Right, the catastrophic development of monopoly capitalism, and the threat to high culture by the rapid emergence of industrial mass culture. The philosophical perspective developed in *Dialectic of Enlightenment* would encourage such a framework. Notably the culture industry chapter with its emphasis on the dangers of mass culture for the concept of individual freedom and subjective reflexivity contains the material for such a reading. The concept of the totally administered society, which plays a significant role in Adorno's later social criticism, would extend this line of thought to Adorno's late work by underscoring the dependent status of cultural institutions with the consequence that modern art finds itself in a feeble and marginalized position. Seen from this vantage point, *Aesthetic Theory* offers a critique of late capitalist consumer culture, a critique that includes traditional high culture. It is not difficult to detect this line of thought in parts of *Aesthetic Theory* as well—for example, in the long section on art and society (AT 225–261). The seeming advantage of this approach would be the creation of a consistent position. A clear direction of Adorno's writings on aesthetic problems could be posited: radical modern art becomes the bulwark against the threat of mass culture.

I have not chosen this approach for several reasons. One of the potential consequences would have been a reading of Adorno's literary and aesthetic theory primarily through the economic category of monopoly or state capitalism, already a past historical reality in the 1970s. Such an approach would undercut the contemporary force of Adorno's critique and deprive it of its future potential—not to mention the fact that Adorno's theory, as it is presented in *Aesthetic Theory,* resists this very kind of generalization. As I have already pointed out, the posthumous work, which the author was unable to complete, subverts the notion of a linear presentation organized in the form of a sequence of logically connected chapters. Instead, it is more helpful, I believe, to understand the work as a sequence of thematically connected large essays that are organized around their individual centers. They gesture toward an ultimate center that is, however, not immediately visible in the text. Foregrounding the essayistic structure of *Aesthetic Theory* explains two important moments of the text, namely its repetitive character, insofar as ideas and themes will reoccur in different sections, but individually modified by the topic and the specific thought process that drive the particular section, resulting in noticeable variations between the individual sections. It appears that Adorno was ultimately less interested in maintaining a consistent overall position than in radicalizing the thought movement of the individual section.

This insight guides the method of reading I have used in this book. Rather than try to harmonize the various parts of Adorno's oeuvre and seek out logical consistency, the approach here has been to focus on specific problems in *Aesthetic Theory* and in Adorno's literary criticism, probing and putting pressure on sections of the book or individual essays. This means, among other things, that my readings pay careful attention to explicit arguments in the text without reducing the meaning of any one text to a single argument that can be accepted or rejected. Adorno himself—for instance, in his defense of the essay—is already aware that his work does not fit into the mold of analytic philosophy. My readings respect this self-understanding of the author as an essential aspect of his work that cannot be overlooked or denied. To be sure, many philosophers would not grant the viability of this position, but I nevertheless believe that it is an essential component to reading Adorno's work. On the one hand, it is important to acknowledge the integrity of the author's intentions, but on the other it is just as important never to presume the outcome of an interpretation.

Following the text sometimes leads to insights that the author might not have embraced or might have even rejected. In other words, while the readings acknowledge and carefully consider the intended meaning of a text, it is not the final horizon of the interpretation.

This principle is especially important when considering Adorno's literary criticism. In every instance these essays were written for specific purposes and therefore cannot be understood without a deeper grasp of the institutional context in which they were written. As mentioned above, Adorno wrote these essays frequently as interventions, sometimes polemical responses to prior interpretations of the same work or author. This context, however, is rarely explained in the text of the essays themselves. They are part of a debate that is typically not disclosed. This debate shapes not only Adorno's arguments but also the style used in each essay, a fact that a reading has to take into consideration. Moreover, the literary text that is the topic of Adorno's intervention must always be considered in its own hermeneutical context. Both for Adorno and his contemporary German readers the works under discussion are part of a highly contested literary tradition. Any textual explication, including Adorno's own, will, either implicitly or explicitly, be influenced by the critical constellation that defines the ongoing debate. It shapes the emphasis as well as the evaluation of the literary text under discussion. At the same time, it is only through careful attention to Adorno's grasp of an individual literary work, a poem or a play, that the intertextual and institutional aspects become legible. For example, the peculiar insistence on the crucial importance of Thoas at the end of his reading of Goethe's *Iphigenia* signals Adorno's protest against the implicit imperialism of the German cultural tradition through its identification with the culture of ancient Greece. The unspoken requirement at this juncture is the need for a new definition of mankind (*Menschheit*), a definition that no longer excludes the ethnic other. Whether Goethe intended this meaning is ultimately irrelevant for Adorno's reading, but it is highly relevant for the impact of Adorno's intervention in 1967 and its evaluation today.

Aesthetic Theory references not only literary works but also, and perhaps even more important, musical compositions and paintings. These references demonstrate Adorno's understanding of his theory as a theory from below that gains its insights from the close encounter with artworks rather than conceptual constructs imposed from above. In truth, it is a theory that hovers between the concept and the individual experience, that is, between the universal and the particular (AT 343), seeking mediation in the moment of critical performance. While these references to artworks are more than mere examples to demonstrate a point, they typically do not evolve into an extensive analysis. They become integrated elements in the movement of the text and it would be problematic to take them out of their immediate context. What is vital for the explication of artworks mentioned in *Aesthetic Theory* is their relationship to the conceptual constellation and the movement of the larger argument. They are chosen to support the argument. At the same time, they are the occasions in the text where Adorno's reflection seeks the connection with the concrete aesthetic phenomenon. Yet the concrete work, when it is mentioned in the text, does not merely affirm the argument; as a complex and unstable artwork it also challenges the conceptual logic, subverting the chain of reasoning. Thus the chain of reasoning becomes unstable and does not show linear progress.

My readings had to consider this structural feature of *Aesthetic Theory,* which, as I have alluded to above, discourages a summary of the argument as a way of opening up the substance of the work. Consequently, the three chapters dealing with *Aesthetic Theory* vary in their approach. They focus on Adorno's encounter with Kant's aesthetic theory, the function of a concept (the ugly), and the role of an idea (the absolute). In each instance the method of reading had to be adapted. The Kant chapter required not only attention to the status of Kant in the German philosophical tradition but also a detailed recognition of the complex interplay between Adorno's theory and Kant's Third Critique. Adorno's peculiar way of engaging Kant becomes the object of my analysis because it reveals essential features of Adorno's theory. In other words, the reading had to move outside the text in order to open it up. Similarly, the chapter on the section of *Aesthetic Theory* devoted to the ugly had to negotiate the role of this concept in post-Kantian aesthetics and in Adorno's use. At the same time it had to grapple with the growing importance of the ugly in modern art and the cultural debates about the meaning of the ugly as an aesthetic and cultural category. While it is not difficult to recognize the centrality of the ugly for modernism and a modernist aesthetic theory, for Adorno the stakes become much higher when the concept of the ugly is brought into contact with the category of the primitive, including its political connotations. Here the aesthetic discussion moves beyond the aesthetic sphere and points to a problematic border.

Adorno's discussion of the ephemeral moment of the artwork and its relationship to the idea of the absolute similarly challenges the familiar notion of aesthetic autonomy commonly connected with Adorno's theory. Yet Adorno's affirmation of the artwork, while strongly stated in some parts of *Aesthetic Theory*—for example in the section on the theory of the artwork (AT 175–199)—is not unqualified. Only a close look at Adorno's critique of the notion of the artwork's timeless status and his foregrounding of the ephemeral and fleeting moments of works of art, which seemingly lower their value, brings into focus that the category of the absolute as a counterweight, although not an aesthetic category itself, plays a significant role in Adorno's thought about the status of art. While the two chapters come to Adorno's theory from different vantage points and do not create a unified conceptual framework, they point to critical aspects of Adorno's theory that challenge preconceived notions.

Finally, it is necessary to turn again to the question of Adorno's significance for the present aesthetic discourse. I first raised this question in the introduction, arguing for the relevance of Adorno's theory by providing a map of the contemporary discussion, a map on which Adorno's place could be marked. Now it is time to look back at this question from the vantage point of the previous chapters. There is no claim to systematic completeness. In each instance, however, the goal is to make visible the strength and intellectual energy of his writings. The force of Adorno's texts, their radical nature, is, I believe, the result of the dialectical thought process, the relentless persistence of his language that is not satisfied with presentable dogmatic results. There is always a next turn that questions what has been established. One misunderstands Adorno, I believe, if one wants to determine a stable position, including the notion of aesthetic autonomy. The core is the process. This, by the way, is the reason why Adorno's polemics against perceived enemies are ultimately unsatisfactory, since they tend to attack other positions and thereby potentially lose their moment of self-reflexivity. The term "negative dialectics" gives only a rough approximation of the subtle work that Adorno's language has to perform in order to reach its conceptual goal. Its elevated radical rhetoric, a persistent problem for his translators, drives the thought process in spiral movements until it finds a moment of rest before it continues its unending labor. What appears to be a statement that can be looked at and judged separately is in fact always already part of a movement that transcends the level of a statement.

This intensity, the relentless pursuit of his topics in *Aesthetic Theory* without finding a final systematic resolution, is by all means part of Adorno's importance and relevance. Still, this formal argument would not by itself guarantee an irrefutable significance of his theory in the present discourse.

As I have argued in the introduction, Adorno's late work does not fit neatly into the contemporary aesthetic discourse. *Aesthetic Theory* was untimely in 1970 and may well be untimely again, despite the valuable efforts of Adorno specialists to reconstruct and preserve his work. Yet this untimeliness can also be its strength as a provocation for the contemporary discourse. Therefore I suggest that the question of Adorno's significance should be reconsidered in different terms. The claim of unmediated relevance is possibly the wrong approach because it forces us to repress the historical distance between the 1960s and today. Neither a pure reconstruction of Adorno's ideas nor the insistence on the unmediated relevance of Adorno's writings within the spectrum of contemporary philosophical positions, resulting in the teaching of a neo-Adornian dogma, would be the answer. Instead, the engagement would focus on the labor of theoretical thought, in our case the questions that Adorno posed when he engaged art. One of these questions that deserves our renewed attention is the complex and problematic relationship of philosophy and art, the way each needs the other and depends on the other, as well as the way that each remains distant from and incompatible with the other. It is a question that, at least among philosophers, is not very popular right now because it is commonly assumed that philosophy is in control.

Once we have considered the concept of mediated relevance it becomes more difficult, if not impossible, to think simply of a number of features of Adorno's aesthetic theory that should be preserved for contemporary discussion. One would have to look at this question more in terms of general directions and tendencies rather than specific claims. I believe that Adorno's persistent focus on the concrete artwork and its specific historical situatedness is more fruitful than new versions of Platonism or abstract transcendentalism, since neither art, as produced by human labor, nor its philosophical assessment stand outside of the process of history. In this context even the old-fashioned but vexing idea of progress through aesthetic differentiation deserves further attention and clarification. Moreover, it goes almost without saying that the concept of aesthetic autonomy, as much as Adorno problematized it, cannot be given up as a decisive moment of aesthetic quality. It is worth defending it against a comparative cultural theory that denies the universal validity of the claim and therefore challenges Adorno.[5]

This critique, while it rightly underscores the need for a global perspective and attention to the institutional and cultural situatedness of art, is hasty for two reasons. First, it postulates that Adorno is unaware of the peculiar nature of the Western tradition with respect to the development and definition of art and literature and therefore makes (naive) universal claims. But Adorno consciously restricts himself to those parts of the Western tradition with which he is familiar and refuses to make universal claims in terms of content. In his discussion of lyric poetry, for instance, he even excludes medieval European poetry from his considerations, since it may well have had a different cultural function from modern poetry.[6] Moreover, he refuses to consider Japanese poems because they are culturally different and therefore resist subsumption under the category of (autonomous) poetry. Second, the culturalist polemic against Adorno's theory remains inadequate in its exclusive emphasis on a dogmatically constructed concept of autonomy without acknowledging Adorno's own critique of the Western tradition, especially in his discussion of classicism and his assessment of the ephemeral nature of the artwork. In short, this judgment underestimates the critical and self-reflective force of *Aesthetic Theory.* Using a very broad brush, namely the notion of the Western tradition, this polemic ends up with a relatively distorted definition of Adorno's theory and its place in the history of aesthetics.

Cultural criticism might possibly respond by arguing that the charge against Adorno is more basic and therefore untouched by the specific structure of *Aesthetic Theory.* Yet this argument overlooks the very nature of Adorno's theory as a fundamental critique of the Western tradition. When Timothy Reiss points out that "the conditions that aesthetics takes art to cure, the divisions it judges art to bridge, may be peculiar to modern Western culture(s)" and then concludes, "If so, products of the fictive imagination produced in different cultures will not be art in a modern Western sense at all,"[7] he is stating only what Adorno knew from the beginning. But Adorno refuses to treat aesthetics—because of its cultural borders—as a purely discursive phenomenon, since that perspective flattens and empties out the specific cultural importance and aesthetic truth content within the cultural tradition to which it belongs. Ultimately, therefore, the misplaced challenge from the vantage point of comparative cultural theory can only sharpen the definition of Adorno's theory. It also underlines the problematic nature of a simplified reception of Adorno's theory with an exclusive and dogmatic stress on aesthetic autonomy. By perceiving Adorno as a typical representative of Western philosophy, cultural theory misreads *Aesthetic Theory* as an affirmative theory that simply states and maintains the value of the artwork as derived from the idea of aesthetic autonomy.

This critical reassessment of Adorno's concept of aesthetic autonomy could be part of a broader program that includes a discussion of Adorno's emphasis on the human production of art, the fact that for Adorno all artworks are the result of human labor under changing historical and cultural conditions and are therefore finite. Acknowledging the materialist component of Adorno's theory, which has become unfashionable, would guard against a purely idealistic reception of *Aesthetic Theory* that deems the material aspect as no longer crucial for aesthetics.

NOTES

Introduction

1. Theodor W. Adorno, *Ästhetische Theorie,* ed. Gretel Adorno and Rolf Tiedemann, 4th ed. (Frankfurt am Main: Suhrkamp, 1980). References to this edition are given in parentheses as ÄT. The first English edition, translated by C. Lenhardt, was published in 1984 by Routledge & Kegan Paul (London). This translation was superseded by Robert Hullot-Kentor's translation: Theodor W. Adorno, *Aesthetic Theory* (Minneapolis: University of Minnesota Press, 1997). All English quotations are based on this edition (AT).

2. Christoph Menke, *The Sovereignty of Art: Aesthetic Negativity in Adorno and Derrida,* trans. Neil Solomon (Cambridge, MA: MIT Press, 1998).

3. Elaine Scarry, *On Beauty and Being Just* (Princeton, NJ: Princeton University Press, 1999); Peter de Bolla, *Art Matters* (Cambridge, MA: Harvard University Press, 2001).

4. Scarry, *On Beauty,* 57.

5. Ibid., 86–93.

6. Ibid., 92.

7. De Bolla, *Art Matters,* 12.

8. Ibid., 139. In his later work de Bolla perfected his affective approach to art but also slightly changed his method by giving more room to the formal elements of the artwork. His 2009 interpretation of Gerhard Richter's painting *Betty* (1988), while not forcing a formalist analysis, is highly attentive to its composition as well as its use of color. The detailed record of the experience of the viewer (obviously a trained art historian) is actually based on a subtle reading of specific

formal moments of the portrait. Thus the unlocking of the affective aspect has to consider the structure of the painting. At the same time, there can be no doubt that de Bolla's intention remains significantly different from Adorno's method, since for de Bolla the truth of the painting fully discloses itself in the experience of the viewer, whereas for Adorno the discerning gaze and subsequent experience of the viewer only prepares the disclosure of the truth content, which is not identical with the experience. For these reasons de Bolla's encounter with *Aesthetic Theory* can succeed only up to a point. See Peter de Bolla, "Facing Betty's Turn," in Peter de Bolla and Stefan H. Uhlig, eds., *Aesthetics and the Work of Art: Adorno, Kafka, Richter* (New York: Palgrave Macmillan, 2008), 222–240.

9. Jonathan Loesberg, *A Return to Aesthetics: Autonomy, Indifference, and Postmodernism* (Stanford: Stanford University Press, 2005), 8.

10. Pierre Bourdieu, *Distinction: A Social Critique of the Judgment of Taste,* trans. Richard Nice (Cambridge, MA: Harvard University Press, 1984). See also Jonathan Loesberg, *Return to Aesthetics,* 218–225.

11. For Adorno this relationship is the very core of his dialectic. For him it is equally true that modern aesthetic concepts such as Kant's notion of disinterested pleasure are theoretically indispensable and that they are conditioned within and by the broader historical process.

12. Robert Stecker, *Aesthetics and the Philosophy of Art: An Introduction* (Lanham, MD: Rowman and Littlefield, 2005); Noël Carroll, *The Philosophy of Art: A Contemporary Introduction* (London: Routledge, 1999).

13. Albrecht Wellmer, *The Persistence of Modernity: Essays on Aesthetics, Ethics, and Postmodernism,* trans. David Midgley (Cambridge, MA: MIT Press, 1991), 16–17.

14. A good example of this critique can be found in the essay "Der mißbrauchte Barock," in Adorno, *Ohne Leitbild: Parva Aesthetica* (Frankfurt am Main: Suhrkamp, 1967), 133–157.

15. Theodor W. Adorno, "Trying to Understand *Endgame*," in Adorno, *Notes to Literature,* trans. Shierry Weber Nicholsen (New York: Columbia University Press, 1991), 1:241–275.

16. Wellmer, *Persistence of Modernity,* 23.

17. Ibid., 29.

18. Menke, *Sovereignty of Art,* xi.

19. Ibid.

20. In a later essay Menke posits in stronger terms not only the compatibility of Adorno and Derrida but also their methodological proximity, since in both instances the certainty of the subject and the conditions of transcendental knowledge are subverted, leading to a pattern of aporetic thought. This shift implicitly underlines the difference between Adorno and the second generation of the Frankfurt School, a difference that the early Menke played down. See Christoph Menke, "Subjektivität und Gelingen: Adorno – Derrida," in Eva L. Waniek and Erik M. Vogt, eds., *Derrida und Adorno: Zur Aktualität von Dekonstruktion und Frankfurter Schule* (Vienna: Turia & Kant, 2008), 189–205.

21. See Lambert Zuidervaart, *Adorno's Aesthetic Theory: The Redemption of Illusion* (Cambridge, MA: MIT Press, 1991); Tom Huhn and Lambert Zuidervart, eds., *The Semblance of Subjectivity: Essays in Adorno's Aesthetic Theory* (Cambridge, MA: MIT Press, 1997); Simon Jarvis, *Adorno: A Critical Introduction* (Cambridge: Polity Press, 1998); J. M. Bernstein, *Adorno: Disenchantment and Ethics* (Cambridge: Cambridge University Press, 2001); Nigel Gibson and Andrew Rubin, eds., *Adorno: A Critical Reader* (Walden, MS: Blackwell, 2002); Gerhard Richter, ed., *Language without Soil: Adorno and Late Philosophical Modernity* (New York: Fordham University Press, 2010).

22. See David Pan, *Primitive Renaissance: Rethinking German Expressionism* (Lincoln: University of Nebraska Press, 2001).

23. Adorno, "Cultural Criticism and Society," in Adorno, *Prisms,* trans. Samuel Weber and Shierry Weber (Cambridge, MA: MIT Press, 1981), 17–34.

24. Hans Magnus Enzensberger, "Berliner Gemeinplätze," in Enzensberger, *Palaver: Politische Überlegungen (1967–1973)* (Frankfurt am Main: Suhrkamp, 1974), 13–17.

25. Adorno, "On Lyric Poetry and Society," in Adorno, *Notes to Literature,* 1:37–54.

1. Human Freedom and the Autonomy of Art

1. Adorno, *Kant's "Critique of Pure Reason,"* ed. Rolf Tiedemann, trans. Rodney Livingston (Stanford, CA: Stanford University Press, 2001), 4. Cited in parentheses as KC.

2. Adorno, *Kants Kritik der reinen Vernunft (1959), Nachgelassene Schriften,* Abteilung IV: Vorlesungen, vol. 4, ed. Rolf Tiedemann (Frankfurt am Main: Suhrkamp, 1995), 34. Cited in parentheses as KK.

3. Immanuel Kant, *Critique of Pure Reason,* trans. Norman Kemp Smith (New York: St. Martin's Press, 1965), 125. Cited in parentheses as CPR.

4. Adorno, *Ästhetik (1958/59): Nachgelassene Schriften,* Abteilung IV: Vorlesungen, vol. 3, ed. Erhard Ortland (Frankfurt am Main: Suhrkamp, 2009), 320. Translations are mine. Cited in parentheses as Ä.

5. Kant, *Critique of the Power of Judgment,* § 42, ed. Paul Guyer, trans. Paul Guyer and Eric Matthews (New York: Cambridge University Press, 2000), 178. Cited in parentheses as CJ.

6. Kant, *Kritik der Urteilskraft,* B 116, A 115, in Kant, *Werke,* 6 vols., ed. Wilhelm Weischedel (Darmstadt: Wissenschaftliche Buchgesellschaft, 1957), 5:358. Cited in parentheses as KU.

7. Adorno, *Ästhetische Theorie,* ed. Gretel Adorno and Rolf Tiedemann, 4th ed. (Frankfurt am Main: Suhrkamp, 1980). Cited in parentheses as ÄT.

8. Andrea Esser, *Kunst als Symbol: Die Struktur ästhetischer Reflexion in Kants Theorie des Schönen* (Munich: Fink, 1997).

2. The Ephemeral and the Absolute

1. A strong restatement of this position we find in Fabio Akcelrud Durão, "Adorno Thrice Engaged," *Cultural Critique* 60 (Spring 2005): 261–276.

2. See, for instance, Albrecht Wellmer, *The Persistence of Modernity: Essays on Aesthetics, Ethics, and Postmodernism,* trans. David Midgley (Cambridge, MA: MIT Press, 1991); David Roberts, *Art and Enlightenment: Aesthetic Theory after Adorno* (Lincoln: University of Nebraska Press, 1991).

3. See, for example, Christoph Menke, *The Sovereignty of Art: Aesthetic Negativity in Adorno and Derrida,* trans. Neil Solomon (Cambridge, MA: MIT Press, 1998); Eva Geulen, "Reconstructing Adorno's 'End of Art,'" *New German Critique* 81 (Autumn 2000): 153–168; Carsten Strathausen, "Adorno; or, the End of Aesthetics," in *Globalizing Critical Theory*, ed. Max Pensky (Lanham, MD: Rowman & Littlefield, 2005), 221–240.

4. For a discussion of Adorno's position on religion, see John Hughes, "Unspeakable Utopia: Art and the Return to the Theological in the Marxism of Adorno and Horkheimer," *Cross Currents* 53 (Winter 2004): 475–492.

5. J. M. Bernstein, "'The dead speaking of stones and stars': Adorno's *Aesthetic Theory,"* in *The Cambridge Companion to Critical Theory*, ed. Fred Rush (New York: Cambridge University Press, 2004), 139–164, here 141.

6. Ibid., 145.

7. Ibid., 146.

8. Ibid., 147.

9. Theodor W. Adorno, *Aesthetic Theory,* trans. and ed. Robert Hullot-Kentor (Minneapolis: University of Minnesota Press, 1997), 29; all subsequent quotations from this edition will be cited in parentheses as AT.

10. Bernstein, "'Dead speaking of stones and stars,'" 157.

11. See chapter 3 in this volume.

12. In *Negative Dialectics* Adorno explicates the philosophical problematic of the concept of the absolute. As part of metaphysics the concept has to be thought as part of a system. "Although dialectics allows us to think the absolute, the absolute as transmitted by dialectics remains in bondage to conditioned thinking. If Hegel's absolute was a secularization of the deity, it was still the deity's secularization; even as the totality of mind and spirit, that absolute remained chained to its finite human model" (Adorno, *Negative Dialectics,* trans. E. B. Ashton [New York: Continuum, 1973], 405). While the project of metaphysics, Adorno insists, has failed, the concept of the absolute as a point of reference remains legitimate for the examination of the crisis of modernity and specifically for the reflection on given metaphysical needs.

13. For an excellent example, see Rose Rosengard Subotnik, "Adorno's Diagnosis of Beethoven's Late Style: Early Symptoms of a Fatal Condition," *Journal of the American Musicological Society* 29, no. 2 (Summer 1976): 242–275.

14. Adorno, *Philosophy of Modern Music,* trans. Anne G. Mitchell and Wesley V. Blomster (New York: Seabury Press, 1973), 133.

15. Michael Pauen, *Dithyrambiker des Untergangs: Gnostizismus in Ästhetik und Philosophie der Moderne* (Berlin: Akademie Verlag, 1994), 381.

16. Ibid., 383.

17. From a different perspective Eva Geulen has drawn our attention to the apocalyptic tone in *Dialectic of Enlightenment.* In her discussion of the topic of the end of art she points to the strong similarities between genuine art and the culture industry in the author's description. The supposed opposition collapses in light of the presumed end of history. "The epistemological pattern of this all-encompassing knowledge . . . is grounded in the spectacle of the apocalypse" (Geulen, "Reconstructing Adorno's 'End of Art,'" 160). What is not stressed in Geulen's assessment is the affinity to Gnosis. For this reason she interprets as process what can be read as a fundamental pattern that determines the understanding of empirical reality and the process of history in general. In Gnostic thought the end of history (and by extension art) is already found in its origin. The depravity of the material world can be shown but does not have to be proved in empirical terms.

18. See Pauen, *Dithyrambiker des Untergangs,* 383.

19. Frederic Jameson, *Late Marxism Adorno; or, the Persistence of the Dialectic* (London: Verso, 1990), 1–12.

20. It seems that Geulen, in her attempt to understand the logic of endings in Adorno, merges the aesthetic and the ethical dimension and thereby conflates Adorno's ethical challenge, which was immediately misunderstood by contemporary critics as a historical indictment, with the intrinsic aesthetic problematic. Adorno's extreme formulations encourage such conflation, since they do not carefully mark the range of their meaningful application (Geulen, "Reconstructing Adorno's 'End of Art,'" 155–156).

21. John Hughes tends to be a rather sympathetic reader of Adorno's and Horkheimer's critique of Christianity, and he provides a good interpretation of their position, which he defines as Jewish Enlightenment focused on a negative dimension of messianic expectation. Ultimately, however, Hughes means to rescue Christian theology from Adorno's overly negative critique (Hughes, "Unspeakable Utopia," 490–492).

22. Adorno, *Minima Moralia: Reflections from Damaged Life,* trans. E. F. N. Jephcott (London: Verso, 1978), 247.

23. I follow the more accurate translation of the text by Gerhard Richter in his essay "Aesthetic Theory and Nonpropositional Truth Content in Adorno," *New German Critique* 97 (Winter 2006): 119–135, here 126.

24. Adorno, *Minima Moralia,* in the translation of Richter, 126.

25. Ibid.,127.

26. Richter, "Aesthetic Theory and Nonpropositional Truth Content," 131.

3. Aesthetic Violence

1. See Christoph Menke, *The Sovereignty of Art: Aesthetic Negativity in Adorno and Derrida*, trans. Neil Solomon (Cambridge, MA: MIT Press, 1998); David Roberts, *Art and Enlightenment: Aesthetic Theory after Adorno* (Lincoln: University of Nebraska Press, 1991).

2. See Günter Oesterle, "Entwurf einer Monographie des Häßlichen," in *Zur Modernität der Romantik: Literaturwissenschaft und Sozialwissenschaft*, vol. 8, ed. Dieter Bänsch (Stuttgart: Metzler, 1977), 217–297; I. M. Bernstein, *The Fate of Art: Aesthetic Alienation from Kant to Derrida and Adorno* (University Park: Pennsylvania State University Press, 1992).

3. See Siegfried J. Schmidt, "Der philosophische Begriff des Schönen und des Häßlichen in Adorno's Ästhetischer Theorie," *Zeitwende* 43 (1972): 94–104; Thomas Huhn, "Diligence and Industry: Adorno and the Ugly," *Canadian Journal of Political and Social Theory* 12 (1988): 138–146.

4. See Albrecht Wellmer, *The Persistence of Modernity: Essays on Aesthetics, Ethics, and Postmodernism* (Cambridge, MA: MIT Press, 1991).

5. See Robert Hullot-Kentor, "The Philosophy of Dissonance: Adorno and Schönberg," in *The Semblance of Subjectivity: Essays on Adorno's Aesthetic Theory*, ed. Thomas Huhn and Lambert Zuidervaart (Cambridge, MA: MIT Press, 1997), 309–320.

6. Theodor W. Adorno, *Philosophy of New Music*, ed. and trans. Robert Hullot-Kentor (Minneapolis: University of Minnesota Press, 2006), 29. Subsequent citations are given in parentheses as PMM.

7. See Andreas Huyssen, "Adorno in Reverse: From Hollywood to Richard Wagner," *New German Critique* 29 (Spring–Summer 1983): 5–29.

8. Carl Einstein, *Werke*, ed. Rolf-Peter Baacke (Berlin: Medusa, 1980), 1:245; all translations are mine.

9. For a general discussion of primitivism, see Robert Goldwater, *Primitivism in Modern Art* (New York: Random House, 1938); Colin Rhodes, *Primitivism and Modern Art* (London: Thames and Hudson, 1934); also David Pan, *Primitive Renaissance: Rethinking German Expressionism* (Lincoln: University of Nebraska Press, 2001).

10. Einstein, *Werke*, 1:254–261.

11. Ibid., 1:254.

12. Ibid., 1:256.

13. Ibid., 1:258.

14. Ibid., 1:259–260.

15. Max Horkheimer and Theodor W. Adorno, *Dialectic of Enlightenment*, trans. John Cumming (New York: Herder and Herder, 1972), 52. Subsequent citations are given in parentheses as DE.

16. Theodor W. Adorno, *Aesthetic Theory*, trans. and ed. Robert Hullot-Kentor (Minneapolis: University of Minnesota Press, 1997), 325–331. Subsequent citations are given in the text as AT.

17. See Peter Uwe Hohendahl, *Prismatic Thought: Theodor W. Adorno* (Lincoln: University of Nebraska Press, 1995), 75–104.

18. Sigmund Freud, *The Standard Edition*, trans. J. Strachey (London: Hogarth Press, 1955), vol. 13, here 90.

19. Friedrich Nietzsche, *The Birth of Tragedy and Other Writings,* trans. Raymond Geuss and Ronald Speirs (Cambridge: Cambridge University Press, 1999), 21. Subsequently cited as BT in the text.

20. Friedrich Nietzsche, *Human, All Too Human,* trans. R. I. Hollingdale (Cambridge: Cambridge University Press, 1996), 100.

21. Ibid., 101.

4. Reality, Realism, and Representation

1. For a discussion of the concept of realism in Lukács and Adorno, see Peter Uwe Hohendahl, "The Theory of the Novel and the Concept of Realism in Lukács and Adorno," in *Georg Lukács Reconsidered: Critical Essays in Politics, Philosophy and Aesthetics*, ed. Michael J. Thompson (New York: Continuum, 2011), 75–98.

2. Adorno, *Notes to Literature,* trans. Shierry Weber Nicholsen, 2 vols. (New York: Columbia University Press, 1991–1992), 1:37–54. Subsequently cited in the text as NL.

3. For a general discussion of the concept of representation in literature, see Elaine Scarry, *Resisting Representation* (New York: Oxford University Press, 1994); William G. Tierney and Yvonne S. Lincoln, eds. *Representation and the Text: Re-Framing the Narrative Voice* (Albany: State University of New York Press, 1997).

4. Georg Lukács, *Balzac und der französische Realismus* (Berlin: Aufbau, 1952).

5. Friedrich Engels, Brief an Miss Harkness, in Fritz J. Raddatz, ed., *Marxismus und Literatur: Eine Dokumentation* (Reinbek: Rowohlt), 1:157–159.

6. For a more complete understanding of Lukács's theory of realism, see Lukács, *Essays über den Realismus,* vol. 4 of *Werke* (Neuwied: Luchterhand, 1971).

7. Adorno, *Prisms,* trans. Shierry Weber Nicholsen and Samuel Weber (Cambridge, MA: MIT Press, 1981), 243–271. Subsequently cited as Pr in the text. There are frequent scattered references to Kafka in the volumes of *Notes to Literature*.

8. The diversity is particularly evident in the earlier scholarship. See Wilhelm Emrich, *Die Weltkritik Franz Kafkas* (Wiesbaden: Steiner, 1958); Bert Nagel, *Franz Kafka: Aspekte zur Interpretation und Wirkung* (Berlin: Erich Schmidt, 1974); Heinz Politzer, *Franz Kafka: Parable and Paradox* (Ithaca, NY: Cornell University Press, 1966); Erich Heller, *Franz Kafka* (Princeton, NJ: Princeton University Press, 1982); Stanley Corngold, *Franz Kafka: The Necessity of Form* (Ithaca, NY: Cornell University Press, 1988).

9. Hohendahl, "Theory of the Novel," (n. 1, above).

10. In the culture war between the Federal Republic of Germany and the German Democratic Republic during the 1950s and 1960s the distortion of reality as a symptom of decadent Western art and literature is central to the orthodox Communist attack against West German culture. In part, Adorno's defense of Kafka aims at the Stalinist position of East German literary criticism.

11. There were (unauthorized) voices within East German criticism that were sympathetic to Adorno's position, among them the philosopher Wolfgang Heise, who engaged in a productive dialogue with Adorno's literary theory. See Helmut Pillau, "Adorno in der DDR: Zur kritischen Rezeption seiner Ästhetik bei Wolfgang Heise," in *Adorno im Widerstreit: Zur Präsenz seines Denkens,* ed. Wolfram Ette et al. (Freiburg: Karl Alber, 2004), 518–533.

12. Theodor W. Adorno, *Aesthetic Theory,* trans. Robert Hullot-Kentor (Minneapolis: University of Minnesota Press, 1997). Subsequently cited in the text as AT.

13. Coming from a different perspective Ulrich Plass arrives at a similar conclusion. See Ulrich Plass, *Language and History in Theodor W. Adorno's "Notes to Literature"* (New York: Routledge, 2006), 56–57 and 142–146.

14. Concerning Adorno's engagement with the contemporary novel, see David Cunningham, "After Adorno: The Contemporary European Novel," in *Adorno and Literature,* ed. David Cunningham and Nigel Mapp (New York: Continuum, 2006), 188–200.

15. Adorno, *Ästhetische Theorie,* ed. Gretel Adorno and Rolf Tiedemann, 4th ed. (Frankfurt am Main: Suhrkamp, 1980), 53. Subsequently cited in the text as ÄT.

16. In this respect the comparison with Erich Auerbach's concept of mimesis is instructive, although there is no evidence that Adorno read Auerbach's groundbreaking study *Mimesis* (1946). Auerbach views and evaluates modern realism in the nineteenth-century novel against the

background of the classical tradition of stylistic levels and the Christian tradition of figural interpretation. Thus modern realism is predicated on the Christian tradition. Adorno remains blind to the earlier forms of realism in the Middle Ages. For Adorno early modern realism in the novel is connected to the emergence of modern capitalism and science in England. It is treated as aesthetically inferior. The concept of aesthetic autonomy and the theory of the artwork as a monad make it considerably more difficult for Adorno to integrate realism into his aesthetic theory.

5. A Precarious Balance

1. "On the Classicism of Goethe's *Iphigenia*" can be read as a companion piece to Adorno's essay "Parataxis" (1964), a polemic against Martin Heidegger's interpretations of Friedrich Hölderlin. Indeed, the polemic in "Parataxis" ultimately transcends even the question of an appropriate reading of the late poems of Hölderlin.

2. Rolf Wiggershaus, *The Frankfurt School: Its History, Theory, and Political Significance,* trans. Michael Robertson (Cambridge, MA: MIT Press, 1994), 619–621; Lorenz Jäger, *Adorno: Eine politische Biographie* (Munich: Deutsche Verlags-Anstalt, 2003) 276–279.

3. Theodor W. Adorno, *Notes to Literature,* 2 vols., trans. Shierry Weber Nicholsen (New York: Columbia University Press, 1992), 2:305–308. Hereafter cited as NL 2.

4. Wolfgang Albrecht, *Literaturkritik* (Stuttgart: Metzler, 2001), 43–44; Stefan Neuhaus, *Literaturkritik: Eine Einführung* (Göttingen: Vandenhoeck & Ruprecht, 2004), 66–67.

5. Theodor W. Adorno, *Ohne Leitbild: Parva Aesthetica* (Frankfurt am Main: Suhrkamp, 1967), 29. Hereafter cited as OL (translations here and following are mine).

6. Karl Robert Mandelkow, *Goethe in Deutschland: Rezeptionsgeschichte eines Klassikers,* 2 vols. (Munich: C. H. Beck, 1980–1989).

7. Arthur Henkel (1915–2005) studied German literature, philosophy, and art history in Leipzig, Marburg, and Cologne. Later he moved to Graz, where he received his PhD in 1941 with a dissertation on Novalis. It took him more than a decade to complete his *Habilitation*, which he received in 1952 with a study of Goethe's concept of *Entsagung*. Henkel's academic career progressed relatively slowly. His first academic appointment, at the University of Göttingen in 1956, was followed by a position as associate professor at the University of Heidelberg in 1957. From 1958 until his retirement in 1980 he taught German literature as a full professor in Heidelberg. Initially Henkel was strongly influenced by Max Kommerell, although his plan to write his dissertation under Kommerell was unsuccessful because of hostile political interventions. At that time Henkel was close to the oppositional circle around the theologian Bultmann and the philosophers Ebbinghaus and Gadamer. Henkel distinguished himself primarily as an innovative Goethe scholar. Although Henkel did not reach the same national and international visibility as Staiger, he had a significant impact on the field of German literature through a large number of students.

8. Emil Staiger (1908–1987) became the leading Swiss academic critic of German literature after the war. He received his PhD in 1932 with a dissertation on Annette Droste-Hülshoff and his *Habilitation* in 1934 with a study on Schelling, Hegel, and Hölderlin, which was published in 1935. Apart from major theoretical interventions, among them his *Grundbegriffe der Poetik* (1946), his publications focused on the literature of the late eighteenth and the nineteenth centuries. His Goethe study (3 volumes, 1952–1959) became canonical. His distance from modern literature remained more implicit, until 1966 when he provoked the so-called *Züricher Literaturstreit* with a public lecture entitled "Literature and Public Sphere" (December 17, 1966). Staiger denounced contemporary German and European literature as nihilistic, calling instead for a return to positive values as they were expressed in the literature of the past. The following heated public discussion framed Staiger as an openly reactionary critic, a turn of which Adorno must have been aware when he wrote his *Iphigenia* essay.

9. Johann Wolfgang Goethe, *Plays,* ed. Frank Ryder (New York: Continuum, 1993), 112.

10. Emil Staiger, *Goethe,* 3 vols. (Zurich: Atlantis, 1952–1959), 1:367.

11. Arthur Henkel, "Iphigenie auf Tauris," in *Das deutsche Drama vom Barock bis zur Gegenwart,* 2 vols., ed. Benno von Wiese (Düsseldorf: Bagel, 1964), 1:170–194 (hereafter cited as IT; translations here and following are mine).

12. Max Horkheimer and Adorno, *Dialectic of Enlightenment,* trans. John Cumming (New York: Herder and Herder, 1972), 43. Hereafter cited as DE.

13. For a more extended discussion, see Mandelkow, *Goethe in Deutschland,* 2:30–33.

14. Walter Benjamin, *Selected Writings,* 4 vols., ed. Michael W. Jennings (Cambridge, MA: Harvard University Press, 1996–2003), 2:379.

15. Ibid., 2:382.

16. Max Kommerell (1902–1944) was next to Friedrich Gundolf the most important literary critic of the George Circle. He became a member in 1921 and remained close to George until 1930. Among his academic teachers were Gundolf, Ernst Robert Curtius, and Friedrich Wolters (also a member of the Circle). He received his PhD in 1924, with a dissertation on Jean Paul, and his *Habilitation* in 1930 at the University of Frankfurt, where he taught during the following decade. Although strongly recommended, he did not get a chair in Frankfurt in 1938. It was only in 1941 that he was offered a chair at the University of Marburg. Notwithstanding his relatively slow academic career, Kommerell became a major intellectual figure in the late 1920s, especially after the publication of his pathbreaking book, *Der Dichter als Führer in der deutschen Klassik,* which Benjamin reviewed in 1930. While the number of his students remained small during his lifetime (Arthur Henkel among them), his impact on German criticism after 1945 was significant, and by no means exclusively among conservatives.

17. *Adorno-Benjamin Briefwechsel 1928–1940,* ed. Henri Lonitz (Frankfurt: Suhrkamp, 1994), 72–73.

18. Paul Fleming, "Forgetting — Faust: Adorno and Kommerell," in *Adorno and Literature,* ed. David Cunningham and Nigel Mapp (London: Continuum, 2006), 133–144.

19. Max Kommerell, *Der Dichter als Führer in der deutschen Klassik* (Berlin: Bondi, 1928), 152.

Epilogue

1. In the case of Heidegger, see Adorno, "Parataxis: On Hölderlin's Late Poetry," in *Notes to Literature,* trans. Shierry Weber Nicholsen, 2 vols. (New York: Columbia University Press, 1991–1992), 2:109–149.

2. For an extensive discussion of Adorno's reading of Heine, see Peter Uwe Hohendahl, *Prismatic Thought: Theodor W. Adorno* (Lincoln: University of Nebraska Press, 1995), 105–118.

3. See Eva L. Waniek and Erik M. Vogt, eds. *Derrida und Adorno: Zur Aktualität von Dekonstruktion und Frankfurter Schule* (Vienna: Turia & Kant, 2008). For most of the contributors to this volume deconstruction rather than negative dialectics is the point of orientation.

4. Adorno, "Trying to Understand *Endgame,*" in *Notes to Literature*, 1:241–275.

5. See, for example, Timothy J. Reiss, "Aesthetics and the Fully Emancipated Subject: Culture, Histories and the Fictive Imagination," in *Aesthetics and the Work of Art: Adorno, Kafka, Richter*, ed. Peter De Bolla and Stefan H. Uhlig (New York: Palgrave Macmillan, 2009), 71–91. Reiss challenges Adorno's theory and especially the claim for aesthetic autonomy as a typical Western attitude toward art that cannot be universalized in the way Adorno supposedly argues. For Reiss, Adorno's theory is more or less an extension of the Western philosophical tradition. In the West, Reiss maintains, the separation of cognitive spheres has aided the understanding of art as something special, as something that eludes normal comprehension. Thus Adorno's suggestion that the artwork remains ultimately incomprehensible only marks him as a Western philosopher trapped in a precritical cultural slumber.

6. See Adorno, "On Lyric Poetry and Society," *Notes to Literature,* 1:37–54.

7. Reiss, "Aesthetics and the Fully Emancipated Subject," 79.

INDEX

absolute: Adorno and concept of, 22, 59,
70–74, 163, 170n12. *See also* theological
dimension
Adorno, Theodor: as academic teacher vs.
critic, 24, 34; comparative cultural theory
on, 165–66; as conservative vs. progressive,
3, 24; discovery of posthumous work of,
1; essayistic nature of writings of, 10–11,
28, 152; interdisciplinary nature of work
of, 154; as isolated figure, 25; method of
reading of, 160–61; and postwar cultural
restoration, 135; relevance today, 2, 9, 10,
163–64; types of writings of, 152–53. *See
also specific themes and titles of works*
aesthetic/aesthetics: Adorno's doubts about,
7, 154; countercritique of, 7–8; de Bolla's
defense of, 5; modern art and challenge
to, 6–7; and politics, unresolved tension
between, 85, 129–30; return to, 4, 9, 18,
19; Scarry's defense of, 4–5; and social
phenomena, Adorno on, 13, 15–16; in

today's cultural debates, 3, 5, 7–8. *See also*
aesthetic experience; aesthetic theory;
dialectical aesthetics; philosophical
aesthetics
aesthetic autonomy. *See* autonomy of art
aesthetic experience: vs. cognition, Kant
on, 46–47; immediacy of, 5, 8, 19;
transformation into philosophical
thought, 66
aesthetic judgment, Kant's notion of. *See*
judgment of taste
aesthetic production. *See* production
aesthetic reconciliation. *See* reconciliation
aesthetic theory: Bernstein's definition of,
59–60; Hegel and, 3, 35, 43, 53; history and,
123; Kant and, 3, 6, 20–21, 41–42, 46, 52, 53,
55, 153; philosophy and, 8; vs. philosophy
of art, 2; reason and, 60; traditionalism vs.
radical subjectivism and, 6; turning point
in history of, 51. *See also* aesthetic theory,
Adorno's